Digital and Social Media Regulation

Sorin Adam Matei · Franck Rebillard ·
Fabrice Rochelandet
Editors

Digital and Social Media Regulation

A Comparative Perspective of the US and Europe

palgrave
macmillan

Editors
Sorin Adam Matei
Sorbonne University
West Lafayette, IN, USA

Fabrice Rochelandet
Sorbonne University
Paris, France

Franck Rebillard
Institut de la Communication des Médias
Université Sorbonne Nouvelle
Paris, France

ISBN 978-3-030-66758-0 ISBN 978-3-030-66759-7 (eBook)
https://doi.org/10.1007/978-3-030-66759-7

Cover image: HollenderX2/Getty images
Cover design by eStudioCalamar

This Palgrave Macmillan imprint is published by the registered company Springer Nature Switzerland AG
The registered company address is: Gewerbestrasse 11, 6330 Cham, Switzerland

Foreword and Acknowledgments

Great minds think alike! Or, maybe, it is not minds that attract each other, but ideas. A great idea attracts another great idea, which invites another still. This volume is the product of several years of transatlantic intellectual collaboration of the issue of new media regulation for diversity. It emerged through the common work of the US-based Purdue University Global Communication Program sponsored by the Online M.A. program in Strategic Communication and the French Laboratory of Excellence in the Study of Cultural and Artistic-Creative Industries (also known as the LabEx ICCA) funded by the French National Agency for Research (CNRS). The chapters were selected from the papers submitted to the International Communication Association pre-conference (May 2019) *Riding or Lashing the Waves: Regulating the Media of Diversity in a Time of Uncertainty*. Held at the National Press Club in Washington, DC, the conference brought together, besides the contributors to this volume, academics and writers from a broad spectrum of interests, including David Weinberger, the author of several seminal books on the digital revolutions, including the most recent, *Everyday Chaos* (Weinberger 2019). The conference was organized both by the LabEx ICCA and by the Purdue Global Communication Program, the latter financially supported by the Purdue College of Liberal Arts.

The story of this collaboration is worth retelling as it highlights how a strong interest in interdisciplinary and experiential research and teaching can generate remarkable results.

In 2016, at the peak of the US Presidential campaign, Joseph Daniel, the author of La Parole Presidentielle (Daniel 2014) and a former professional political communicator was invited at Purdue University to participate in a series of events about political communication in twenty-first century. Dr. Daniel was invited by Dr. Sorin Adam Matei, who was in the process of launching the Global Communication Program, whose goal was to take Purdue students abroad to study the intricacies of the business, political, and cultural policies that shape the world of international digital communication. Dr. Daniel, a master analyst and storyteller, proved to be more than an informed observer of the US and French political spaces. He showed himself a generous thinker and connector, eager to share his knowledge and intellectual network. Upon his return to France, Dr. Matei visited him in the Fall of 2016, being introduced by Dr. Daniel to Dr. François Moreau, the director of the scientific advisory board of the ICCA LabEx and Drs. Francoise Rebillard, and Fabrice Rochelandet, the last two serving as co-editors of the present volume and core research leaders in the ICCA LabEx. The meeting led to the launch of the Purdue Global Communication Study Abroad program. The program was, from the beginning, imagined as a roving, on-the-spot experience, focused on in-person visits and discussion at major French media and regulatory organizations. Among them: the Superior Council for Audiovisual Media (CSA), the Commission for Information and Liberties (CNIL), the French Senate and National Assembly, DailyMotion, Google France, or the National Library. In addition, each iteration of the program included day-long academic seminars, some hosted by a third partner, the American Graduate School in Paris, at which the students and the researchers from both sides of the Atlantic presented papers and discussed emergent research projects. Some of the papers presented at the 2019 conference, including Dr. Curien's, Dr. Benhamou's, Dr. Matei and Kilman's chapters, were written as active acts of reflection toward the emerging program of research and education forged across the Atlantic since 2016.

A note about the historical context of our collaboration is also needed. The program of collaboration and research of the two organizations, ICCA LabEx and the Purdue Global Communication Program, emerged at a time of continental drift between the USA and European Union. Despite the fact that the two economic, political, and cultural areas share much of the same ideological, economic, and emerging international legal infrastructure, tensions and punitive measures have come about on both sides which threaten an increasing separation between these two global partners. We hoped that both our work together could be a model of collaboration and working together through the major and serious problems of our day.

Finally, we would like to acknowledge the following individuals and organizations for the unwavering support they provided to our initiative and program: David Reingold, Dean of the Purdue College of Liberal Arts was a strong supporter of the project, providing directly or indirectly the material support for the 2019 conference. The institutional leadership of the LabEx ICCA, including its scientific board, also provided financial support for the conference. Dr. Daniel's visit to Purdue and Dr. Matei's trip to Paris, in 2016, was supported by a Purdue University Global Synergy grant. The events in Paris would've not been possible without the unwavering support and time investment of Julie Gibellini, Councilor at the French National Assembly and a remarkable intellectual property scholar, Geoffrey Delcroix and Regis Chatellier, who opened the doors to the innovative research laboratory at CNIL (the Liberties and Informatics Council), David Dieudonné, from Google France. These individuals, among many others, have taught us many valuable lessons about the surplus of similarities and minimal differences between the scholarly and regulatory regimes in the France and the USA. In the USA, many thanks are owed to Bart Collins, the director of the Online M.A. Program in Strategic Communication, who has facilitated the recruitment and integration of the course taught in France in the regular curriculum of his program, co-sponsoring the Global Communication Program in Paris.

We are not only grateful to these individuals and organizations for their past support, but also the future commitment made to the continuation of our common work.

Dr. Sorin Adam Matei
Associate Dean of Research, College of Liberal Arts
Professor of Communication
Brian Lamb School of Communication, Purdue University
West Lafayette, USA

Dr. Francois Moreau
Director of the Scientific Advisory Board of LabEx ICCA
Université Sorbonne Paris Nord
Villetaneuse, France

Dr. Franck Rebillard
Université Sorbonne Nouvelle—IRMÉCCEN (Institut de
Recherche Médias, cultures, communication et
numérique—Research Institute on Media
Culture and Digital Communication) & LabEx ICCA
Paris, France

Dr. Fabrice Rochelandet
Université Sorbonne Nouvelle—IRCAV (Institut de Recherche
sur le Cinema et l'Audiovisuel—Cinema and Audiovisual Media
Research Institute) & LabEx ICCA
Paris, France

References

Daniel, Joseph. 2014. *LaParole présidentielle: De la geste gaullienne à la frénésie médiatique*. Paris, France: Seuil.

Weinberger, David. 2019. *Everyday Chaos: Technology, Complexity, and How We're Thriving in a New World of Possibility*. Harvard Business Review Press.

The original version of the book was revised: Chapters 1, 6 and 7 was previously published as non-open access, which has now been changed to open access under a CC BY 4.0 license. The correction to the book is available at https://doi.org/10.1007/978-3-030-66759-7_11

The original version of the book was revised: The incorrect author's name has been updated in Chapters 1, 3, 8 and Front matter. The correction to the book is available at https://doi.org/10.1007/978-3-030-66759-7_10

Contents

Notes on Contributors

Françoise Benhamou is a Professor of Economics at Sorbonne Paris Nord University and Sciences Po, Paris. She was a member of the board of ARCEP, the regulator for electronic communications and postal services in France (2012–2017). Among other positions, she is currently a member of the Laboratory of Excellence Cultural Industries & Art Creation, of the Cercle des Economistes, of the Committee of programs of the TV channel ARTE, of the scientific board of the CSA, the French regulatory body for audiovisual services in France. She chairs the Ethic Committee of Radio France. She wrote numerous books, papers, reports on the economics of media, culture, and digitization.

Maud Bernisson is a Ph.D. candidate at Karlstad University, in Sweden. She also holds a Master's degree in Media and Communication from the University of Toulon, in France. Before enrolling in a media and communication Ph.D. program, she worked in communications for public and non-governmental organizations. She is specializing in EU public policies concerning digital media and, more specifically, privacy and the public interest.

Nicolas Curien (graduated from École Polytechnique and Mines Paris Tech, Ph.D. Université Paris 6) is an expert in the economic and social impacts of the digital transition. He wrote several books and many articles in this field. He is emeritus professor of Conservatoire national des arts et métiers (Paris), where he held the chair "Telecommunications economics and policy." He currently is a member of the board of CSA, the French regulatory body for audiovisual services. He sat before on the board of ARCEP, the regulator for electronic communications and postal services in France. https://ncurien.fr.

Fabienne Graf is a graduate of the Duke University School of Law and an Academic Assistant at the University of Lucerne, Switzerland.

Larry Kilman has a privileged position in the evolving media world. After a long career in journalism, notably with The Associated Press, Agence France-Presse and Radio Free Europe/Radio Liberty, Larry spent 18 years with the World Association of Newspapers and News Publishers (WAN-IFRA), becoming Secretary General in 2012. Since leaving WAN-IFRA in 2016, Larry spent two years as Director of the American Graduate School in Paris, where he continues to teach NGO Management. He continues his work in the media sector through the Institute for Media Strategies, Upgrade Media and UNESCO.

Inna Lyubareva (Ph.D., Paris Nanterre University; M.A., B.A., National Research University Higher School of Economics, Moscow) is an Associate Professor of Economics at the Graduate Engineering School École nationale supérieure Mines-Télécom Atlantique in France. Her research interests include the areas of creative and cultural industries and their transformation under the impact of digital technologies. She studies business models and quality of information in media sector; communities and echo chambers dynamics in social media.

Sorin Adam Matei (Ph.D., University of Southern California, Annenberg School of Communication; M.A., Fletcher School of Law and Diplomacy; B.A., Bucharest University, History and Philosophy) studies the social implication of technologies in individual and group affairs. He is the author of books on social media and knowledge creation. He is a Professor of Communication in Brian Lamb School of Communication and the Associate Dean of Research and Graduate Education in the College of Liberal Arts at Purdue University, in West Lafayette, Indiana.

Marko Milosavljević Ph.D is a Professor in the Department of Journalism at Faculty of Social Sciences at University of Ljubljana, Slovenia. He is a vice-chair of the Committee of experts on media environment and reform (MSI-REF) at the Council of Europe. He is a member of the Core Experts Group for Media and Culture, advising European Commission, and the chair of Communications Law and Policy section of European Communication Research and Education Association (ECREA). He is a member of Horizon2020 project EMBEDDIA, researching artificial intelligence in the media and newsrooms, where he is the regulation and ethics manager.

Philip M. Napoli (Ph.D., Northwestern) is the James R. Shepley Professor of Public Policy, and Senior Associate Dean for Faculty and Research, in the Sanford School of Public Policy at Duke University (NC, USA).

Iva Nenadić, Ph.D.studies democratic implications and media pluralism in content moderation policies of online platforms and engages in policy debates over the same issues. Nenadić is an instructor at the Faculty of Political Science of Zagreb University, Croatia, and a research fellow at the European University Institute in Florence, Italy. She supervises the implementation of the EU Media Pluralism Monitor in the area of Political Independence and is a member of the European Digital Media Observatory. She is also a member of Horizon 2020 project MEDIADELCOM, researching the transformations of the European media landscape considering risks and opportunities for deliberative communication.

Franck Rebillard is a Professor of Media Studies at Sorbonne Nouvelle University, Paris, where he leads the IRMÉCCEN research team (Research Institute on Media, Culture and Digital Communication) within the LABEX ICCA (Laboratory of Excellence about Cultural Industries). His own works deal with the socioeconomics of the Internet and discourse analysis of online news. He is the author of three books (in French) dedicated to the Web 2.0 (2007), media diversity (2013), and digital culture (2016), and of several articles published in national and international journals such as *Media, Culture & Society* or *New Media & Society*.

Fabrice Rochelandet (Ph.D., Université Paris 1 Panthéon-Sorbonne), is a Professor of Communication Science at the Arts & Media Faculty at Université Sorbonne Nouvelle, France. He is a member of the Institut de Recherche sur le Cinéma et l'Audiovisuel and Laboratory of Excellence Cultural Industries & Art Creation. His main current fields of research are the economics of creative industries, digital innovation and regulation. He has published in the areas of copyright and privacy regulations, cultural diversity and digital platforms, online press, business models and crowdfunding.

List of Figures

Linking Theory and Pedagogy in the Comparative Study of US–French Media Regulatory Regimes

List of Tables

Introduction: New Paradigms of Media Regulation in a Transatlantic Perspective

Sorin Adam Matei, Franck Rebillard, and Fabrice Rochelandet

The original version of this chapter was revised: The chapter has been changed from non-open access to open access and the copyright holder has been updated. The correction to this chapter is available at https://doi.org/10.1007/978-3-030-66759-7_11

The original version of this chapter was revised: The spelling of the author name has been changed from "Fabienne Graff" to "Fabienne Graf". The correction to this chapter is available at https://doi.org/10.1007/978-3-030-66759-7_10

S. A. Matei (✉)
Purdue University, West Lafayette, IN, USA
e-mail: smatei@purdue.edu

F. Rebillard
Institut de la Communication des Médias, Université Sorbonne Nouvelle, Paris, France
e-mail: franck.rebillard@sorbonne-nouvelle.fr

F. Rochelandet
Sorbonne University, Paris, France
e-mail: fabrice.rochelandet@sorbonne-nouvelle.fr

S. A. Matei et al. (eds.), *Digital and Social Media Regulation*,
https://doi.org/10.1007/978-3-030-66759-7_1

To claim that communication technology and practices have undergone a tremendous shift over the past 30 years is a self-evident understatement. However, the same cannot be said about our regulatory framework—the product of political and economic ideas several centuries old. Thus, the worlds of communication practice and communication policy-making often are at odds. While it would be easy to claim new material forces demand new laws, the reality is our traditional media customs and laws are rooted in values, needs, and long-term projects that cannot be changed without impacting our entire way of life. Many facets of everyday life rely on this existing framework: individual autonomy, creativity, rule-based interactions, and fairness. A core challenge for technologists, legislators, and policymakers is to integrate new ways of communicating within the existing framework of values and practices in such a way that current values are preserved while specific regulatory practices are updated to match today's technological, economic, and cultural norms.

This volume examines these issues from a specific lens: that which intends to preserve diversity of production systems and respects the variety of consumption patterns. In doing so, we cover four core regulatory issues: intellectual property (copyright, especially), privacy, media diversity, and freedom of expression. The contributors to this volume examine the evolution of regulatory domains and their rules under the pressure of social-cultural practice, technological innovation, economic mechanisms, and legal constraints. More importantly, our contributors offer new cross-cultural approaches, grounded in our modern discourse, to processing and challenging the interplay between these social, legal, and economic forces (Schwanholz et al. 2017).

The authors propose several emerging solutions for re-aligning regulation with practical realities defined by technology, economics, and politics. In this context, we must emphasize that regulation is not seen only as a narrow set of limiting rules or enforceable laws that prescribe strictly and punitively certain behaviors, possible paths of development, or resource allocation, rights, and obligations. This collection insists: Regulation can be more broadly defined as the structural embedding of communication practices and technology in a certain framework of values and principles. Effective regulation should be based on rules and guidelines that are socially acceptable while creating adequate incentives for individuals and organizations to respect and apply them. In this sense, regulation facilitates social, productive interaction; it is not a constraining force. Because of this, the chapters included in this volume may imagine regulation as a collection of self-regulatory, co-regulatory, or directive regulatory practices and legal structures. More importantly, regulation is seen as a necessary means toward a self-sufficient end, which is free, thriving societies in which individuals and communities can learn, do business, and express themselves in a pluralistic way to the benefit and cultural enrichment of all human beings. Values such as diversity and richness of perspectives, a creative new way to think about the present and the future, fair and supportive mechanisms for the full realization of all human beings are of paramount importance for the regulatory mechanisms analyzed in this volume (Bertot et al. 2012).

A complex problem demands an approach to match. The perspectives offered by the authors span a broad array of experiences, domains, and levels of abstraction. This heterogeneity is intentional. As we will emphasize below, the authors were selected to include basic and applied research, regulatory, educational, and practical journalism experiences. As a dual intellectual and policy-practical approach, a diversity of opinions offer a clearer picture of what the future of digital and social media regulation should or can be (Forrest and Cao 2010).

Before summarizing the individual contributions—and given the theoretical concerns that inform this volume—let us categorize the issues decided on by this volume's authors, issues that undergird media and communication regulation in the twenty-first century. These choices are domain-specific. The contributions to the volume discuss regulation in the context of four key issues: intellectual property, privacy, freedom of expression, and media diversity. The significance of each of these issues demands both a diachronic and synchronic perspective. We must look back at the origins of these issues, their recent history, and their simultaneous interplay with technologies and communication practices. Also, as social media has been through a tremendous political upheaval during the last decade, especially in the USA, where accusation and counter-accusations of abuse and censorship abound, we need to look at the emergence of these problems in context (Brannon 2019). A good overview of these issues has been provided in the literature, which not only precedes but informs our work (Napoli 2019; Picard 2020).

To better understand the emergence of communication industry issues, we need to go back in time three decades ago (Picard 2020). The 1990s represented a major technological advancement, legislative change, and political questioning of media regulatory regimes worldwide. The liberation of the Communist nations and economic liberalization of China after 1989 opened the floodgates of communication within those nations and across borders. More important, these exchanges were turbocharged by technological innovation and economic globalization. During the 1990s, worldwide content industries abruptly switched from analog to digital dissemination of information through open and free networks, integrated into the global Internet. New markets for media products and processes spread across continents.

The immeasurable flow of digital information (and the devices that made them possible) challenged every single regulatory regime on the planet. Data started moving across media and between people, often dissolving the border between the two entities. States' ability to consistently enforce copyright laws dwindled. Privacy expectations were affected similarly. The common consumer used mass-interpersonal media—with vast, unplumbable databases of user data—to broadcast their personal brand to anyone else who would listen. The era of newsgroups, email lists, and chatrooms evolved into social media; Twitter, Facebook, Instagram, TikTok, Snapchat, Tinder, and others centralized millions of address books. Partly unintentional, partly by design, personal information from these social vectors became a new type of fuel for marketing and advertising campaigns.

Simultaneously, governments worldwide have begun to mine this information for their own purposes—preventing, sometimes inciting, violence. Yet, despite even the most ham-fisted attempts to control the media, freedom of expression evolved due to the Internet into a truly universal de facto practice. Until 1990, freedom of expression was, at the global level, a mere desideratum, inscribed in the Universal Declaration of Human Rights. For many nations, receiving or sending information was limited to interpersonal conversations. In some, other means of communication, such as typewriters in Communist nations like Romania, were controlled or registered by the government. After 1990 due to the Internet expansion, freedom of expression has become a common practice, especially and counter-intuitively in countries that pre-Internet could easily clamp down on non-governmentally approved public conversations. From China and Russia to Iran or Cuba, information has started to flow in and out via computers, cell phones, thumb drives, satellite, and VPN networks. While a boon for well-intended activists, this freedom of expression also aided ill intended ones. The explosion in militantism and the rapid spread of violent movements on a global scale that shook the world after 9/11, 2001 couldn't have been possible without easy and cheap access to worldwide exchanges of information via social media and content sharing platforms. In the past decade, social media campaigns have become the weapons in the global war of influence via propaganda campaigns targeting electoral processes, instigating cross-border violence, or confounding the public via fake or spun news. All these evolutions have muddied the tasks of media regulation. On the one hand, digital innovation and practices have generated endogenous social norms. For instance, with the proliferation social media-based innovation, individual users and online service providers continuously redefine the social norms of privacy, making it hard to stabilize and efficiently enforce privacy rules. On the other hand, reinforcing one key aspects of media regulation (e.g., privacy or copyright) could threaten or weaken others (e.g., freedom of speech or media diversity). Media regulation increasingly resembles a sudoku-like magic square, in which the rows and columns should add up to the same amount, a task increasingly difficult to solve.

Within this volume, the chapter authors will make reference to variable degree to a tetrad of regulatory challenges: intellectual property, privacy, freedom of expression, diversity and richness of content, and production sources. The changes in these spaces, both positive and negative, as many values in the proverbial sudoku magic square, need to be briefly recapitulated to better contextualize their contributions to the volume.

1 Intellectual Property

The abrupt switch from analog to digital content—including from broadcast to online electronic communication—deeply upset the intellectual property industry. The quasi-intangible nature of digital content raised the issue of its ownership and forced everyone to reconsider the issue of licensing IP rights. In an analog world, a physical copy of a unit of content (e.g., a CD) had material value that the owner could benefit from, including by resale. In a digital world, an mp3 song does not have any material resale value. In fact, the song is simply licensed to the user for personal use. But users did not know nor cared to know about that. In fact, the industry at-large abandoned one model of music distribution, the CD, for new forms of music consumption, such as streaming. The emergence of music sharing through peer-to-peer networks, combined with the lack of portability of legal DRM (digital management rights), and the high prices of CDs, lead the explosion of music on demand via fixed subscription services like Spotify. However, this did not solve the problem of copyright infringement. Entire movie libraries, especially of lesser known productions or popular television shows, were moved by innocent users to YouTube. A reflection of the changing public understanding of copyright, many of these illegal copies are accompanied by naïve disclaimers such as "I do not take credit for this content" or "I am sharing this content for public entertainment only, without any material gain." Such claims ignore that it is not the money or the credit the sharer accrues or not, but the loss of revenue and control it is inflicted on the original copyright holder that matters. Furthermore, global copyright violation enterprises such as the now-defunct (but revived in other forms by other operators) Megaupload, while potentially having positive impacts such as increasing the taste for culture among Internet users, tended to counter the effort to monetize content across borders of many established and newly arrived companies.

In brief, ease of reproducing and disseminating content by non-owners of Intellectual Property fundamentally changed the way traditional licensing schemes were enforced. Laws upon laws and regulations across the world have tried to stave off the onslaught of business models and individual practices that treated copyright almost as a thing of the past, virtually unenforceable. Some of the contributions to this volume, notably Matei and Kilman, consider how the changing nature of practices and de facto arrangements has led to fundamental social and cultural changes which regulatory practices still trail.

2 Privacy

For the past several centuries, most markedly in the Western hemisphere, privacy was considered a right born out of an understanding of individual autonomy that dates to the Renaissance. Privacy is the right to withhold certain information about one's person and private affairs. In the US context, privacy is enshrined in the Fourth Amendment, which reads: "the right of the people to be secure in their persons, houses, papers, and effects, against unreasonable searches and seizures." This right was restated and expanded by the US Supreme Court (Griwsold vs. Connecticut, 1965). In France, it is enshrined in the Civil Code, Article 9 stating everyone has a right to respect for their private life, while the Criminal Code prescribed specific punishments including prison time for willful violation of privacy. In addition, with the emergence of computerized systems and centralized databases, a comprehensive data privacy law (Loi "informatique et libertés") was adopted in 1978 to regulate the collection, storage, processing and use of personal data. While being quite close to the US Privacy Act of 1974, the French regulation is much more comprehensive and uses a more compulsory approach.

In essence, in the US/European tradition privacy is reducible to the proposition that individuals have the right to control if and what to disclose about oneself or one's private life. Materially, this means that behaviors, intimate personal details, and the documents describing them that exist on one's person or property were not to be revealed unless there was a legally justified reason (such as a search due to a criminal investigation). Furthermore, information shared with certain official or commercial institutions are protected either by laws or contractual obligations—often in the form of a Non-Disclosure Agreement. The emergence of social media, where a precondition of access is to fill out a profile with details of one's intimate life, changed all this. Even more significant, social media communication is premised on the idea of sharing and doing things in the public view or at least in semi-public communities. While protected by legally valid and binding user agreements, the public component of social media interactions puts a lot of information in the hands of commercial enterprises. Although terms of use and other conventional means of ensuring the "privacy" of such data are provided, in all reality the information leaks out as soon as the post is made or the tweet is sent. Once materially shared on a given social medium, data from media interaction is legally admissible (read as: commercially exploitable) to copying and sharing by third parties via other media. Even when and if social media platforms come with "privacy" settings, their true nature and limitations are poorly understood. For example, the fact that content is shared only with "some friends" does not mean that the friends of those friends or for that matter the rest of humanity cannot get screenshots of one's musings or compromising photos. Similarly, deleting content is seldom permanent, as some of the content might've already leaked through a network or has been archived. Many compromising tweets posted by famous or not-so-famous public figures restored from the many Twitter archives testify to this. One of the fundamental issues of the current definition of online privacy is that the current definition tends to ignore the old materiality of personal space defined by one's own person, house, or personal possessions. Further, that these conditions cannot be entirely reproduced online. The materiality of online communication is enshrined in networks, which are by-definition shared spaces, in which privacy is hard if not impossible to protect. The contributions to this volume, including Bernisson, Curien, or Matei and Kilman, highlight these issues directly, suggesting that the industry of privacy is in flux. While the General Data Protection Regulation issued by the European Union did create a "de facto" global privacy regime, this is at the mercy of international politics. This collection proposes some ideas for regulating social media for the future, illustrating original, stimulating avenues by which to accomplish this feat (Curien, Napoli and Graf).

3 Freedom of Expression

The modern political and civic concept of freedom of expression—as recorded in the US or French constitutions—rests on the radical proposition that individual thought and speech should be protected. This means to preserve the right of every individual to seek, access, form, hold, and express ideas, even if those ideas clash with current beliefs or political arrangements. Despite some differences, these two models have created cultures of lively personal expression. One difference is the conceptual leaps made between the US Constitution First Amendment, which denies the right of the government to pre-emptively regulate print media to the French Press Law, which includes provisions that can limit some speech. This culture was, at least after World War II, adopted by many governments and memorialized in the United Nations Declaration of Human Rights. Yet, in material practice, the ability of many people to even seek—let alone expressing freely—ideas contrary to those espoused by their governments or by the majority of the people in their nations was severely limited during the Cold War. When knowledge was bound to hard-copy books or newspapers and when radio waves were limited by frequency allocations and power limits, information could be easily denied, filtered, or ignored by gatekeepers. Similarly, expressing opinions could be easily denied by controlling the access to the enterprise-grade printing plants and broadcasting infrastructures. Digital media and global Internet fundamentally changed the rules of information exchange. As a "connectless" series of networks, the Internet is infinitely expandable. Any new local network can join the global Internet with a simple router and connection to the nearest node. Practically, even if the national infrastructure is controlled by a governmental entity that aims to limit access to some of the content, the task is so onerous it is rarely fully enforced. Despite multiple attempts, the Chinese, Iranian, or Russian Internets remain porous through a variety of technology subterfuges, from VPN and proxy gateways to spoofing IP addresses and other hacking techniques. Even though such opportunities are primarily available to technically astute users, they constitute an alternative to state-controlled media.

The ability of governments to control public discourse and to reprimand those that infringed local laws has declined significantly. The ability of citizens to protect their privacy and of governments to assist them has equally decreased. Commercial transactions across borders have expanded, at times challenging the ability of governments to levy taxes or punish tax cheats. Simultaneously, commercial transactions in the gray or underground illegal space of national and international economies have increased in frequency and the ability to control them evaporates more every day. More worrisome, the new digital, open, international order of communication allowed state and non-state actors to engage in massive operations of cross-border influence: propaganda, espionage, and at times open cyber-warfare interfere with basic utility services. In our collection Nenadić and Milosavljević monitor the efforts of the governments to keep track of and implement rules that cross borders, while Kilman and Matei analyze the challenges in imagining a trans-border regulatory regime for these issues.

4 Diversity and Richness of Content and Production Methods

The values and practices related to individual intellectual property, privacy, and freedom of expression were not adopted independent of greater social goals. One of the most important objectives was and remains: encouraging a diversity of opinions, perspectives, and creative visions. Modern social structure relies on diversity to adapt to new challenges and explore new dimensions of human life. The emergence of digital, networked global social media has created opportunities for plurality and diversity of opinions, but also challenges. The greatest net asset of the newly found digital global environment is that it encourages person-to-person communication. Indeed, one can describe the Internet as a mass-personal medium, blurring the lines between immediate, interpersonal, and mass communication. The new environment encourages many-to-many interactions, instead of one-to-many flows of content and knowledge, which has unleashed seismic waves of public and private expression. Emails, blogs, instant TV channels facilitated by YouTube, mass-viewed esports events; the number of voices and their authority to speak about matters of public importance has increased immeasurably over the past 30 years. Alongside consecrated professional commentators, journalists, entertainers, politicians, and other publicly recognized celebrities, we now have influencers—social media celebrities. Gigantic social movements have emerged from seemingly nowhere—think the Arab Spring or #metoo—expressing new points of view, advancing the common discourse. At the same time, this diversification of opinions has come at the cost of reduced visibility of individual opinions due to the fact that a narrowing range of channels and platforms disseminate these opinions. A few global platforms, mostly based in the USA (Facebook, Amazon, or Apple), have cornered various delivery markets, turning themselves into unavoidable conduits for expressing the newfound global conversation. The geographic, political, and commercial needs of these corporations raise important questions about diversity of choice and voice. While anyone can tweet, Twitter has become an arbiter of what can or should be tweeted. While any publication can be registered with Google News, Google's algorithm decides which publications are more or less visible. The contributions to this volume, most notably by Lyubareva and Rochelandet's, as well as Nenadić and Milosavljević's ones, emphasize the need to reconsider the trend of "platformization" and the implicit cost in the trend for authentic diversity of both production and consumption.

5 Contributions

The specific questions our collection asks and the answers it provides about the changing nature of regulation in the global media environment occupy a necessary thematic and geographic space. The themes include: theoretical grounding for regulation (Napoli and Graf), policy-practical propositions for future regulations (Curien, Benhamou), in-depth analyses of specific regulatory practices (Bernisson, Nenadić and Milosavljević), and structural challenges present in contemporary communication structure (Lyubareva and Rochelandet, Matei and Kilman). The chapters brought together by this volume include the following contributions:

Dr. Nicolas Curien, a commissioner of the Conseil Supérieur de l'Audiovisuel of France, an organization whose role is similar to that of the US Federal Communication Commission or the British Ofcom, proposes in his chapter "The Audiovisual Industry Facing the Digital Revolution: Understanding the Present and Inventing the Future" two propositions for understanding the current global regulatory climate. Dr. Curien is both a traditional French intellectual—a mathematician and an economist, Professor Emeritus of one of France's Grandes Ecoles, Conservatoire national des arts et métiers—and a policy maker, a rare species in field dominated by professional politicians or lawyers. He proposes that the world media environment is as seamless as the world ocean. The Internet that makes the global media process possible might be fragmented into local subnetworks, like as many separate oceans, but their value comes from their ability to connect to the global network of networks—in the end, all one body. However, this is not to say that there are no local regulatory entities. They do exist and work to regulate the production and consumption process of the citizens or corporate entities found within the boundaries of one nation or another. However, Curien sees the local regulators as fishbowls sunken in the ocean. The communicative ocean denizens—corporations—as often hide in these waters as they venture outside: at times forgetting to come back or growing too big to return to the small local fishbowls from which they hail.

The second, perhaps more powerful, proposition offered by Dr. Curien is that: given the rapid change and the difficulty of enforcing inflexible regulations, such as those meant to guide responsible use of social media, we need to rely more and more on nudging rather than on interdicting or giving permission for certain activities. He calls this process "co-regulation," which is an innovative way to use the old idea of relying on personal choice and sense of responsibility as a surer way to create peer-pressure for inducing expected behaviors. While Dr. Curien does not promote co-regulation as the only form of regulation, his idea is a fresh approach that strikes a middle ground between administrative enforcement of regulatory regimes and self-regulation. His plea for innovative approaches to regulation is more than a breath of fresh air, it is a truly new way to think about the future of structuring constrains and incentives in an era of rapid change and technological challenges.

Dr. Phil Napoli, James R. Shepley Professor of Public Policy at Sanford School of Public Policy, and Fabienne Graf, LLM, Duke University propose in the chapter "Revisiting the Rationales for Media Regulation: *The* Quid Pro Quo *Rationale and the Case for Aggregate Social Media User Data as Public Resource*" a new way to conceptualize the public nature of networks and their data, implying the necessity of future regulatory strategies. The chapter asks if we can consider data aggregated by social media as a type of public resource, and if this new perspective can be used as a *quid pro quo* rationale to regulate it in the manner used for regulating broadcasting. Then, the chapter explains how and why this rationale can be applied to social media. The concluding section considers the implications of this argument specifically for contemporary diversity-related policy objectives. Overall, the chapter proposes that regulation may carry over many concepts and principles from older to newer technologies. While not prescriptive directions, instead an angle of philosophy, this contribution offers the necessary abstract thinking about the nature of data and regulation.

Maud Bernisson, a Ph.D. candidate at the University of Karlstad, Sweden, contributes the chapter "GDPR and New Media Regulation: The Data Metaphor and the EU Privacy Protection Strategy," in which she continues Napoli and Graf's exploration of social media as a public goods creator, diving deeper into the specific meaning attached to "data" when utilized in EU regulatory actions and documents. She proposes that while there are tangible referents for the "data" concept used in privacy regulations, such as the General Data Protection Regulation (GDPR) directive issued by the European Union, the meaning of the concept tends to be structured more like a metaphor. Seeing data as a metaphor, Bernisson suggests that regulation and regulators have quite a bit of creative leeway in imagining new methods to think about and regulate privacy.

Drs. Iva Nenadić (University of Zagreb) and Marko Milosavljević (University of Ljubljana) continue the examination of European Union regulatory instruments seeking, as the title of their chapter suggests, to study the effectiveness of "regulating for media pluralism." Their goal is to discover the limits and possibilities intrinsic in major European Union regulations, including the better-known ones, such as GPDR, but also some that are less known, such as the Open Internet Access rules or the Audio-Visual Media Services directive. The chapter uses the Media Pluralism Monitor (MPM) framework to assess media pluralism in the EU member states as a means to prevent possible threats and violations of fundamental rights. The chapter's goal is to determine if the directives and policies have the intended efficacy at the national level. This type of investigation is very necessary because it is the responsibility and privilege of national governments to implement the directives and until they act, EU directives remain just that. The chapter concludes that, in the future, the European Commission should get a stronger role in the process of securing regulatory unity in media diversity at the European Union level. At the same time, governments should be encouraged and supported through unifying documents and rules, following the model set by GDPR. The authors also convincingly argue that one of the best ways to connect the supranational (EU) and national (state) levels of regulation would be the transnational working groups of regulations authorities as the ERGA (European Regulators Group for Audio Visual Media Services).

Drs. Inna Lyubareva (IMT Atlantique) and Fabrice Rochelandet (Sorbonne Nouvelle University and Labex ICCA) examine another facet of the media diversity debate in their regulation chapter "From News Diversity to News Quality: New Media Regulation Theoretical Issues." The chapter is an in-depth investigation of the manner in which the emergence of social media platforms—a new, privileged avenues for disseminating news produced by traditional media organizations—has affected the quality of the news production. The authors identify more than one axis of impact, including heterogeneity, originality, presence of critical analysis, and general rhetorical quality. The authors conclude that, in most of these modes, media platformization can lead to lower quality. The problem is made more complex by the fact that the "platform effect" is not perpetuated only by the production mechanism, but also by the consumption patterns. Social media posts are expected and are consumed as "quick snacks," which does not allow in-depth development of the content along academic, philosophical, or political registers.

Dr. Françoise Benhamou's chapter, "The Stakes and Threats in the Convergence Between Media and Telecommunication Industries," reflects on the dramatic economic and technological shift represented by the emergence of telecommunications companies, such as the American AT&T or French Orange. As an academic economist with an appointment at University of Sorbonne Paris Nord, with vast experience in media regulation—she was a commissioner of the French Telecom Regulator ARCEP—she provides a practical view on what is possible in the world of media industries, while contrasting opposition to what is desirable. Starting from the fact that convergence is a growing phenomenon, she questions the efficiency of the infrastructure available and its ability to overcome its early limitations. Dr. Benhamou also investigates the new business models created by convergence, which are rooted in mining personal data and consumption. From a regulatory perspective, she proposes that new regulatory tools should be created, including those that focus on non-discrimination (much like Net Neutrality) within media diversity.

Dr. Sorin Adam Matei (Professor of Communication and Associate Dean of Research, Purdue University) and Larry Kilman (Professor, American Graduate School, Paris) investigate in the chapter "Linking Theory and Pedagogy in the Comparative Study of US—French Media Regulatory Regimes" the core regulatory research and educational topics that can be most profitably studied across the Atlantic. Relying on rich experiences in teaching graduate courses that bring US students to study media practices and regulation in France, the authors examine the core areas of regulation that connect the chapters of this book: intellectual property, privacy, and freedom of expression. The authors propose that one of the most profitable manners of investigating these issues and teaching about them at the graduate level is to emphasize the growing hybridization of the US and European media industries. Long considered distinct regulatory regimes, one more libertarian (USA) and the other more statist (EU), the last three decades have taught us that neither position is tenable within its old contours. The globalization of media affairs, the fact that most US social media companies make a significant amount of money in Europe, and the truth that Europe depends on US media markets to reach out to the world with its own content, has led to convergent approach in regulation. The unexpected smooth and successful emergence of GDPR as a de facto common regulatory regime for most US social media companies, regardless of the area of operation, highlights this development very well. Citing learner insights collected from the papers written for the professional graduate courses they taught, the essay demonstrates the degree to which this convergence process has advanced in the minds of professional practitioners while still allowing for significant differences. Meanwhile, the chapter proposes new ways to think about developing new pedagogical and research approaches to explore this possibility in the future. The chapter's conclusions are strengthened by the students: are mid-career professionals, who in great majority, are US communication professionals and media opinion leaders.

The volume's concluding chapter "Short and Long-Term Scenarios for Media Regulation" engages in anticipatory analysis of critical trends and issues in the space of mediated communication. While the future is and will forever be as unpredictable as the weather, it does have, just like atmospheric phenomena, a certain climate determined by fundamental, institutional realities. The final chapter asks the volume contributors to reasonably speculate about institutional media developments in the near and distant future, including propositions for regulating or deregulating media to facilitate those development that are positive or to prevent the ones that may be negative. The chapter extrapolates from what is known to what is completely unknown, revealing some unexpected hopes, fears, and possibilities.

Our hope is the current volume provides a forward-looking vision of the issues that regulation and regulators need to pay attention to in the future through its contemporary scholarship and the caliber of the contributors. We believe that the pluralistic vision of the volume has created new frameworks to consider about media regulation. Some of these frameworks include: proposing new and justified motivations for regulating the potential deleterious effects of media platformization, creating legislations that make sense for the heterogeneous members of the UE, and encouraging media organizations and their users to be partners in a process of co-regulation. These and many other yet-to-be-revealed challenges and opportunities make the study of media transformation and regulation at this historic crossroad a rich territory of research, through which this volume has only blazed one trail of exploration.

References

Bertot, John Carlo, Paul T. Jaeger, and Derek Hansen. 2012. The Impact of Polices on Government Social Media Usage: Issues, Challenges, and Recommendations. *Government Information Quarterly* 29 (1): 30–40.

Brannon, Valerie. 2019. Free Speech and the Regulation of Social Media Content. R45650. Washington, DC: Congressional Research Service. https://doi.org/10.1201/b22397-4.

Forrest, Ed, and Yong Cao. 2010. Opinions, Recommendations and Endorsements: The New Regulatory Framework for Social Media. *Journal of Business and Policy Research* 5 (2): 88–99.

Napoli, Philip M. 2019. *Social Media and the Public Interest: Media Regulation in the Disinformation Age*. Columbia University Press.

Picard, Robert G. 2020. *Media and Communications Policy Making: Processes, Dynamics and International Variations*, 1st ed. 2020 edition. Palgrave Macmillan.

Schwanholz, Julia, Todd Graham, and Peter-Tobias Stoll (eds.). 2017. *Managing Democracy in the Digital Age: Internet Regulation, Social Media Use, and Online Civic Engagement*, 1st ed. 2018 edition. Springer.

The Audiovisual Industry Facing the Digital Revolution: Plunging the Predigital Fishbowl into the Digital Ocean

Nicolas Curien

1 Introduction

The main purpose of this article is to understand the transformations presently at work in the audiovisual industry and its regulation as being part of the more global process of digital transition. Once we emphasize this inclusive pattern, we then aim to identify what the collective invention of a desirable digital audiovisual future could look like.

In Sect. 2, we discuss the main features of the digital transition. Unpredictability and pervasiveness of digital usage and technologies generate a global and immersive ecosystem, within which economic and social players are fully embedded (2.1). As it alters cognitive and not only operational capabilities, the digital transition is before all a cognitive revolution, differing in this regard from the previous industrial revolutions of the eighteenth and nineteenth century based on mechanics and chemistry (2.2). Expected impacts are substantial and hit all aspects of human activities and concerns: economy, society, governance, ethics… (2.3). Section 2 aims to give an overview of the global digital context; it might be skipped by readers mainly interested in evolutions within the audiovisual industry.

N. Curien (✉)
Académie des Technologies, Paris, France

S. A. Matei et al. (eds.), *Digital and Social Media Regulation*,
https://doi.org/10.1007/978-3-030-66759-7_2

In Sect. 3, we contemplate the particular case of the audiovisual industry. We first analyze the two industrial and cognitive dimensions of the ongoing audiovisual transformations (3.1). These are mainly driven by the increasing influence of online platforms as matchers of content requests and proposals and as audience aggregators (3.2). Platforms challenge both competition and content regulatory bodies, respectively, because of their dominant market position and their prescriptive orientation of consumer choices (3.3). In this fastly moving environment, audiovisual regulation must itself evolve and adapt in two different directions: extending its scope to digital players, and adopting more flexible and adaptive methods, based on soft law rather than just coercion as in the past (3.4).

In Sect. 4, we assert that, in the digital era, the future must be proactively invented rather than passively predicted. After a short historical perspective of the principles and methods of future analysis over time (4.1), we characterize two contrasting attitudes when facing the future: fore-acting versus forecasting (4.2). A tentative application of the fore-acting approach to the evolution of the audiovisual industry is then carried out, resulting in three scenarios: (i) a neutral idle line one in which tomorrow's audiovisual sector globally resembles today's, except for some expectable and non disruptive effects of technological progress; (ii) a desirable and symbiotic scenario, in which the "fishbowl" of incumbent audiovisual actors is smoothly embedded into a global "digital ocean" where historical players cooperate and share value with pure players through win-win deals; (iii) a catastrophic and divide scenario, in which the digital ocean would become an hostile and dangerous ecosystem dominated by a narrow oligopoly of gigantic platforms providing poor audiovisual content and aiming to their own private interest rather than promoting public welfare. It is indeed up to us, through making relevant present decisions, to make the desirable future eventually happen as the actual future (4.3).

The predigital fishbowl plunged into the digital ocean!

2 The Main Features of the Digital Transition

Digital Is Both Unpredictable and Pervasive

Two stories illustrate the unpredictable and pervasive nature of the digital world. The first story refers to Vinton Cerf, one of the pioneers of the Internet. Once asked about the opportunity of "ruling" the Internet, he answered something of the kind:

- Are you claiming that the Internet could be ruled? To achieve such a crazy purpose, you should know in the first place what is going on in the Internet! Imagine a bowl of spaghetti. Imagine this plate placed in a working washing machine. Imagine this washing machine embedded inside the rotor of a concrete mixer. And finally imagine this whole system hanging from a rope bridge during an earthquake. Now, be honest with me: could you tell what is the exact equation describing the dynamics of the sauce?

Such is the very essence of the Internet, being a continuous creation by the crowd of its users in a permanent "impermanence"! The blood running in the veins of the network is not merely a flow of bytes. It is much more than that, namely a torrent of bursting innovation. The main attribute of the Internet is to be a "cauldron of creativity". And such is the only relevant formulation as any other definition of the

Internet's "essence" would immediately be violated by Internet's "existence". Contrary to most familiar objects, the Internet definitely cannot be reduced to a predefined menu of its potential usages, since it is the place for an open and bottom-up innovation process, emanating from the user base. The only manual of Internet usage is the user herself!

The second story reports a discussion between a baby boomer and his grandson or granddaughter. The grandfather is showing to the young millennial old pictures from the times of his own childhood. Looking at it, the child is surprised by the total absence of personal computers, digital tablets, mobile phones, and other electronic devices. Then, he asks:

– Hey, Granddad, you had no computers at that time?

With a touch of secret satisfaction and retrospective relief, Granddad answers:

– This is perfectly true, my dear, we had no such devices!

The child's reply is immediate and guided by an irrefutable logic:

– Then, Granddad, how did you surf the Internet?

In the eyes of a digital native, a world without Internet is just an unconceivable world that never could have been real, for the simple reason that a digital native "thinks", and thus "is", through the Internet. He or she chats with friends through instant messaging, listens to music downloaded from sharing platforms, socializes via social networks, learns from Wikipedia, etc. Human cognitive functions are today all affected and altered by Internet usage, in such a way that those born in the "matrix" cannot even imagine any preexisting system.

The Digital Transition Is Both Industrial and Cognitive

Bringing together the messages from the above two stories yields an important key to better understand what really is the so-called digital transition and why it differs in depth from the two previous industrial revolutions that occurred in the eighteenth and nineteenth centuries. The latter gave birth to material objects such as the plane, the train, or the car, which certainly changed drastically the economic and social organization, but left the cognitive dimensions of human life unchanged.

Of course, on the one hand, the penetration of digital technologies and the rolling out of electronic networks are the driving forces of a third industrial revolution, since they generate deep and transversal mutations in the way of designing, providing, distributing, and consuming economic goods and services. On the other hand, this industrial revolution also is a cognitive one, as information and communication technologies are not reducible to mere machine tools and rather generate a surrounding environment in which individuals do speak out, exchange, establish links, work, and entertain... in brief in which they "are".

In this respect, information technologies exhibit a feature that technologies issued from the progress of mechanics or chemistry do not. The Internet is not just a tool made by the human hand in order to be used as its prosthetic extension. It rather constitutes a "global object" in the philosophical sense, *i.e.*, an artifact relative to which we are both in an external and internal position, since we all elaborate and post on the Internet the creations of our minds in a continuous process. The global object named Internet may indeed be seen as a prosthetic extension of the brain rather than of the hand; or, more exactly, as a collective and shared extension of all human brains, literally a "noosphere", *i.e.*, a sphere of the minds. In short, whereas past industrial revolutions operated in the "technosphere", made of material items, the digital transition operates in the "noosphere", made of cognitive items.

The neologism "noosphere" is by no means a recent one. At the beginning of the twentieth century, far before the invention of the Internet, two geologists, Vladimir Vernadski and Pierre Teilhard de Chardin, invented the concept of brains' interconnection all over the planet, and they called it the "noosphere" (Teilhard de Chardin 1955). In the vision of Teilhard, who also was a Jesuit theologian, the noosphere, coming after the biosphere, coming itself after the geosphere, constitutes the third and last step in a cosmogony bringing the Universe from its starting point Alpha of pure matter to its ultimate point Omega of pure spirit. Teilhard, who did foresee the noosphere as a kind of biofilm, surrounding the atmosphere, would likely today be astonished to "discover his invention" under the appearance of a spider's web named Internet, made of electronic routers and optical fibers. In his vision, he certainly missed the physical shape of the noosphere but he was perfectly relevant as regards its function: bringing human brains together into a "collective mind".

Of course, the noosphere did not emerge from scratch with the apparition of the Internet. It has existed for long but evolved at a much slower pace in the past. About 5 million years seem to separate the birth of humanity from the use of articulated speech, which probably occurred around 500,000 years ago. The first paintings in grottos date back to 50,000 years ago, the first written texts back to 5,000 years, the first printed book back to 500 years, the invention of Internet back to 50 years ago, the first development of the Internet of things to 5 years ago… What is fascinating here is the logarithmic character of this time scale: what has been realized in the Internet arena during the last five years likely compares to the improvement of cognitive capabilities of *homo erectus* during the five hundred thousand years going from the first speech to the first rock painting.

This does not mean, however, that we are about to reach some "S" point of singularity. It just means that big data, mobile connectivity, cloud computing, and social networking do exponentially increase the pace of occurrence of "digital events" in a given frame of time. In other words, all these phenomena increase the density of the noosphere along the timeline. It also means that neutral connectivity becomes as essential to humankind as drinkable water, so that countries which deny net neutrality by restricting open access to the Internet sin heavily against civilization… sadly recalling, in a way, the censorship achieved by the Inquisition in the times following Gutenberg's invention.

Any major seism occurring in the noosphere enforces transformations in all the aspects of human organization and activity. Economy is changed, society is transformed, political governance is altered, the guidelines of moral and ethics move as well. Let us give a very rough view of the main driving forces at work in these four different "orders".

Some Major Impacts of the Digital Transition

In the economic order, the main impact of the digital revolution consists in a "flattening" of costs and utilities, which do no longer depend significantly on the supplied and consumed quantities, but quasi-exclusively on the conditions of access. In an electronic network, the additional cost of transporting and managing an extra byte is almost zero, the main cost being the fixed initial cost of installing the network's capacity. Symmetrically, from a web user's standpoint, the utility derived from an extra byte is almost deprived of sense, as what mainly matters is the utility of acceding to an "all you can eat" information corpus. Behind the flatness of costs and utilities lies a revolutionary agent: since increasing the quantity of information costs and benefits almost nothing at the margin, economic theory states that the efficient price of a byte is zero!

This, of course, does not imply that information, as an economic good, should be delivered free of charge, but it implies that the access to information should be provided against a lump sum payment, such as a subscription fee. Fixed costs and utilities do imply fixed prices. One should pay when entering the Ali Baba's digital grotto but, once entered, one should be offered free disposal of all digital jewels present in the magical place. The digital economy is an economy of profusion. This has a major impact on cultural industries (books, music, movies), which have built their pre-digital business model upon the sale of units, rather than upon the sale of access. These industries now face the need to adapt their model, which has been made obsolete by digital technology and which cannot survive for long, even with the "help" of ephemeral legal devices to maintain the ancient system.

In the social order, what the Internet has essentially brought about is a ubiquitous and immediate one-to-one interconnection. Although social scientists rightly point out that most often "friends" on social networks are not real friends, and that the number of people with whom one maintains close links has not changed very much with Internet usage, it would be a severe mistake to draw the conclusion that information technologies did not move the lines of social linkage. In this regard, the Internet gave rise to three important phenomena, namely "instrumental intimacy", "serendipity", and "long tail".

(i) Although my friends on social networks are not intimate friends, they are indeed "instrumental relationships", posting on the Web a myriad of data that do help me to retrieve more accurate information, to get better value from my professional curriculum, to consume in a more advised way, and so on. Precisely because those friends are not real friends, one may "use" them as "resources" without complying to the rituals of standard sociability.

(ii) Going erratically from one "friend" to another may generate unexpected findings during a free surfing on the Web, just in the way the Lords of Serendip, according to the tale, ride from discovery to discovery through the antique Perse.

(iii) Because most of my friends online are not my real friends, they and I build and share on the Web a "long tail" of data: each unit of content bears an infinitesimal value when considered separately, but all units make up altogether a huge corpus of an inestimable utility, as each of us may get out of it what happens *hic et nunc* to be the most relevant.

Such is the cognitive power of the crowd. The blogosphere on the Net is nothing else but Teilhard's noosphere!

In the political order, the Internet challenges the modalities of governance, at every level.

Often mentioned is the ability of the Net, as a worldwide network ignoring geographical borders, to generate behaviors that stand out of the direct control of the States: The Internet is accused of bypassing national laws, creating fiscal evasion, violating trade settlements, harming intellectual property, dispatching fake news, hosting hatred speech… in brief creating a cyber-criminality which proves very difficult to fight through standard means of the pre-digital world.

Often mentioned too, is the electronic tribune that the Net offers to political leaders, enabling them to increase considerably their audience, an opportunity which is counterbalanced by the capacity of citizens to create online efficient lobbies and influential communities, or to post informational "leaks" which may become highly explosive electronic bombs.

At first view, the growing impact of these phenomena seems to call for an Internet "regulation". But which form such a regulation could well take? How one could regulate the random dynamics of the bowl of spaghetti so nicely described by Vinton Cerf, without wasting at the same time the special flavor of the pasta? In other words, how to find the way off the following paradox:

To regulate amounts to reducing uncertainty.
The very richness of Internet is to be unpredictable.
Hence, regulating the Internet means downgrading the Internet.

The solution lies in finding a new path for regulation, a path which might be summarized in the following "commandments".

- To move progressively from a prescriptive regulation, which forbids and punishes, to a regulation inspired by the Socratic maieutic, which is based on incentives.
- To give up a regulation in which the regulator dictates to the princess which frog she should kiss in order to make her prince appear, and rather adopt a regulation in which the regulator prepares the most favorable scenery for creative kisses to occur!
- To forget, to a certain extent, about the administrative in vitro regulation centered on problem solving and promote a regulation in vivo, based on the delivery of solutions by the market players themselves.
- To move, whenever possible, from a centralized regulation toward a self-organized regulation, *i.e.,* an auto-regulation, however possibly supervised.
- To move from a compartmented regulation toward a shared and cooperative regulation, *i.e.*, a co-regulation associating several regulatory bodies in a same economic sector or in interrelated sectors.

In the ethical order, the Internet affects the conditions in which fundamental human rights are respected, especially freedom of speech and privacy. Online practices may generate conflicts between these two rights. For instance, while aiming to secure personal data or to protect fragile audiences from undesirable content, one may, at the same time, restrict freedom of expression by implementing insufficiently targeted remedies. Conversely, permitting an unconditional liberty of expression on the Web would cause damage, as it would hinder the eradication of obnoxious content favoring radicalization, promoting xenophobia and discrimination or exhibiting pedophilia.

The enforcement of these fundamental rights may also conflict with the defense of a variety of other rights. For instance, free file sharing online does harm intellectual property. Another example, administrative interceptions requested by the Police or Justice authorities for the sake of national security impact the privacy of citizens.

Thus, the pervasive irruption of the Internet in everyday life and social behavior shifts the balance between different rights, resulting in disputes. Besides the legal settlement of these disputes in a continued process, an ethical approach is imperative in order to analyze the evolution of practices and to better define what is deemed as being acceptable and desirable in a democratic society.

The link between digital technologies and sustainable development is too often reduced to the sole Green IT issue. This legitimate specific aspiration must not make us forget that information technologies being themselves a constitutive part of development, not to say the engine of it, they chiefly contribute to the building-up and to the preservation of our welfare. The "digital ecology", *i.e.*, the study and the monitoring of evolutionary digital ecosystems, thus appears to be a critical problematic. We all are co-responsible for—and co-regulators of—the quality of our digital environment, an imperious necessity at the dawn of the upcoming era of robots and artificial intelligence.

3 Digital Transformation of the Audiovisual Industry

The Audiovisual Industry Stands at the Core of the Two-Pronged Digital Transition

The digital transition has led to the imposing omnipresence of a new socio-economic ecosystem centered on communication, information, and knowledge with the binary digits as the universal reference system. In this regard, we have seen above the extent to which the Internet is both similar to the steam engines and to printing. The steam engine drove the industrial revolution that transformed business models across all economic sectors, while printing was the catalyst of a cognitive revolution that disrupted the conditions of access to cultural and information content as well as the modes of creating, publishing, distributing, and sharing that same content.

By its very essence, the audiovisual industry is located at the confluence of the industrial and cognitive currents of the digital transition (see Fig. 1).

- On the industrial side, the audiovisual sector has reconstructed itself. First, it has done so with advent of the new actors who have emerged from the digital economy: Over the top (OTT) service providers, online distributors, and publishers, such as Netflix, Roku, or Apple TV, search engines, app stores, social media, video sharing sites.

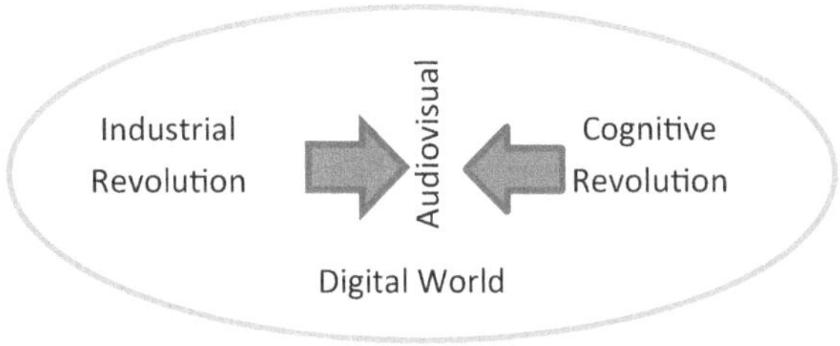

Fig. 1 The digital transition: two revolutions in one

Second, it has done so with the progressive blurring of the borders of what until now had been the separable functions of content production, publishing, broadcasting, and distribution.

- On the cognitive side, audiovisual content, strictly speaking, has been itself submerged in the immensity of a "digital ocean", plunged into a collection of much broader, multimedia content types that hybridize texts, sounds, and images in a mix of work by professionals and amateurs. This protean collection of content is increasingly accessible on demand in non-linear viewing formats and becomes available for viewing almost "seamlessly" on a variety of mobile, portable, and non-portable device screens.

The Dual Role of Platforms: Matching Processors and Audience Aggregators

"Platforms" occupy a singular position in the transformed landscape of the digital era. Expressed in a stylized fashion, these online intermediaries, as suppliers of audiovisual content, play a very similar role to that of a village market. They offer a space where consumers and merchants are put in contact with one another. This contact space generates "cross-side network effects": the larger the number of consumers using the platform, the greater the number of providers who are drawn to being present on it and to offering richer, more varied content. Reciprocally, the presence of many suppliers attracts more consumers. At that point, the platform manager can take advantage of the synergy loop linking its two client "sides", which, in turn, causes a dynamic snowballing of growth, possibly reinforced by introducing asymmetrical pricing, which benefits the side whose greater numbers create the greatest gain to the actors on the other side.

To qualify a platform's business activity, economic theory uses the term: "two-sided market", where the word "market" should be understood as a marketplace, that is, as the support for an intermediation. Two-sided markets came into existence before the digital era. In particular, free television is a two-sided market that came out of the pre-digital era and created a relationship between television viewers and advertisers. Like this emblematic model that founded the media economy, most platforms that supply content online have advertisers as a third player. These advertisers bring in money from selling ad space, and the revenue subsidizes access to the platform of the first two players, namely the content providers and content consumers, and, most often, enables users to access content completely free of charge.

In short, digital platforms appear as three-sided structures (see Fig. 2), or more precisely, they are "doubly two-sided", setting up an initial relationship between publishers and users where the platform acts as a "matching processor" while a second two-sided relationship connects users to advertisers as an "audience aggregator". In particular, this scheme prevails for the YouTube video sharing platform and, increasingly, for the social network Facebook, both of which have become major actors worldwide in the distribution of audiovisual content in the broad sense.

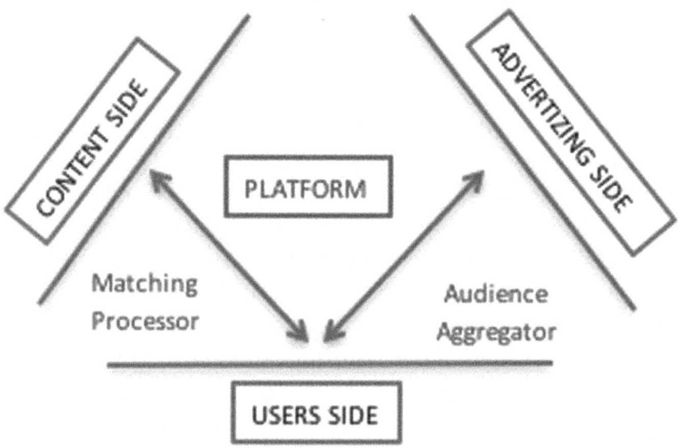

Fig. 2 Digital platforms are multi-sided systems

Platforms Challenge Competition Law and Sectoral Regulation

Characterized in this manner, online platforms appear as key actors in the audiovisual sector's digital transition, from both industrial and cognitive viewpoints.

- As regards the industrial aspect, due to the economies of scale derived from their high fixed costs, and to the network effects that give rise to them and then feed their dizzying growth, platforms tend to be gigantic. Their huge sizes confer on them a solidly advantageous position in their relationships with other parties, and with regard to the revenue-sharing rules they negotiate with partners on the different sides of the marketplaces they shape: content providers, advertisers, or even mere online users.
- As regards the cognitive aspect, to carry out their role as a processor of matches, platforms act as artificial intelligence agents, matching content requests to content offers. To do so, they use software algorithms to orient demand through the hyper-offer maze and thereby significantly influence the structure of cultural content consumption. Whether they are used by platforms or on-demand audiovisual media services, it is advisable to guarantee the "loyalty" of these algorithms and ensure they are not excessively biased toward business interests. Also, care must be taken not to enclose consumers in a bubble that exploits their usual transactions but that does point them toward exploration of new cultural horizons serendipitously.

As an emerging phenomenon, the growing power of platforms in the audiovisual business landscape raises a series of novel problems for fair competition authorities and audiovisual industry regulators.

First, from the point of view of competition law, the planet-wide scale of platforms, their force as market oligopolies or, even monopolies, engenders the non-negligible risk of abusing their ultra-dominant positions. This explains the necessity for competition authorities to maintain the "contestability" of multi-sided intermediary markets, that is, by lowering entry barriers, reducing costs for consumers of switching to another supplier, incentivizing innovation, and, in short, creating a situation that ensures that these "Colossuses with feet of clay" operating in the market places may only keep their supremacy in a transitory manner as long as they remain more innovative and efficient than potential rivals.

Second, from the point of view of regulating the audiovisual sector, the soaring development of platforms has created many additional challenges that can be summarized by the twelve questions below according to a study carried out by the CSA in 2016 (CSA 2016).

1. How are publishers of audiovisual works to be guaranteed fair and effective exposure on platforms?
2. Upstream from platform business activity, does the framework for applying the net neutrality principle need adaptation to ensure content providers have non-discriminatory access to electronic communication networks?
3. Should content indexing conditions, as normally practiced by platforms, be improved?
4. How is the "biodiversity" objective in the production and consumption of culture best achieved in an ocean of digital content? How can diversity be strengthened when non-linear individual selection of content, which is desired by consumers and facilitated by existing prescriptive algorithms, paradoxically constitutes a factor of uniformization under the guise of being customization?
5. How does one, to the advantage of the consumer, act as a catalyst for innovation and spur greater variety within a range of services and applications, where a situation of concentration of operating systems exists that might lead to an impoverishment dynamic via a homogenization effect?
6. What fair balance should be struck between the fundamental rights of freedom of expression and consumer protection? Are the current modalities of online moderation adopted by platforms sufficiently satisfying in this regard, and are they sufficient in and of themselves?
7. Do the present legal framework and resources currently deployed by platforms provide useful, effective protection to those entitled to these rights? What fair balance may be struck between the broadest possible access to content and distribution of works that adheres to copyright and intellectual property?
8. Does user targeting, or even hyper-targeting, as allowed by programmatic advertising, represent a premium for the consumer or is this an intrusive practice? Can this targeting, by improving

consumer experience, be a countermove to the development of ad blockers?

9. Is programmatic advertising likely to extend the reach of a computer, tablet, or portable device to the living room's TV screen? And if it does, what impact will it have on the historical business model of free broadcast television?
10. The capture of data usage by platforms, and the processing and possible transfer of this data, mark a new stage in audiovisual consumption in its coming out of the age of anonymity. What will be the societal consequences, and, above all, the economic consequences, in an era when data has become "the 21st century's black gold"?
11. Collecting data that has a value will inevitably raises the question of sharing it. In this regard, are business relationships between platforms and traditional audiovisual actors likely to lead spontaneously to balanced sharing among the various parties along the value chain?
12. The last, but no less critical challenge, is: Should the system for financing audiovisual content and film production be reformed in the long term? How, and under what type of arrangement, should OTT actors, particularly digital platforms, contribute to financing creation?

Audiovisual Regulation Should Become Incentivizing, Cooperative, and Reflective

The challenges above are related to a series of three major problems. The first is the exposure of content, its indexing, and promotion of cultural diversity (see items 1 to 5 above). The second is protection of consumers and content rights holders in a context of responsible control for, and of, personal data (items 6 to 10), and the third is value sharing and content and network access financing (items 11 and 12). For each of these issues, the difficulty is not so much about coming up with new and original arrangements, but is rather disencumbrance from past tendencies such that a transition path acceptable to all the parties involved is possible. How does one then subject these actors, with their worldwide grip on the Internet, to an assortment of adapted measures, which, necessarily, will strongly clash with a regulatory system that was conceived in a national framework and pre-digital era?

Furthermore, the issues reveal that the audiovisual regulator—as well as those who regulate electronic communications, the protection of personal data, and the distribution of works over the Internet—are not outside of the scope of their own complementary regulations, but are, on the contrary, bound by, if not embedded in, the dynamic of digital transition, in the same manner as the very business actors they are regulating. Regulators, too, are seeing a shift in the center of gravity of their activities; they, too, must react with agility in response to the two-pronged industrial and cognitive earthquake shaking their own terrains so strongly.

In terms of the audiovisual regulator in particular, a double "worksite" has already been started at the national and European levels dealing with both the scope of the material and geographical competencies of regulation and its procedural methodology:

- Extension of the domain of competencies is necessary because the digital world opens up new virtual territories without clear-cut borders. Historical regulations cannot be exported "as is" into them but, inversely, the digital spaces must not totally ignore fundamental goals set by public policies, particularly, in matters of freedom of expression, the protection of personal data and the promotion of creating works and enhancing cultural diversity (see above).
- Concomitantly, there must be an evolution in methods and procedures because the very fast pace of change of, and in, technologies and usages require regulators to have greater flexibility and adaptability. This must translate into making greater use of soft law; more co-regulation with other actors in the sector; strengthened cooperation with other regulatory bodies acting in the content and infrastructure sphere; and limitation of the prescriptive framework to the strictest necessary perimeter while implementing a plan of incentivizing measures.

In a constantly changing digital universe where technologies and its uses are being transformed by a Darwinian model ruled by innovation and disruption, regulation must take into account this structural uncertainty by becoming more adaptive and more "reflective". Reflective regulation first consists of anticipating the likeliest scenarios that will develop in the sector, and second, it is about accompanying the actors on their self-chosen development path with the goal of guaranteeing the most efficacious forward movement, both socially and business-wise. And, third, it consists of adapting regulatory schemes to give them greater flexibility and the capacity to resist to inevitable occurrence of unforeseen events. Anticipate, Accompany, and Adapt are the sign of a "Triple A" reflective regulation.

4 Inventing the Future

A Short Perspective About Future Analysis

During antiquity, forecasting was not a scientific practice. Only Gods were supposed to know about the future and they could be consulted through oracles, such as the famous Delphic oracle, Pythia. Forecasting then consisted in the interpretation of oracles, which were generally ambiguous messages, as when Pythia told Croesus: "If you make war, then a big empire will be destroyed"... In this oracle, a critical point remained undetermined: Which empire will be destroyed? On the basis of an optimistic interpretation, Croesus attacked Cyrus... and he realized *ex post*, once defeated, that although the oracle was right, he had misinterpreted it.

Scientific progress then brought about the deterministic view of a future lying in the continuity of the present and the past, naturally leading to the idea that scanning what already happened might help to predict what will occur... as this is ideally the case in physics for a system of material bodies subject to the fundamental laws of mechanics: assuming that one perfectly knows the present state of such a system, then all future states are perfectly determined as well.

Over time, the elaboration of more and more sophisticated quantitative tools, based on the statistical analysis of past and present data, allowed forecasters to build more and more likely "models" of the future and to propose them to the wise appreciation of decision makers, as oracles of the modern times. Nevertheless, despite of their increased relevance, the scientific instruments for exploring the future structurally suffer from two major drawbacks.

- First, the reliability of models is strongly limited since the past and the present, not only future, are very imperfectly known, and predictive algorithms prove to be very sensitive to even small variations in the uncertain data used as inputs: the models show a chaotic behavior which makes predictions very fragile beyond a certain horizon of time.

- Second and not least, by very construction, one may only predict what is *ex ante* located in the set of "expectable" outcomes. Unexpected outcomes are necessarily out of the scope of forecasting. For instance, the Fukushima nuclear accident in 2011 could not be expected from the set of available data, as this set excluded the very possibility of an accumulation of the exceptional factors which altogether led to the catastrophic outcome.

Dramatic events are far from being the only ones that fall into the traps of forecasting. Indeed, what occurs in daily social or economic life is most often what was unexpected, as beautifully expressed in the title of a novel by André Maurois: "Toujours l'inattendu arrive" (Maurois 1943). The usage of telephone and Minitel in France was unforeseen and even wrongly foreseen, not to speak of the Internet, the world champion of unpredictable technologies. In the digital era, *i.e.*, in a world of permanent innovation, unpredictability is indeed a structural and beneficial feature... which makes standard forecasting irrelevant by nature. Just remember Vinton Cerf's striking image of the spaghetti bowl!

To overcome the curse of unpredictability, an alternative approach to forecasting, called "Prospective" or "Future Analysis", was developed after the Second World War in France, with the works of Gaston Berger and Bertrand de Jouvenel (Berger 1964; Jouvenel 1967). In this approach, the future is no longer considered as an object of prediction, but rather as an object of desire. A desirable future, a "futurable" is "selected" from a number of possible scenarios and it is set as a goal to be reached at some given horizon of time. Then, reversing the arrow of time, the back path from this projected future toward the present time is carefully examined in a retrospective way, trying to answer this question: Which key issues will have to be solved at different critical intermediary stages, in order to make the desired futurable eventually occur as the real future, when the natural direction of time is restored? Following this logic, fore-acting is substituted for forecasting.

Contrary to forecasting, the aim of which is to provide decision makers with a quantified vision of the future relying upon "scientific neutrality", future analysis and the consequent fore-acting is a proactive, reflective, and mainly qualitative discipline: the decision-making process is included inside the very analysis, as a part of a same loop of thought, in which cognition and action are tightly associated. This mental loop breaks up the linear and causal sequence going from expertise to decision, which is present in the two frameworks of the Delphic oracle and of the standard forecasting approach.

Two Ways of Facing the Future: Forecasting vs. Fore-Acting

The difference between forecasting and fore-acting is not just a question of methodology. It expresses a fundamental divergence of attitudes toward the future, as enlightened by the Newcomb's paradox, an experience of thought due to Harvard professor of sociology Robert Nozick (1993) and popularized in France by the philosopher Jean-Pierre Dupuy (2004).

An infallible predictor presents two boxes X and Y and invites you to take either box X only or both boxes X and Y. Box Y is open and it contains a visible $1,000 check. Box X is closed and, the predictor says, either it contains $1,000,000 if the predictor guessed that you will take box X only, or it contains nothing if the predictor guessed that you will take both boxes X and Y. The content of the closed box X has been chosen by the predictor before you came and there is no way it can be changed. Then, what is your choice? Are you a 1-boxer or a 2-boxer? (see Fig. 3).

On the one hand, a rational standard forecaster will take the two boxes, on the basis of the following rationale: as the content of box X won't change anyway, whatever it might be, an extra $1,000 is most welcome... and as the predictor is infallible, then box X contains nothing, which is

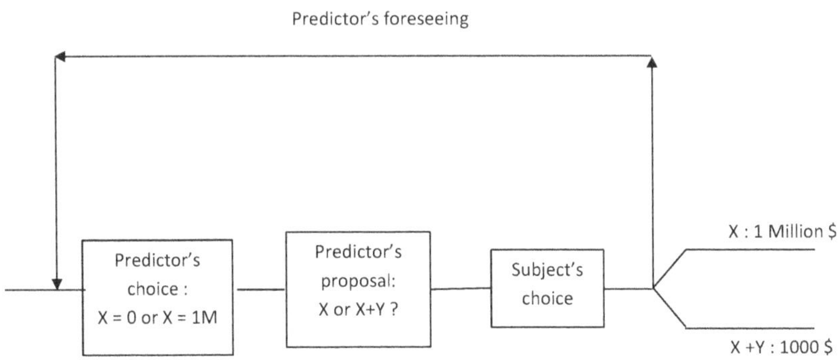

Fig. 3 The Newcomb's paradox

the only consistent forecast… a very convincing final argument for getting \$1,000 by taking the two boxes rather than getting nothing by taking only box X.

On the other hand, a fore-actor will take box X only, thus getting \$1,000,000… since the predictor is infallible. This is indeed a much better outcome than getting \$1,000 only, by taking the two boxes…

In the eyes of the forecaster, there exists only one line of time and the challenge is to predict rationally what this line is made of, before playing. In the eyes of the fore-actor, there are two potential lines of time, respectively, associated with the two possible contents of box X and the challenge is to play so as to "select" the most favorable line.

In the fore-acting perspective, the future is seen in the same way as the famous "Schrodinger's cat" of quantum mechanics, enclosed in its box, dead or alive. Just as the quantum state of the cat, the future is not "uncertain", it is rather "undetermined" or, more precisely, not yet determined. While the forecaster aims to reducing uncertainty through rational thinking before playing, the fore-actor reduces indetermination through his own decision making, *i.e.*, by playing. This shows the way to a "quantum decision theory", which would be to standard decision theory what indetermination is to uncertainty.

A game theorist would see in the Newcomb's paradox a strategic game exhibiting two perfect Bayesian equilibria: the 1-box equilibrium, in which the strategy of taking box X only is consistent with the belief that 1,000,000 \$ are enclosed in this box, and the 2-boxes equilibrium, in which the strategy of taking both boxes X and Y is consistent with the belief that box X contains nothing. In this formalized setting, the delicate issue of selecting a particular equilibrium is solved differently by the fore-actor and by the forecaster: whereas the latter is imprisoned in the "poor" 2-boxes equilibrium, because of his excess of rationality ($X + 1{,}000 > X$), the former refuses such a fatality and keeps the freedom of choosing the "rich" 1-box equilibrium, a freedom which is indeed left to him by the rules of the game, such as these are stated by the predictor.

Interestingly enough, when the game is played experimentally among a group of students, about half of them are 1-boxers and the other half, 2-boxers. Each of the two sub-groups is convinced that the other one behaves in a crazy way: the 2-boxers accuse the 1-boxers of practicing magic thinking, while the 1-boxers accuse the 2-boxers of mere stupidity!

This discussion brings us to the dialectic opposition between determinism and free will. In this regard, the Newcomb's paradox may be rephrased in terms of a cinematographic metaphor: although a movie is pre-written by its director, characters seem to act freely, as if alternative potential movies existed, in which they could act differently. This view reconciles in some way determinism and free will, as it allows the two to coexist at two different levels, namely determinism at the director's level and free will at the characters' level... just as does the presence of two potential lines of time instead of a single one, in the Newcomb's paradox. If we imagine that we are the characters, not in an ordinary movie, but in the big "movie of the Universe", then we are ready to behave as fore-actors.

To summarize, two distinct attitudes are possible when facing the not already existing future and contemplating action. On the one side, the "forecaster" thinks of himself as being a neutral "decoder" of the future and, on the other side, the "fore-player" stands as an engaged "architect" of the future: he does not try to guess an unknown future but rather succeeds in making a desirable one occur!

Today, the transition from decoding the future toward shaping it is enforced by the increasing dynamic complexity of economy and society in a digital world. In this upcoming world, innovators reign and they definitely are fore-actors, guided by their confidence in their success... just as in a fairy tale where the princess kisses the frog to make the prince appear. Frog kissing is the archetype of fore-acting!

Change is insidious and it always catches the forecaster off-guard but the fore-player, never!

A Tentative Application to the Audiovisual Sector

Within the CSALab, a think-tank created in 2016 by the CSA, the French regulator of the audiovisual sector, an exercise of future analysis has been carried out (Curien and Sonnac 2018), observing the general principles mentioned above and using a methodological framework designed by Michel Godet in his handbook of prospective (Godet 2007). The analysis was conducted in four steps.

In the first step, about forty experts were consulted about the strategies of major players in the sector, historical ones as well as new digital comers. Main stakes and challenges were identified for each player in the chain of value, and the inter-relationships across players were scrutinized.

In the second step, the panel was requested to analyze all cross-influence patterns inside a system of about seventy key factors driving the sector and related to the economic environment, the technological change in networks and devices, the evolution of content provision and usage and the scope of public and regulatory policies.

In the third step, based on the outcomes of the two first ones, three contrasted long-term scenarios at horizon 2030 were built up (see Fig. 4).

The middle line scenario

In this intermediate scenario, tomorrow's world globally resembles today's. Only the technological context and usage habits have changed, but in a non-disruptive way. The current debates within the audiovisual industry are still active as they have not yet reached clear conclusions. Historical players have adapted their organization in order to resist the growing power of the large, domineering Internet media companies, known as GAFA (Google, Apple, Facebook, Amazon), with which they try to negotiate a more favorable sharing of the value.

The symbiotic scenario

In this "desirable future", the "fishbowl" of the historical audiovisual sector lives in symbiosis with the digital ocean, inside which it is now completely embedded. Network and device technologies offer a neutral access to all content, be it linear or non-linear. Seen from the users, the

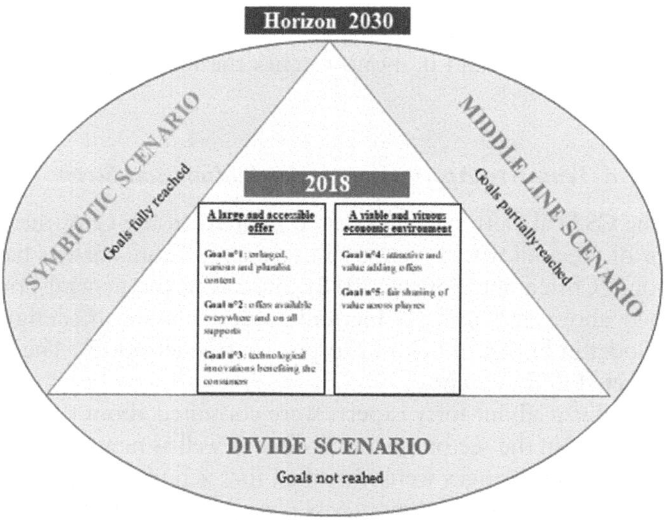

Fig. 4 Three contrasted scenarios at horizon 2030

audiovisual supply looks like a seamless fabric. And as regards the industry's organization, the players preexisting in the fishbowl, and those native from the digital ocean do nicely coexist in a virtuous ecosystem, in which win-win deals have been found for sharing the value of data.

The divide scenario

In this catastrophic Orwellian scenario, the digital world has become a hostile and dangerous one, split out by technological and social divides, a world in which the audiovisual industry has failed to preserve its identity and values. GAFA have swept out the traditional players and these giants reign as absolute masters on the provision of content, the quality of which is definitely out of hand. A significant fringe of the population, having no access to fiber and 5G fixed and mobile services, is offered downgraded services. Final usage is manipulated by opaque algorithms and A.I. agents, serving private interests and harming social welfare.

In the fourth and last step, the collective task of the panel of experts consisted in retropolating from the future backward to the present, in order to determine which key conditions should be fulfilled in the short and medium range, under the monitoring of public policy and regulation, to make the symbiotic scenario occur by 2030 rather than one of the two others. Two main necessary conditions have been identified in this perspective: (i) the audiovisual offer must be rich and available to all; (ii) all market players, i.e., right holders, publishers, distributors, network operators, and platforms, must compete and/or cooperate in a healthy and virtuous economic ecosystem. These conditions were then refined in five objectives for public payers and for the industry.

Objective 1: Encouraging the provision of rich, diversified, and pluralist content.

Authors and producers are the source of creativeness and quality of audiovisual programs, which publishers finance at a significant level. To make the content provision altogether rich, various and pluralist, a right balance across these different players should be sought for, in order to guarantee authors' independency and to increase the investment capacity of those who finance creation. Reaching this objective requires three levers of action:

(i) The obligations imposed to providers of audiovisual services to finance and to distribute programs issued locally by independent production firms should be maintained for the sake of diversity and pluralism.

(ii) These obligations should be adapted and harmonized across the different players, in order to erase regulation asymmetries as today exist between linear and non-linear services, between services using hertzian spectrum and those delivered through IP platforms, or between domestic and foreign services.
(iii) A reflection about the public utility missions of government-owned broadcasters in the digital age must be undertaken.

Levers (i) and (ii) were operated in December 2020 when transposing the AMS European directive into French law. Lever (iii) is currently in progress.

Objective 2: Making content available and easily findable everywhere and on all supports.

To reach this objective, the rolling out of broadband and ultra broadband networks, the coverage of white zones, as well as observing the net neutrality principle are necessary but not sufficient conditions. Complementary levers must be operated.

(i) Maintaining a free and universal TV and radio broadcasting platform is essential as other distribution platforms bill a subscription fee and don't offer a uniform quality of service all over the country. Accordingly, the hertzian terrestrial platform must be upgraded in order to fit new usage behaviors and market standards, especially as concerns interactivity and programmatic advertizing. The 2024 Olympic Games in Paris could be an important milestone in the broadcast modernization process.
(ii) Rules framing net neutrality and the opening of consumer devices and operating systems have to be considered. Such rules should be set in a way not to harm innovation; nor forbid all type of exclusive deals, which would be detrimental to the production of premium content and thus to consumer's welfare. This issue is presently being discussed among european regulators.
(iii) In this context, developing cooperation across different regulatory bodies at the national and european levels, in order to adopt aligned positions and avoid inconsistent decisions, is a key prerequisite.

Objective 3: Stimulating user-centric technological progress.

Investment in technology and in consumer interface is necessary to offer users the best possible experience. Whatever their needs and habits of usage, they should have access to the whole audiovisual offer in a nice and friendly digital environment. The use of algorithms and artificial intelligence for the presentation and delivery of audiovisual content must comply with transparency and fairness principles applying to service providers and users. Combining several actions will efficiently ensure consumer protection and accessibility of works.

(i) Media literacy and education to the digital world proves to be an appropriate lever to orient users toward a wise consumption of audiovisual content online. Endeavors already made in this direction should be encouraged, increased, and pursued at a larger scale.

(ii) The platforms' weak obligations to disclose the inner mechanism of their algorithms must be strengthened, in the view of a clear and transparent understanding of the origin of content recommendations online. In this regard, although it does not address all societal concerns brought about by platforms, the implementation of the European rulings for the use and protection of personal data (GDPR) is a crucial stake for the years to come.

Objective 4: Generating maximal value from content through attractive audiovisual offers.

Generation of value proceeds through advertizing revenues as concerns free TV offers or through subscription fees as concerns pay TV and VOD services.

(i) Restoring a path of growth in the audiovisual advertizing market requires virtuous practices to sanitize relationships between players while offering the consumer less intrusive and more acceptable adds. To this purpose, professional auto-regulation has so far been successful and should continue to be.

(ii) However, one-sided decisions and «private police» behaviors should not occur. To avoid this danger, a desirable regulation design should rely upon concentrations bringing together all the economic stake holders. In this regard, co-regulation which instills soft rule making into the game appears as an efficient instrument, reconciling the economic goals of players with public interest considerations and warranting operational effectiveness. Designing such a supervision device is a today's priority.

(iii) Drastic obligations presently imposed to publishers in terms of advertisement volumetric caps, exclusion of some products, or prohibition of segmented and geolocalized messages should be significantly relaxed in order to facilitate the ongoing sector's mutations and to enable publishers to face on a level playing field the strong competitive pressure coming from online companies which currently drive the major part of the growing advertizing revenues.

(iv) A better understanding by the users of the sustainable business models at work in the cultural industries could contribute to develop willingness to pay for content and to reduce the incentives to consume illegally. Here again, media literacy is a precious tool.

(v) Last but not least, IP-TV offers should match the heterogeneous expectations of consumers who differ with respect to their respective budget constraints and patterns of preferences. Public authorities might incentivize the development of both supply and demand: by decreasing the publishers' charges on the supply side (e.g., through tax credits) and by subsidizing the access of audience to content on the demand side.

Objective 5: Fully benefiting from the upcoming economy of data through a fair sharing across players.

The balance of power between historical players and platforms should be shifted, in order to prevent the decline of the former to the benefit of the latter and to ensure the funding of creation upstream of the value chain. Such a shift is also necessary to preserve investment of telcos in the rolling out of broadband and ultra broadband networks all over the national territory. To reach this objective, two main levers of action must be operated.

(i) Tools for measuring audience, assessing performance, and collecting data of usage should be developed and made more efficient, transparent, and harmonized.
(ii) A global reform of the legal status of different categories of players, such as publishers, distributors, or hosts, is necessary, as well as a clarification of the respective obligations attached to each of these particular status. This should reduce asymmetries due to the inadequation of the present regulatory framework. The national transposition of the AMS european directive in December 2020 made a major step in this direction.

* * *

In the audiovisual industry as in any other, little by little, the noospheric spider weaves its cobweb. What tomorrow will be made of? The answer is indeed: it will be made of what we all shall make it!

References

Berger, Gaston. 1964. *Phénoménologie du temps et prospective*. Paris: PUF.

CSA. Sept. 2016. «Plateformes et accès aux contenus audiovisuels». http://www.csa.fr.

Curien, Nicolas, and Nathalie Sonnac. 2018. *Avenir de l'audiovisuel: construire le meilleur*. Paris, France: Conseil Supérieur de l'Audiovisuel. https://www.csa.fr/Informer/CSA-lab/Les-publications/Avenir-de-l-audiovisuel-construire-le-meilleur.

Dupuy, Jean-Pierre. 2004. *Pour un catastrophisme éclairé. Quand l'impossible est certain*. Seuil: Points Editions.

Godet, Michel. 2007. *Manuel de prospective stratégique* (2 tomes), Tome 1 "L'indiscipline intellectuelle", Tome 2 "L'art et la méthode". 3ème edition. Dunod: Dunod.

Jouvenel, Bertrand (de). 1967. *The Art of Conjecture*. New York: Routledge.

Maurois, André. 1943. *Toujours l'inattendu arrive: contes et nouvelles*. New York, NY: Éditions de la Maison française.

Nozick, Robert. 1993. *The Nature of Rationality*. Princeton: Princeton University Press.

Teilhard de Chardin, Pierre. 1955. *Le phenomene humain*. Paris: Edit. du Seuil.

Revisiting the Rationales for Media Regulation: The *Quid Pro Quo* Rationale and the Case for Aggregate Social Media User Data as Public Resource

Philip M. Napoli and Fabienne Graf

1 Introduction

When we think about why we regulate media, it is important to recognize that there are two components to how we answer that question. The first component has to do with the underlying *motivations*. By motivations we mean the underlying problems being addressed and/or principles being pursued. Media regulations have, of course, been implemented on behalf of a wide range of motivations, ranging from protecting children from

This research was made possible in part by grants from the Carnegie Corporation of New York and the John S. and James L. Knight Foundation. The statements made and views expressed are solely the responsibility of the authors.

The original version of this chapter was revised: The spelling of the author name has been changed from "Fabienne Graff" to "Fabienne Graf". The correction to this chapter is available at https://doi.org/10.1007/978-3-030-66759-7_10

P. M. Napoli (✉)
Sanford School of Public Policy, Duke University, Durham, NC, USA
e-mail: philip.napoli@duke.edu

F. Graf
School of Law, University of Lucerne, Lucerne, Switzerland

S. A. Matei et al. (eds.), *Digital and Social Media Regulation*,
https://doi.org/10.1007/978-3-030-66759-7_3

adult content, to preserving and promoting competition, to protecting domestic cultural expression, to (the focus of this volume) enhancing the diversity of sources and content available to media users (see Napoli 1999, 2011).

In countries with very strong legal impediments to government intervention into the media sector (such as the United States, with its strong First Amendment tradition), motivations alone are seldom adequate for facilitating regulatory interventions. These motivations must be accompanied by compelling *rationales*. Rationales, in this case, refer to technologically derived justifications for imposing regulations that, to a certain extent, infringe on media outlets' speech rights. The logic here is that certain characteristics of a medium may justify a degree of regulatory intervention. The underlying premise of this approach is that particular characteristics of a medium may warrant a greater emphasis on collective speech rights over individual speech rights; or that the medium may have a capacity for influence or harms that make some intrusion on speech rights permissible. These rationales serve as a mechanism for pursuing regulatory objectives within the context of a free speech tradition that is intrinsically hostile government intervention, regardless of the broader public interest values that these interventions might serve.

So, for instance, electronic media regulation in the United States has been justified by a wide range of medium characteristics. Broadcasting (and, to a lesser extent, cable television) has been regulated in part on the basis of these media being "uniquely pervasive" (Wallace 1998). Failed efforts were even made to apply this uniquely pervasive characterization to the Internet back in the 1990s, when Congress was attempting to impose strict indecency regulations on online content providers (Napoli 2019a). Within these contexts, the notion of pervasiveness appears to relate to the distinctive reach, ease of access, and/or impact that certain media may have—particularly in relation to allowing children to be exposed to adult content. Media such as cable and satellite television have been regulated on the basis that their functionality is "reasonably ancillary" to the functionality of other, more heavily regulated media (i.e., broadcasting). The logic here is that, to the extent that one medium serves an important role in the distribution of—and audience access to—another, more heavily regulated medium, then that more heavily regulated medium's regulatory framework may, to some extent, be imposed on the other medium. Looking specifically at broadcasting, the most frequently utilized (as well as most frequently criticized) rationale for regulation is the notion that broadcasters utilize a "scarce public resource" (see Logan 1997). Here, the key contention is that broadcasters' use of the broadcast spectrum represents the use of a publicly held resource for which there are more parties seeking access than the spectrum can accommodate—thus justifying a governmental role in allocating the spectrum and, to some extent, dictating behavioral guidelines for those privileged few granted access.

These rationales that have justified the regulation of previous generations of media have, over the years, been analyzed and critiqued in-depth (see, e.g., Krattenmaker and Powe 1994; Spitzer 1989). Most of them do not hold up particularly well under scrutiny—a pattern that would suggest that the typical approach to media regulation is for policymakers to move forward on regulatory interventions on behalf of specific motivations, with the consideration and articulation of rationales being something of an afterthought to buttress these regulatory interventions against critiques of government overreach and any accompanying legal challenges.

Today, many governments across the world have moved forward with regulatory interventions into the operation of social media platforms (see, e.g., Australian Government 2019; Department for Digital, Culture, Media, and Sport, 2020). At the same time, nations such as the United States continue to ponder, evaluate, and investigate possible regulatory interventions (Napoli 2019a). However, there has been very little robust discussion of the underlying rationales that might justify such interventions. Much of the discussion to this point has focused on motivations—the concerns about disinformation, hate speech, privacy, and violence that have compelled policymakers to pay attention and, in some cases, take action. Recent developments such as the global coronavirus pandemic have provided renewed fuel—and additional complexity—to ongoing deliberations related to social media regulation; particularly given the extent to which these platforms have proven to be an effective mechanism for distributing life-threatening misinformation, hoaxes, and conspiracy theories (see, e.g., Goldsmith and Woods 2020; Newton 2020).

However, in many ways this situation—in which policy deliberations focus on the concerns at hand and the possible mechanisms for addressing them—mirrors what we've seen with previous generations of media, where much of the meaningful exploration of regulatory rationales took place post hoc and, to some extent ad hoc. For example, when we look at the history of broadcast regulation in the United States, we see a history of the courts often casting about for reasons to justify particular regulatory interventions, and thus accumulating over the years a patchwork of rationales that have been applied in an inconsistent manner, and that often come across as somewhat half-baked and vulnerable to critical analyses highlighting their flawed logic and inconsistent application (see, e.g., Evans 1979; Spitzer 1989). That the courts have behaved this way is telling evidence that—at least within the US context—the necessary rational foundations for government intervention were not robustly and explicitly laid out by Congress or the Federal Communications Commission.

It would be ideal if this mistake were not repeated within the context of social media regulation. Metaphorically, if the cart was not—once again—to precede the horse, but rather at least operate in parallel. It is toward this end that this chapter focuses on the question of the established rationales that might be brought to bear to regulate social media platforms—whether on behalf of diversity or other pressing concerns such as disinformation or hate speech. Such an exercise seems of particular importance at this point in time, given the movement within some national contexts to "harmonize" the disparate regulatory frameworks that have developed, somewhat piecemeal, across different media platforms. These approaches involve creating "level playing fields" across the different media sectors, or crafting "platform-neutral" regulatory frameworks (see, e.g., Australian Competition and Consumer Commission 2019; Australian Government 2019; Data Ethics Commission 2019; Savin 2018). Ultimately, this process involves bringing a more consistent regulatory approach across both "legacy" and newer media.

Such efforts represent a fairly recent philosophical shift—a move away from treating newer media such as social media as profoundly and fundamentally distinct from previous generations of media; so much so that the very label of "media" may not even apply; or, at the very least established regulatory frameworks should be considered completely irrelevant (Napoli and Caplan 2017). However, the pendulum now seems to be swinging the other way, to some extent. Policymakers and policy researchers are beginning to recognize the points of intersection and overlap between legacy and newer media (see, e.g., Napoli 2019a; Samples and Matzko 2020). Any efforts to build such harmonized regulatory frameworks require a detailed examination of where continuity with legacy models does/does not make sense

This chapter is an effort to make a fairly narrow contribution within this broader endeavor. The goal here is not to provide a detailed overview and analysis of the wide range of rationales that have been brought to bear to justify media regulation in the United States, and to consider their potential applicability to the social media context. I have conducted that exercise elsewhere (see Napoli in press). The goal here, rather, is to provide a deep dive into one potentially viable rationale, to explore its origins and applications, and to consider its potential applicability within the distinctive context of social media platforms, in a way that builds upon and extends prior preliminary inquiries in this area (Napoli 2019a, in press).

Specifically, this chapter is concerned with the application of the public resource—or, as it is sometimes referred to—the *quid pro quo* rationale of broadcast regulation to the seemingly incompatible context of social media. In doing so, this chapter articulates points of commonality between the broadcast spectrum that serves as the foundation of the broadcast industry and the aggregate user data that serve as the foundation of the social media industry.

In addressing these goals, the first section of this chapter outlines the public resource/quid pro quo rationale that has developed within the context of broadcast regulation. The second section lays out how and why this rationale merits being ported to social media context. The third section considers critiques and counterarguments to this proposal. The concluding section considers the implications of this argument specifically for contemporary diversity-related policy objectives.

2 The Public Resource/Quid Pro Quo Rationale for Media Regulation

We begin then, somewhat ironically, by revisiting a medium that is of steadily diminishing importance within the contemporary media ecosystem—terrestrial broadcasting. In an era of 500+ cable networks, online streaming of music and video, and mobile device applications, broadcasting represents a shrinking slice of the overall media pie. Broadcasting as a means of accessing media content is practically alien to young people today (try explaining rabbit years to a university undergraduate). Viewers of broadcast television are, for the most part, approaching or past retirement age. Even these viewers are, in most cases, not even accessing broadcast signals directly, but rather through an intermediary such as a cable service provider, making the broadcast transmission largely superfluous. Indeed, most of the content that is distributed over the broadcast spectrum today is frequently accessed through other means. Television broadcasts can be accessed not only through cable (linear or on-demand), but also through online streaming platforms. Much of broadcast radio is now livestreamed online and/or made available in the form of podcasts. So it is, admittedly, a bit odd to be looking to broadcasting for guidance as to how to—or more specifically, why—regulate social media, a medium that would seem to have little in common with broadcasting.

But within the vast array of differences between broadcasting and social media there are also some important similarities. Each, at their peak, has represented the most far-reaching and immediate distribution platform available. From a structural standpoint, each represents a model in which substantial gatekeeping authority is invested with a fairly limited number of gatekeepers. And the early history of each is inextricably intertwined with some of modern history's most significant advances in technically driven propaganda campaigning (broadcasting in the case of the rise of Nazi Germany [see Bytwerk 2004] and social media in the case of election interference in the United States, the UK, and many other national contexts [see Napoli 2019c]). Therefore, looking to the broadcast medium for guidance may not be as outlandish as it initially seems.

In the United States, what may be the most sound and resilient rationale that has been put forth for the regulation of broadcasting is the notion that broadcasters utilize a publicly owned resource, and as privileged users of this publicly held resource, must abide by certain fiduciary responsibilities that take the form of government-crafted and enforced public interest obligations. These public interest obligations can take the form of impositions on broadcasters' speech rights, but such impositions are, to some extent, permissible as conditions of access to the resource to which the broadcasters have been granted. As articulated by Logan (1997), "in return for receiving substantial benefits allocated by the government, broadcasters must abide by a number of public interest conditions that, in the absence of government allocation, would be found unconstitutional" (p. 1732). This model is built upon the well-established notion that the broadcast spectrum is "owned by the people" (Berresford 2005).

This public resource, or *quid pro quo* rationale, as it is sometimes called (see, e.g., Graham 2003; Spitzer 1989) has been described as being "overshadowed" (Logan 1997, p. 1691) in legal discussions evaluating the constitutionality of broadcast regulation by scholars' and critics emphasis on dissecting the logic of the associated scarcity rationale. It is important to distinguish between this scarcity rationale and the related public resource/quid pro quo rationale. As much as the two rationales are interconnected through the notion of the broadcast spectrum as a "scarce public resource," it is important to emphasize that the public resource rationale can operate independently of the scarcity rationale. That is, as much as the logic of regulating a medium on the basis of its use of a resource that is "scarce" is subject to a wide range of critiques (exploring these critiques is beyond the scope of this chapter; but see, e.g., Krattenmaker and Powe 1994; Spitzer 1989), the logic of regulating the medium on the basis of its use of a resource that is publicly owned is inherently much more sound.[1] Even staunch opponents of media regulation acknowledge that the public resource rationale is fundamentally stronger than the range of other, more specious, rationales that have been proffered over the years (see, e.g., Krattenmaker and Powe 1994).

Of course, the logic of the resource (spectrum) being publicly owned in the first place remains open to challenge (see, e.g., Evans 1979; Spitzer 1989), particularly if the logic for public ownership is based upon the resource's scarcity. However, as the next section will illustrate, when we transfer this public resource/quid pro quo regulatory rationale to the social media context, the notion of public ownership of the resource is much more inherent in the very nature of the resource (aggregate user data) in the social media context than it is in the broadcast context (spectrum), and operates largely independently of any contentions of scarcity.

3 Translating the Public Resource/Quid Pro Quo Rationale to Social Media

Given that social media platforms make no use of the spectrum, the logic of applying the public resource/quid pro quo rationale to them is not intuitively obvious. These platforms do, however, similarly build their businesses upon a resource that, when evaluated thoroughly, may very well best be thought of as a public resource. The public resource within the context of social media platforms is the *aggregate user data* that serves as their economic foundation. As is well understood at this point, the business model for virtually every large social media platform is to develop a massive user base, compile all of the demographic, geographic, psychographic, and behavioral user data that can be harvested through users' interaction with the platform, oftentimes impute additional data points from the data that have been gathered, and monetize these data—primarily in the form of delivering targeted advertising services to advertisers; though there are certainly other ways these aggregations of user data can be monetized as well (Albarran 2013).

To understand how and why these aggregate user data are best thought of as a public resource, we need to briefly delve into ongoing policy deliberations about the appropriate property status of user data. These deliberations are an outgrowth of ongoing concerns about the privacy and security of user data. This is a much larger and complex topic than can be fully addressed here, but for the purposes of this analysis, the most relevant aspect of these deliberations is the extent to which many stakeholders see both a model in which the platforms have outright ownership of their data and the model in which individuals have outright ownership of their data as problematic for various reasons (for more detail on this issue, see Napoli in press). Conceptualizing aggregate user data as a collectively owned public resource thus represents an intermediate solution point (Napoli in press)—one that also (as will be illustrated) best reflects the unique characteristics of user data as a resource.

A useful starting point for this argument is that, whatever the exact nature of one's individual property rights in one's user data may be, when these data are aggregated across millions of users, their fundamental character changes in such a way that they are best conceptualized as a public resource. It is in this massive aggregation that the economic value of user data emerges. As renowned policy scholar Shoshana Zuboff (2015) notes, "Individual users' meanings are of no interest to Google or other firms… Populations are the sources from which data extraction proceeds" (p. 79). The real value in user data only emerges through large aggregations, which allow predictive analytics and behavioral targeting. Individually, a person's data gleaned from a social media platform may be worth about $5 a month (Hart 2019). Collectively, such data are incredibly valuable.

This scenario represents a case of the whole being greater than the sum of the parts. Privacy scholars have utilized this notion of the whole being greater than the sum its parts to advocate for the application of an "emergent properties" approach to data privacy (see, e.g., Esayas 2017). The notion of emergent properties here refers to the idea of looking "beyond the properties of individual components of a system and understand[ing] the system as a single complex" (Esayas 2017, p. 139). While Esayas (2017) applies this logic to the various components of a platform's data gathering enterprise (each part of which contributes to a larger whole), the logic seems equally applicable to how we think about the user data themselves, and the need to think not in terms of the individual user's data, but the larger data complex constructed through the aggregation of individual data.

Another reason for thinking about user data as what Tisne (2018) terms a "collective good" is that collective benefits arise when individual-level data are aggregated. Such aggregation allows for the observation of broader patterns that might otherwise go unnoticed, or the formulation of generalizable insights. Thus, in this collective formulation of a valuable resource, it makes sense to embrace a form of collective ownership that parallels, to some extent, the notion of the public as owners of the airwaves.

Reflecting this position, some privacy advocates have suggested that recent legislative proposals to require platforms to determine and disclose to individual users the value of their data (Designing Accounting Safeguards to Help Broaden Oversight and Regulations on Data Act 2019) are fundamentally problematic. Instead, they propose a collective negotiation model, in which individuals band together to form a "privacy union" of sorts to collectively negotiate the value of their aggregate data and the terms and conditions for its use (Barber 2019). As Zuboff (2019) has argued, "Data ownership is an individual solution when collective solutions are required." The argument being put forth here essentially takes this perspective and pairs it with a philosophically compatible regulatory rationale.

Consider that, from a property standpoint, spectrum has been characterized as a common asset, or what the Romans termed *res publica* (Calabrese 2001). This concept serves as the foundation for the *public trust doctrine*. The key point of the public trust doctrine is that "because of their unique characteristics, certain natural resources and systems are held in trust by the sovereign on behalf of the citizens" (Calabrese 2001, 6).[2] This characterization seems particularly well-suited to aggregate user data as well, given the unique resource characteristics of user data described above. In both cases, there is a public character to the resource. Also in both cases, there is no expectation that this resource is legitimately accessible by the entirety of the public. Rather, the access limitations inherent in the resource require that public service obligations be imposed upon those who do obtain access, in order that the public accrue benefits from their collectively held resource. This is an important point, as it underscores the fact that the argument being put forth here is not intended to support any notions that the data aggregations compiled by social media platforms should be publicly accessible. This is why the analogy at use here is broadcast spectrum, not publicly accessible public resources such as waterways or parks.[3]

However, the analogy with the mechanics (though not the spirit) of broadcast spectrum regulation does break down somewhat in terms of the notion of ownership by the people. Fortunately, this analogy breaks down in way that is actually truer to the spirit of broadcast regulation than broadcast regulation itself. Specifically, in the model being proposed here, the "substantial benefits" being allocated are not being allocated by the government through the allocation of broadcast licenses, but rather by the collective of social media users, who are making decisions to allow a privileged few platforms to accumulate massive aggregations of user data. In this way, the notion of the public resource being "owned by the people," which has been more rhetorical stance than reality in the realm of broadcast regulation, is more legitimately the case within the context of social media regulation. Whereas the federal government essentially owns and allocates the broadcast spectrum on behalf of the public, it is the public that owns aggregate user data. This is an important distinction, as it helps to make explicit that the argument being put forth here is not intended to justify any form of federal licensing of social media platforms.

However, just as government ownership and allocation of the broadcast spectrum justified a quid pro quo in the form of public interest obligations, so too can public ownership of aggregate user data justify such a quid pro quo. In both cases, it is the issues of ownership and privileged access that provide the basis for the quid pro quo. Imagine, then, a scenario in which, just as individual social media users accept terms of service associated with our use of these freely provided platforms, the platforms themselves had to acknowledge a parallel set of *terms of access* that represent the obligations that they accede to in exchange for the right to gather and monetize such large aggregations of collectively owned user data.

And while the logic of the government's proxy ownership of the broadcast spectrum is often considered to be a function of the spectrum's perceived scarcity, and also sometimes argued to be an invalid role for the federal government to assume (for a summary of these arguments, see Graham 2003), these particular vulnerabilities do not characterize the aggregate user data as public resource argument being put forth here.

This argument is not premised on the notion of aggregate user data being in any way scarce.[4] Rather, it is premised on the notion of these user data being—inherently—the property of the collective of users who have made the decision to allow certain platforms to have access to it and to build commercial enterprises upon it. Further, the notion of aggregate user data as a public resource places ownership within the collective of social media users, and does not in any way mandate or infer that these data then become any kind of quasi-property of the federal government (the way the broadcast spectrum has). Rather, the government simply becomes the agent for the collective in terms of articulating and enforcing the public interest obligations that must be met as the quid pro quo for this privileged access to this collectively owned resource.

4 Counterarguments and Critiques

The argument being put forth here represents quite a radical departure from how policymakers have, to this point, thought about both data policy and social media regulation. Consequently, this argument can be critiqued from a wide range of perspectives. The goal of this section, then, is to address these potential critiques in a way that hopefully further clarifies and refines how the proposal has been described thus far.

One concern that has been expressed in response to this proposal is that it essentially provides *carte blanche* for government intervention.[5] However, one need only look to the history of broadcast regulation in the United States to see that, while the broadcast spectrum's status as a public resource has facilitated a more aggressive regulatory framework than can be found in print or online; it has not facilitated massive government intrusions into the speech rights of broadcasters. Broadcasters retain substantial editorial autonomy—an autonomy that has only expanded over the years as regulators have scaled back the parameters of broadcast regulation in a variety of ways. As Logan (1997) states, "The quid pro quo rationale does not give the government unlimited authority" (p. 1734).

Nor is this argument meant to justify the regulation of *any* social media firm that aggregates and monetizes user data. Central to this argument is the idea that only at some level of aggregation (the specifics of which still need to be worked out) do user data meet the threshold of a public resource. The idea here is that the public resource/quid pro quo rationale would only apply to platforms of a certain size, leaving smaller, emergent platforms free of the accompanying public interest obligations. Should these platforms grow to reach the designated size/scope in terms of their aggregation of user data, then the rationale and its accompanying public interest obligations would kick in. In this way, the regulatory rationale being outlined here is compatible with the frequently articulated goal of developing a regulatory framework directed primarily (if not exclusively) at the dominant platforms (see, e.g., Esayas 2017).[6]

Another concern that has been raised in response to the proposal put forth here (and that was touched on briefly above) is that it essentially institutionalizes a model of government ownership of the user data aggregated by platforms such as Facebook, YouTube, and Twitter. Any such government ownership naturally raises privacy and security concerns, given that such ownership of course means government access to these data. However, it bears repeating that the argument put forth here advocates for collective public ownership, with the governmental role being one of devising the public interest obligations that merit being generated from this public ownership, but not maintaining proxy ownership of the resource as has been the case with the broadcast spectrum. Building upon this approach, one could even imagine a model in which a government-sanctioned non-governmental organization assumes this regulatory authority, not unlike the way in which Congress mandated that the audience measurement industry create an independent self-regulatory body to oversee that industry (the Media Rating Council—see Napoli 2019b).

Finally, it is important to address the concern that this proposal provides a "slippery slope" to the regulation of all advertising-supported media, or all business enterprises that compile massive aggregations of user data (e.g., Amazon). Starting with the first concern, it is important to acknowledge that the aggregate user data amassed by social media platforms are used primarily to facilitate the sale of advertising. In this way, these platforms are similar to other ad supported media such as television, radio, some print publications, and so many commercial Web sites. From this standpoint, it could be argued that these media also are reliant upon a public resource and should fall under the regulatory framework proposed here. However, there are a number of important differences that work against this argument.

First, traditional ad-supported media have monetized audience data derived from relatively small samples of media users, who have knowingly volunteered to take part in the measurement process and typically receive compensation for doing so (Napoli 2003). This is very different from the social media model, in which all users must agree to the terms of data extraction in exchange for access to an increasingly necessary communications platform, and certainly nobody is receiving financial compensation in exchange for having their data aggregated. Even when the audience measurement systems for other media involve a census rather than a sample (think, for instance, of traffic audits for Web sites), the scope of the user data that can be gathered through such an approach is infinitesimal compared to what can be gathered through social media platforms, given that this approach involves measuring activity through the prism of the site, rather than through the monitoring of actual users (Napoli et al. 2014). Monitoring individual sites, and how users engage with them, provides dramatically less data about the users than monitoring users and their behavior directly.

It is also important to note that the data aggregation for other ad-supported media has traditionally been conducted not by the media outlets themselves, but rather by third-party measurement firms (Nielsen, comScore, etc.), in a long-standing "separation of powers" model that seems to have been dismantled in the social media context. These third parties, it should be noted, are overseen and audited by a quasi-governmental body (the Media Rating Council) created at the behest of Congress (Napoli 2019b). This third-party measurement model is largely missing from the data aggregation and monetization conducted by social media platforms.

Finally, and most obviously, the scale and scope of data gathering that can be undertaken by social media platforms dwarfs what can be achieved in almost any other mediated communication context, given the size of user bases and the breadth and depth of information users provide through the various means of interacting with the platforms. This reflects the way in which select social media platforms have become the gatekeeper of—and thus gateway to—the broader web (Napoli 2019a). Other digital media entities, such as Internet Service Providers (ISPs) and Web sites can't come close to matching the breadth and depth of user data that large social media platforms are able to accumulate. Facebook is reported to have over 29,000 data points on the average user (McNamee 2019). Only Google through its cross-platform data gathering (search, email, YouTube, maps, etc.) extracts comparable amounts of user data and comes in contact with a comparable number of users.

This Google comparison helps to raise the next question/concern noted above—the possibility that this regulatory rationale could extend beyond the social media context that has been the focus of this analysis. Aggregate user data are certainly a vital component of the business models of other digital platforms such as e-commerce sites such as Amazon and search engines such as Google. In the Amazon example, a vitally important point of distinction involves the fact that the user data are used primarily to personalize product offerings to generate sales, with the direct monetization of these data serving as a relatively minor component of the overall business model. Given, then, that the revenue is not directly derived from the public resource at issue, the quid pro quo regulatory framework would not apply. The same argument would apply to digital media distributors such as Netflix, which gather a somewhat limited array of user data in order to provide personalized media content options in exchange for subscription fees. In these cases, aggregations of user data *support* the business enterprise but are *not* the business enterprise.

In a case such as Google, however, a more compelling case could be made that the quid pro quo model could—and perhaps even should—apply. Like social media platforms, Google's business model is primarily oriented around providing free digital products and services in order to gather and monetize massive aggregations of user data through advertising sales, in a manner that differs from more traditional media in many of the same ways that social media platforms' monetization of aggregate user data differs from traditional media (see above). And so, while this analysis was motivated in large part by the concerns about the proliferation of disinformation and hate speech, and the privacy and security of user data that have swirled around social media platforms over the past decade, Google has hardly been immune to these concerns (see, e.g., Nieva 2019; Plasilova et al. 2020). For these reasons, extending the quid pro quo regulatory framework to the search context may make sense, though further exploration of this possibility is beyond the scope of this chapter.

5 Conclusion

This chapter started from the premise that within a legal and regulatory context such as the United States, any efforts to regulate must be built upon a foundation of a robust and compelling technological rationale. Such motivations must be accompanied by a viable rationale. This chapter has argued that treating aggregate user data as a public resource, as a mechanism for triggering the quid pro quo regulatory rationale that has characterized broadcast regulation, represents just such a viable regulatory rationale.

As a concluding point, it is worth briefly considering what the adoption and application of the regulatory rationale proposed here would mean for diversity-motivated regulation of digital platforms. As a starting point, it is perhaps worth pinpointing the most pressing diversity policy concerns related to these platforms, given that diversity-related policy concerns evolve over time and across technological contexts (Napoli 2011).

The first concern is structural, in that there are calls in many quarters for policy interventions that enhance the diversity of platforms available; that would impose structural interventions seeking to diffuse the existing social media user base beyond the select few dominant platforms such as Facebook, YouTube, and Twitter (see, e.g., Data Ethics Commission 2019; Hughes 2019). Here we see intersections (as we have seen in previous generations of media policy) between the diversity and competition policy objectives (Napoli 1999). The second concern is more content-oriented and is directed at the exposure diversity of social media users. Here, the primary concern is with "filter bubbles" (Pariser 2011), and how individuals tend to use social media platforms in ways that inhibit their exposure to diverse sources and perspectives; as well as with how the design and operation of the platforms themselves may further exacerbate such tendencies (Helberger et al. 2018).

Looking at the first concern, it is worth noting how, by many accounts, contemporary antitrust enforcement has been critiqued for failing to adequately account for the distinctive economics (and consequences) of digital platforms that rely on the monetization of aggregate user data (see, e.g., Wu 2018). This is because contemporary antitrust enforcement has been heavily oriented around the analysis of the prices consumers pay for goods and services (Stigler Committee on Digital Platforms 2019). This factor is fundamentally irrelevant to the relationship between consumers and social media platforms—unless, of course, antitrust enforcement pivots effectively to acknowledge the provision of user data as a price paid for service, and integrate this thinking into their analysis.

The alternative (or additional) approach is to lean more heavily on diversity concerns as the motivation for government interventions on behalf of greater structural diversity (i.e., competition) in the social media sector, and to rely on the premise of aggregate user data as a public resource as a means of justifying such interventions. Just as concerns about structural diversity were a component of why the Federal Communications Commission mandated in the early days of the NBC broadcast network that it be broken up into two separate networks (and justified this action on the basis of its regulatory authority over a public resource) (NBC v. U.S. 1943), so too could efforts to break up Facebook or Google be premised on diversity-related public interest principles that are enforceable on the basis of these platforms user data aggregations being a public resource.

Turning next to concerns about exposure diversity and filter bubbles, this takes us into the realm of possible behavioral regulation of digital platforms, particularly in terms of possible requirements related to the operation of curation algorithms. Certainly, any intervention that would impose the integration of exposure diversity objectives, or filter bubble remedies, into the design of social media platforms' content curation algorithms would need to be premised upon a rationale that has an established record of justifying comparable intrusions into the speech rights of media outlets. The public resource rationale meets these criteria and could allow for the development of these or other content-related regulatory requirements that, at this point, lack a compelling regulatory rationale to support them.

Notes

1. And, importantly, the Supreme Court has acknowledged that the public resource/quid pro quo rationale operates independently of the scarcity rationale. As the Court noted in the landmark *Red Lion Broadcasting v. Federal Communications Commission* (1969) decision, "Even where there are gaps in spectrum utilization, the fact remains that existing broadcasters have often attained their present position because of their initial government selection" (p. 400). The key point in this statement is the phrase "even where there are gaps in spectrum utilization." This phrase emphasizes that even in those contexts where the scarcity rationale does not hold up (because there is apparently more spectrum available than there is demand), the public interest regulatory framework imposed by the FCC still applies, on the basis of broadcasters' utilization of a government-allocated resource.
2. For a more detailed discussion of the applicability of the public trust doctrine within the context of the regulatory rationale being developed here, see Napoli (in press).

3. This distinction is particularly important in that it separates the argument being put forth here from seemingly similar—though in reality quite different—arguments for a "data commons," which generally advocate for broader public access to data (see, e.g., Yakowitz 2011).
4. This lack of scarcity in relation to user data is a particularly important point, as it has served one of the primary pushbacks against the widely repeated mantra that "data is the new oil." As critics of this argument have countered, given the rate and scope at which data is generated, data would not seem to have the same scarcity characteristics as oil (see, e.g., Marr 2018). On the other hand, one could argue that data aggregations of the size and scope of those possessed by companies such as Facebook are quite scarce; and given that the value of data lies in its aggregation, perhaps it is appropriate to think about the issue of scarcity in data at the aggregate level as well.
5. When presenting this idea at a conference in London in 2019, one conference participant responded to the presentation by saying "I feel like I am sitting in Beijing." This statement gives a sense of how the argument being put forth here can be perceived as facilitating a massive degree of government control over the social media sector. The reality is that the proposal being put forth here is intended to only facilitate a degree of government oversight comparable to the degree of oversight that we have seen in the broadcast sector. Admittedly, however, this argument could be used on behalf of efforts to engage in overly invasive regulation of digital platforms.
6. As Esayas (2017) notes within the European context, "Under competition law, the trigger for the special responsibility regime is the existence of market power and whether an undertaking occupies a dominant position" (p. 175). This notion of dominant position as trigger is to some extent compatible with the argument being put forth here that user data aggregations of a certain scale would trigger the public resource-derived set of public interest obligations. As Esayas also notes, "One may well ask, 'what criteria ought to be used ... trigger the enhanced responsibility framework?'"(p. 175). Laying out suggestions for the specific criteria that would address this question is the next step of this project.

References

Albarran, Alan (ed.). 2013. *The Social Media Industries*. New York: Routledge.

Australian Competition and Consumer Commission. 2019. *Digital Platforms Inquiry: Final Report*. Canberra, Australia: Author.

Australian Government. 2019. Regulating in the Digital Age: Government Response and Implementation Roadmap for the Digital Platforms Inquiry. https://apo.org.au/node/271556.

Barber, Gregory. 2019. Senators Want Facebook to Put a Price on Your Data. Is That Possible? Wired. https://www.wired.com/story/senators-want-facebook-price-data-possible/.

Berresford, John W. 2005. The Scarcity Rationale for Regulating Broadcasting: An Idea Whose Time Has Passed. *Federal Communications Commission Media Bureau Staff Research Paper*. https://transition.fcc.gov/ownership/materials/already-released/scarcity030005.pdf.

Bytwerk, Randall L. 2004. *Bending Spines: The Propagandas of Nazi Germany and the German Democratic Republic*. East Lansing, MI: Michigan State University Press.

Calabrese, Michael. 2001. Battle over the Airwaves: Principles for Spectrum Policy Reform. Working Paper, New American Foundation.

Data Ethics Commission. 2019. Opinion of the Data Ethics Commission. https://datenethikkommission.de/wp-content/uploads/DEK_Gutachten_engl_bf_200121.pdf.

Department for Digital, Culture, Media, and Sport. 2020. Government Minded to Appoint Ofcom as Online Harms Regulator. https://www.gov.uk/government/news/government-minded-to-appoint-ofcom-as-online-harms-regulator.

Designing Accounting Safeguards to Help Broaden Oversight and Regulations on Data Act. 2019. 116th Congress, 1st Session.

Esayas, Samson Y. 2017. The Idea of 'Emergent Properties' in Data Privacy: Towards a Holistic Approach. *International Journal of Law & Information Technology* 25: 139–178.

Evans, A.C. 1979. An Examination of the Theories Justifying Content Regulation of the Electronic Media. *Syracuse Law Review* 30 (3) (Summer): 871–892.

Goldsmith, Jack, and Andrew Keane Woods. 2020. Internet Speech Will Never Go Back to Normal. *The Atlantic*. https://www.theatlantic.com/ideas/archive/2020/04/what-covid-revealed-about-internet/610549/.

Graham, Daniel. 2003. Public Interest Regulation in the Digital Age. *CommLaw Conspectus: Journal of Communications Law and Policy* 11 (1): 97–144.

Hart, Kim. 2019. Bipartisan Senators Want Big Tech to Put a Price on Your Data. *Axio*. https://www.axios.com/mark-warner-josh-hawley-dashboard-tech-data-4ee575b4--4d05-83ce-d62621e28ee1.html.

Helberger, Natali, Kari Karppinen, and Lucia D'Acunto. 2018. Exposure Diversity as a Design Principle for Recommender Systems. *Information, Communication, & Society* 21 (2): 191–207.

Hughes, Chris. 2019. It's Time to Break Up Facebook. *New York Times*. https://www.nytimes.com/2019/05/09/opinion/sunday/chris-hughes-facebook-zuckerberg.html.

Krattenmaker, Thomas G., and Lucas Powe. 1994. *Regulating Broadcast Programming*. Washington, DC: American Enterprise Institute.
Logan, Charles W., Jr. 1997. Getting Beyond Scarcity: A New Paradigm for Assessing the Constitutionality of Broadcast Regulation. *California Law Review* 85: 1687–1747.
Marr, Bernard. 2018. Here's Why Data Is Not the New Oil. *Forbes*. https://www.forbes.com/sites/bernardmarr/2018/03/05/heres-why-data-is-not-the-new-oil/#7eed77953aa9.
McNamee, Roger. 2019. *Zucked: Waking Up to the Facebook Catastrophe*. New York: Penguin Press.
Napoli, Philip M. 1999. Deconstructing the Diversity Principle. *Journal of Communication* 49 (4): 7–34.
Napoli, Philip M. 2003. *Audience Economics: Media Institutions and the Audience Marketplace*. New York: Columbia University Press.
Napoli, Philip M. 2011. Diminished, Enduring, and Emergent Diversity Policy Concerns in an Evolving Media Environment. *International Journal of Communication* 5: 1182–1196.
Napoli, Philip M. 2019a. User Data as a Public Resource: Implications for Social Media Regulation. *Policy & Internet* 11 (4): 439–459.
Napoli, Philip M. 2019b. *Social Media and the Public Interest: Media Regulation in the Disinformation Age*. New York: Columbia University Press.
Napoli, Philip M. 2019c. What Social Media Platforms Can Learn from Audience Measurement: Lessons in the Self-Regulation of Black Boxes. *First Monday* 24 (12). https://firstmonday.org/ojs/index.php/fm/article/view/10124.
Napoli, Philip M. in press. Beyond Information Fiduciaries: Dominant Digital Platforms as Public Trustees. In *Dealing with Digital Dominance*, ed. M. Moore and D. Tambini. New York: Oxford University Press.
Napoli, Philip M., and Robyn Caplan. 2017. Why Media Companies Insist They're Not Media Companies, Why They're Wrong, and Why It Matters. *First Monday* 22 (5). https://firstmonday.org/ojs/index.php/fm/article/view/7051/6124.
Napoli, Philip M., Paul J. Lavrakas, and Mario Callegaro. 2014. Internet and mobile audience ratings panels. In *Online Panel Research: A Data Quality Perspective*, ed. M. Callegaro et al., 387–407. West Sussex, UK: Wiley.
NBC v. U.S. 1943. 319 U.S. 190.
Newton, Casey. 2020. Coronavirus Misinformation Is Putting Facebook to the Test. *The Verge*. https://www.theverge.com/interface/2020/4/17/21223742/coronavirus-misinformation-facebook-who-news-feed-message-avaaz-report.
Nieva, Richard. 2019. Google AG Probe: States Want Answers on Privacy and Antitrust. *CNET*. https://www.cnet.com/news/google-ag-probe-states-want-answers-on-privacy-and-antitrust/.

Pariser, Eli. 2011. *The Filter Bubble: What the Internet Is Hiding from You*. New York: Penguin.

Plasilova, Iva, Jordan Hill, Malin Carlberg, Marion Goubet, and Richard Procee. 2020. Study for the Assessment of the Implementation of the Code of Practice on Disinformation. *European Commission*. https://ec.europa.eu/digital-single-market/en/news/study-assessment-implementation-code-practice-disinformation.

Red Lion Broadcasting v. Federal Communications Commission. 1969. 395 U.S. 367.

Samples, John, and Paul Matzko. 2020. Social Media Regulation in the Public Interest: Some Lessons from History. Knight First Amendment Institute. https://knightcolumbia.org/content/social-media-regulation-in-the-public-interest-some-lessons-from-history.

Savin, Andrej. 2018. Regulating Internet Platforms in the EU—The Emergence of the 'Level Playing Field'. *Computer Law & Security Review* 34: 1215–1231.

Spitzer, Matthew L. 1989. The Constitutionality of Licensing Broadcasters. *New York University Law Review* 64 (5): 990–1072.

Stigler Committee on Digital Platforms. 2019. Final Report. https://research.chicagobooth.edu/-/media/research/stigler/pdfs/digital-platforms—committee-report—stigler-center.pdf.

Tisne, Martin. 2018. It's Time for a Bill of Data Rights. *MIT Technology Review*. https://www.technologyreview.com/s/612588/its-time-for-a-bill-of-data-rights/.

Wallace, Johnathan D. 1998. The Specter of Pervasiveness: Pacifica, New Media, and Freedom of Speech. CATO Institute. https://www.cato.org/publications/briefing-paper/specter-pervasiveness-pacifica-new-media-freedom-speech.

Wu, Tim. 2018. *The Curse of Bigness: Antitrust in the New Gilded Age*. New York: Columbia University Press.

Yakowitz, Jane. 2011. Tragedy of the Data Commons. *Harvard Journal of Law & Technology* 25 (1): 1–68.

Zuboff, Shoshana. 2015. Big Other: Surveillance Capitalism and the Prospects of an Information Civilization. *Journal of Information Technology* 30: 75–89.

Zuboff, Shoshana. 2019. It's Not That We've Failed to Reign in Facebook and Google. We've Not Even Tried. *The Guardian*. https://www.theguardian.com/commentisfree/2019/jul/02/facebook-google-data-change-our-behaviour-democracy.

GDPR and New Media Regulation: The Data Metaphor and the EU Privacy Protection Strategy

Maud Bernisson

With the development of the information society, EU communications policies have increasingly focused on the convergence of the Internet's infrastructures and data flows with economic liberalization and the protection of civil liberties (Schwartz and Solove 2014). Data came to be at the heart of privacy laws, which exist precisely because of personal data (Schwartz and Solove 2011). In EU privacy laws, the first data protection Directive (95/46/EC) was enacted in 1995. The Directive was highly inspired by the German Bundesdatenschutzgesetz (BDSG, which can be translated as the Federal Data Protection Act). It is one of the first laws to protect personal data considering computer developments (Schwartz 2004). The development of the protection of personal data precedes the rise of Big Data, which occurred in the 2010s. The design of EU privacy laws has been influenced by technological interpretations of reality that inform the myth of Big Data.

The first section of this chapter discusses definitions of data and information. In light of the theory of the metaphor, I compared previous

M. Bernisson (✉)
Department of Media and Communication, Karlstad University, Karlstad, Sweden
e-mail: maud.bernisson@kau.se

S. A. Matei et al. (eds.), *Digital and Social Media Regulation*,
https://doi.org/10.1007/978-3-030-66759-7_4

literature that either focused on definitions per se or on approaches to reality that influence definitions. The theory of the metaphor suggests that several interpretations, which depend on approaches to reality, define a concept in context. Critical Discourse Studies (CDS) offer guidance to *analyze how several interpretations embedded in the metaphor of data contribute to its redefinition in EU privacy policies*. With this method, the analysis focuses on definitions in context, which vary according to different interpretations. The last section encompasses the analysis of several interpretations involved in the metaphor of data in privacy policies, i.e., human rights, technological, and economic.

1 Defining Data and Data as a Metaphor

Data are often defined as electronic information (e.g., van Dijck 2013, 30), and "information" and "data" have been used interchangeably by privacy policies scholars (Schwartz and Solove 2014). Not only differences between data and information seem unclear, but also, focusing on a definition alone would not permit to unravel the meaning of data (or information). As Markham (2018) pointed out, the focus should be on interpretation rather than on data. The theory of the metaphor considers interpretations in addition to definitions per se.

Ricœur (1975) explains that a metaphor[1] is created when a meaning exists in a semantic field but lacks a label. Then, a label from another field is borrowed. The label is aggregated to the meaning together with elements of the approach to reality, which belong to the other field. For example, the folders on our computers work as an analogy of the physical world where folders contain files and are organized quite similarly. Lakoff and Johnson (2003) define the metaphor in a similar way. Not only metaphors derive from "our physical and cultural experience," but also, they influence how we act and experience the world. However, their theories diverge in different respects from Ricœur's. While the latter focuses on the creation of meaning, Lakoff and Johnson do not. The metaphor borrows meaning from semantic fields in interaction (Ricœur 1972), which denotes the process of creation of meaning. This process refers to the living metaphor. When this meaning becomes hidden—i.e., the word has entered everyday language—Ricœur (1972) calls this metaphor dead.

In addition, Lakoff and Johnson (2003) focus on ontological approaches that permit a common understanding shared in cultural groups. Ricœur (1972) explains that the metaphor shapes our actions and our interpretations of reality as well. However, his definition of interpretation aggregates other aspects to consider for analyzing a metaphor. Interpretation depends on the field of application of the metaphor and on the epistemological specificity of the metaphor. Concerning the first characteristic of interpretation, this study applies the metaphor of data to privacy policies. Concerning the second characteristic, several epistemological approaches exist to interpret this metaphor in a similar field of application, as discussed below. In other words, the metaphor of data equates to data interpreted in the context of privacy policies. As I will discuss in this section, the coexistence of different interpretations in the living metaphor of data shows that its meaning is in construction, and somehow blends with the definition of information. First, I compare definitions per se, and then, interpretations of data and information in previous literature.

As Braman (1989) pointed out, more than forty academic fields use the term *information*. They have different definitions of the concept (Machlup and Mansfield in Braman 1989) and different uses of the concept (Capurro and Hjørland 2005). Information science (IS) scholars, Capurro and Hjørland (2005), offer a classification of the word *information* according to scientific fields to show the great differences among definitions. In natural sciences, *information* is "interpreted data" (Mahler in Capurro and Hjørland 2005). From a media perspective, Capurro and Hjørland found that there is no "information-in-itself," and to "inform (others or oneself) means to select and to evaluate" (2005, 373). In information science (IS), *information* depends on its degree of informativeness for the receiver. The authors explain further that the degree of informativeness depends on the capacity of interpretation of the receiver.

In a more schematic way, some scholars use the pyramid of knowledge to define different concepts according to each other. At the top, there is wisdom and understanding that stems from knowledge, which derives from information, which in itself derives from data that lie at the bottom (Kitchin 2014, 10). Kitchin (2014) explains that the order of these concepts is usually uncontested. However, it is unclear in many contexts what the difference between data and information is. For example, the literature on privacy law tends to use information and data interchangeably. Schwartz and Solove (2011) note that information privacy law scholars often use the term *personal information*, "and sometimes interchangeably with PII," i.e., personal identifiable information (2011, 12).

When they (2014) compare the definition of personal information in EU and US privacy laws, they use "personal information," "personal identifiable information," and "personal data" interchangeably as well.

Although there is not one definition of information or data, IS scholars have noted an increase of the use of *information* in IS together with the development of Information Technology (IT) (Hjørland in Capurro and Hjørland 2005). The IT interpretation of information has been strengthened with the emergence of Big Data in the mid-1990s, which became popular in 2013 (Kitchin 2014, 71), and which has certainly helped to blur the distinction between data and information. Big Data has often been defined with the 3V's; Volume, Velocity, and Variety (De Mauro, Greco, and Grimaldi 2014, 101; Kitchin 2014, 71). Its definition has evolved to characteristics such as "value, veracity, complexity, and unstructuredness" (De Mauro et al. 2014, 101). Kitchin (2014) adds to the three Vs: exhaustivity, "fine-grained in resolution," relationality, and flexibility (2014, 72). DeNardis and Hackl (2015) categorize data as follows: "content and accompanying user data such as registration information, identifying information (voluntarily provided by users), and metadata" (2015, 763). Metadata is often defined as data about data (Cheney-Lippold 2017, 39; Kitchin 2014, 10). Following Google's policies, DeNardis and Hackl (2015, 765) provide examples of metadata: location, phone number, device information, cookies, software footprint, IP address, and activity data. These data gain value when aggregated and interpreted. Thus, depending on the context, or field of application, as Ricœur (1972) defines it, definitions vary.

The second characteristic of interpretation to consider is the epistemological specificity of the metaphor. A few scholars have focused on characteristics fairly similar to define data. Boyd and Crawford (2012) add a mythological layer to technological and analytical characteristics of Big Data. That is, "the widespread belief that large data sets offer a higher form of intelligence and knowledge that can generate previously impossible insights, with the aura of truth, objectivity, and accuracy" (2012, 663). In the same vein, Cheney-Lippold (2017) recalls what Haggerty and Ericsson stated: "data are not given; they are made" (2017, 54). For example, data are often collected to be categorized. Following Cheney-Lippold's explanation of common biases in the society, the categories made up online include similar biases to the "offline world," since semi-supervised algorithms include biases[2] (Cheney-Lippold 2017, 60). He provides an example with the classification "man." He questions the criteria that correspond to a male, which are based, among other things, on cultural definitions of gender in society (see 2017, 73). Following this line of thought, it can be said that the categorization of ourselves occurs through patterns. This categorization lies in the register of the resemblance ("as if") rather than the register of the actual evidence ("as") (2017). That is to say, data (as metaphors) are interpreted to make us fit into categories. From a qualitative approach, this is a process of simplification and categorization (Couldry 2017; Markham 2018). Thus, interpretations depend on cultural views, and conceptions and uses of data depend on "those who capture, analyze and draw conclusions from them" (Kitchin 2014, 3). In other words, interpretations of data and methods are intrinsically related.

Thus, epistemological specificities of data are critical. Kitchin (2014) compares two philosophical approaches to data—i.e., essentialist and qualitative—and describes the associated assumptions. The qualitative approach acknowledges elements of contexts and their influence on our interpretations of reality. This qualitative approach assumes that data are necessarily interpreted because they cannot exist without "ideas, techniques, technologies, people and contexts" (Kitchin 2014, 198). Also, the qualitative approach assumes that data are not only a constituent but also constitutive of the social world, which recalls the definition of the metaphor (Ricœur 1975; Lakoff and Johnson 2003).

The essentialist approach assumes that data are objective and neutral (Kitchin 2014). It is close to engineering, technological, and computational interpretations. Boyd and Crawford (2012) explain that the computational interpretation redefines "terrains of objects, methods of knowing, and definitions of social life" (2012, 64). In other words, the traditional scientific approach to reality is being replaced by computational interpretations of elements of reality. In a similar way, Cheney-Lippold (2017) describes that engineering views are used to make sense of the social world as social problems, and by doing so, "they'll find ways to turn these problems into engineering problems, because if you turn them into engineering problems then you can solve them" (2017, 42). Also, there is an interpretation of the visible outputs their tools create. Namely, "we're data," and "we're interpreted by computer networks, governments, and even our friends" (2017, 46). In other words, those who develop the platforms *interpret* who we are through data about us. Their approach to reality, or essentialist approach, influences their interpretations of data about us. The essentialist approach challenges the traditional approach to reality.

The redefinition of data and datafication of the society by an essentialist approach has been called an "ideological shift" (Couldry 2017, 236). Cheney-Lippold (2017) calls this phenomenon a "reessentialisation" (2017, 64). He explains that Big Data leads to "understanding a new version of the world, one previously unavailable to us because in an antiquated era before digital computers and ubiquitous surveillance, we didn't have the breadth and memory to store it all" (2017, 57). This new ideology is based on a technological interpretation of reality, i.e., reality is made of information instead of natural and social phenomena (Mayer-Schönberger and Kenneth Cukier in Couldry 2017, 236), and some call information the "fuel" of Big Data (De Mauro, Greco, and Grimaldi 2014), which makes information or data at the core of the essentialist approach.

To conclude this section, interpretations from different fields, e.g., computational or technological, influence the very definitions of data or information. Whether our data are defined from an economic or human rights interpretations, legal protections can differ much. For example, being considered as a consumer or an individual does not offer the same legal protections. In addition to interpretations, the last characteristic of a metaphor to consider is the field of application, as explained by Ricœur (1972). The application of a specific definition in a field implements its related interpretations, which convey approaches to reality (e.g., essentialist or traditional). The next section focuses on data and information in one field of application, i.e., privacy policies.

The Concept of Data in Privacy Laws

Interpretations of data or information described in the previous section are anchored in epistemological and ontological discussions (respectively, interpretations and approaches to reality). These discussions tend to oppose traditional and essentialist approaches, which classify interpretations in these two broad categories. Privacy policies do not differentiate these categories as clearly. Thus, interpretations are necessarily mixed and have to cohabit.

Braman (1989) distinguishes four types of definition of information in policies. The first is a resource, in the legal context of international trade. Contextualized as such, information can be informed by an economic interpretation, which permits to exclude other interpretations like cultural, social, or political. The second is very close; information is a commodity. The author highlights that if keeping only one definition of information, i.e., economic value, other interpretations might disappear (1989). The third is a perception of patterns, which echoes the technological interpretation as described in the previous section. To exemplify this category, the author provides definitions from computer science, economics, mathematics, engineers, and more. From a human rights interpretation, Hamelink (2003) shows that the classification depends on the use of information, which he calls "patterns for the traffic of information."[3] Human rights provisions tend to address one pattern. Freedom of expression covers dissemination; access to information is associated with consultation; and protection of privacy deals with registration (2003, 155). The human rights interpretation encompasses the risks associated with the advancements in technologies that could harm human rights. In the EU, there is a similar interpretation of personal data. During the redesign of the General Data Protection Regulation (GDPR), the Proposal from the European Commission expressed worries about the capacities of computers toward personal data. For example, it stressed the risks of using "automated" decision-making that can lead to discriminating categories of people (Schwartz and Solove 2014, 894).

The last definition proposed by Braman (1989) is data as a constitutive force in society, and it resembles the broad traditional approach, as described previously. This approach sees information as the main constituent of a social structure. The author specifies that any definition of information can be used ideologically, which makes it necessary to use different definitions to avoid the ideological pitfalls of a single interpretation. The United Nations general assembly resolution from 1973 provides a good example that includes multiple interpretations. The assembly emphasized that scientific and technological developments should be used "to strengthen peace and security, the realization of people's right to self-determination and respect for national sovereignty, and for the purpose of economic and social development" (in Hamelink 2003, 126).

To conclude this section, neither interpretations nor definitions can offer a universal definition of data or information. Analyzing the metaphor of data should include different types of interpretation in their field of application. So far, three types of interpretation have been identified in the context of privacy policies, i.e., technological, economic, and human rights. These interpretations have to be understood as potentially competing to impose a definition in privacy laws because defining data is subjected to power dynamics (Braman 1989). Hence the following research question: *How do several interpretations of the metaphor of data compete to redefine data in privacy policies?*

In this chapter, the metaphor of data permits to focus on interpretations that coexist in privacy policies. Before to conduct the analysis, I explain how Critical Discourse Studies can be used to analyze the metaphor of data in privacy policies.

2 Analyzing Data as a Metaphor with CDS

Defining data[4] in EU regulations is a major concern for data governance, and it depends on their field of application, i.e., privacy policies. Kitchin (2014, 146) recalls that there is an agenda behind the use of data, which denotes the importance of the stakeholders involved. Not only governments shape privacy with policies and laws, but also companies with their privacy policies (Peek 2006). In other words, the privacy policies of the biggest online companies (GAFAM) are critical since the protection of personal data does not only depend on laws but also on privacy policies.

In this study, "defining" includes the different ways of interpreting the metaphor of data in their field of application (i.e., privacy policies). The metaphor can be addressed analytically with an adapted version of Critical Discourse Studies (CDS). One version of CDS divides the analysis into different levels to contextualize the smallest unit of analysis in its broader contexts (Wodak and Reisigl 2016). In this study, there are three levels. The first level concerns the definitions of data alone. The second contextualizes these definitions that connect together within documents and interview transcriptions in English (i.e., laws, privacy policies, and interviews), and which I categorize according to interpretations. The third concerns interpretations of data found in the above literature review, i.e., technological, economic, human rights, and it structures the analysis. This division scrutinizes the impacts of the different interpretations of data on privacy policies.

The material encompasses laws, privacy policies, and interviews. The laws are those in the EU regulatory framework for privacy that concern telecommunications and data directly (i.e., 97/66/EC,[5] and its renewed version 2002/58/EC,[6] and 2016/679[7]). In addition, the data set includes the global privacy policies[8] of the GAFAM (i.e., Google, Amazon, Facebook, Apple, Microsoft). These companies were selected because they are major players among online companies, which play a crucial role to define privacy protections online (Schwartz 2004). Eventually, the data set comprises specific parts of semi-structured interviews[9] with 14 lobbyists and policymakers[10] working on the GDPR or the E-regulation. I made three interviewees categories. The first is "corporate lobbyists" (those who are working or who have worked for one of the GAFAM), and it concerns three interviewees. The second is "policy-makers," which includes seven interviewees. Policymakers work or have worked either for the European Parliament, the European Commission, or the Council. The last category is "lobbyists," and it concerns four persons working for lobbying companies or think tanks.

Once I gathered the definition of data from the different documents and interviews, I could analyze the metaphor of data in privacy policies according to interpretations, as described in the next section.

3 The Interpretations of Data in Privacy Policies

The analysis of the different interpretations embedded in the metaphor of data permits to explore its redefinition. The main interpretations are technological, economic, and human rights. This section explores how they compete or complement each other to impose a definition of data in privacy policies. Before to begin the analysis of the several interpretations of the definitions of data, I describe the field of application of the metaphor of data, i.e., EU privacy policies.

From Internet Infrastructures to the Data Market

There has been a switch of focus from infrastructure to data in EU privacy laws. The current Directive on privacy and electronic communications (2002/58/EC) covers data more broadly than its earliest version. The first version of the Directive (97/66/EC) was targeting the telecommunications sector, specifically. Article 2 of the Directive focused mainly on infrastructures, i.e., "public telecommunications network" and "telecommunications service." Both definitions contain references to the infrastructures, respectively, "transmission systems," and services "whose provision consists wholly or partly in the transmission and routing of signals on telecommunications networks." The latest version (2002/58/EC) widened its scope to the electronic communications sector. Article 2 defines communication as "any information exchanged or conveyed between a finite number of parties by means of a publicly available electronic communications service" (2002/58/EC). This definition focuses mainly on *information*. Together with the definition of communication, two types of data are defined, i.e., location and traffic data. While the early Directive (97/66/EC) focused more on infrastructures, the Directive on privacy and electronic communications (2002/58/EC) focus more on data and information. In Recital 6, the Directive (2002) explains the increase of attention for data: "The Internet is overturning traditional market structures by providing a common, global infrastructure…" and it opens "new possibilities for users but also new risks for their personal data and privacy." The focus on data is accompanied by the endorsement for infrastructures to enable data flows. Recital 6 of the GDPR (2016/679) states that technologies have "transformed both the economy and social life, and should further facilitate the free flow of personal data." These regulations try to combine three interpretations, i.e., economic, technological, and human rights (to address the challenges related to social life transformation).

This change of focus reflects the reality of the market. The number of online services the GAFAM own is huge. To recall, these corporations are merging large numbers of companies from multiple sectors, and the example of Google (or rather, Alphabet) is particularly striking. It owns companies in a multiplicity of sectors like online browsing (Chrome), video sharing (YouTube), smart speakers (Nest), web analytics (Google Analytics), biotechnologies (Calico), smart cities (Sidewalk Labs), etc. The oligopoly and monopolies in services and products, which permit a vast collection of data, result in an oligopoly on the data market. The access to data provides these companies with unrivaled capacities to collect and process them. The multiplicity of sources (not to mention data brokers) results in a high amount of different types of data that are processed altogether. As a consequence, defining key elements of the field of application, i.e., the uses of data, online spaces, and goals to use data, impacts the redefinition of personal data, which is defined from a human rights interpretation in the GDPR.

The Human Rights Interpretation

Economic and technological interpretations challenge the human rights interpretation to redefine personal data. One of the underlying assumptions of the economic interpretation to define data is that they can be considered as goods. A policymaker (January 2018) opposed to this comparison a human rights interpretation of data, which aligns with the definition of personal data in the GDPR. As Schwartz and Solove (2011) pointed out, the fact that personal data are defined (in the legal Acts of the EU legal framework for privacy) as "any information related to an identified or identifiable natural person" makes the definition very broad. In other words, non-personal data can become personal data after processing operations that would permit to identify an individual. On the one hand, the broadening of the definition in the law was necessary to prevent its circumventions by companies. There had been, for example, discussions to categorize an IP address as personal data, which happened to be (Policymaker, November 2009). On the other hand, the broadness of the definition of personal data leads to questioning what non-personal data are. A policymaker (February 2018) explained that their team could not find a definition of non-personal data, which is problematic in contexts different from privacy (e.g., consumer protection). The interviewee (February 2018) noted that it could be interpreted as a non-category because of the potential inexistence of non-personal data. However, the privacy policies of the GAFAM define non-personal data and tend to align with laws.

In its privacy policy (2019), Apple defines non-personal information as "data in a form that does not, on its own, permit direct association with any specific individual," for example, "unique device identifier." Apple's definition enters in conflict with the GDPR, although it adapts to regulation. In the context of "cookies and other technologies," Apple (2019) explains: "to the extent that Internet Protocol (IP) addresses or similar identifiers are considered personal information by local law, we also treat these identifiers as personal information." Also, Google refers to non-personally identifiable information which it defines as "information that is recorded about users so that it no longer reflects or references an individually-identifiable user" (Google, n.d.).

The economic and technological interpretations do not challenge the definition of personal data directly but through key elements of the field of application. Apple provides a good example of the interlinkage of the definition of personal data and the purposes of using personal data. Apple (2019) states: "Aggregated data is considered non-personal information for the purposes of this Privacy Policy." In other words, the definition of data depends on the uses of data, which depends on the goals of using data. Both are defined through technological and economic interpretations.

In addition, the definition of online spaces is at stake to define personal data, as human rights and technological and economic interpretations compete to impose their definition. The human rights interpretation connects personal data to the private sphere. The Directive on electronic communication services (2002/58/EC) defines the private sphere as follows:

> *Terminal equipment of users of electronic communications networks and any information stored on such equipment are part of* the private sphere of the users requiring protection under the European Convention for the Protection of Human Rights and Fundamental Freedoms (Recital 24, emphasis from the author)

The human rights interpretation of the definition of the private sphere aligns with the human rights interpretation of the definition of personal data in the GDPR. Also, in the Directive on privacy and electronic communications (2002/58/EC), the definition of communication is the exchange or conveyed information *between a finite number of parties*. This element of the definition refers to traditional private spaces.

Technological interpretations challenge the definition of the traditional private spheres, which questions the definition of personal data, as defined in the GDPR. A corporate lobbyist (January 2018) explained, "we have a picture (…), we are all enclosed in a personal sphere, where we have our own personal data, and we don't want anyone to enter in that sphere and take that data away from us." However, "this idea of a sphere in which you are a sole person and that nobody enters the sphere is wrong" because "what you are, who you are, your identity is produced by others." The lobbyist linked the private sphere to personal data, and by questioning the private sphere, the person questioned the definition of personal data.

The definition of different types of information or data depends on the definition of different types of spaces, whether public or private. For example, the privacy policy of Facebook (2018) redefines public information based on public spaces, as shaped by its services. It defines this category as information that "can be seen by anyone, on or off our Products, including if they don't have an account." This category of information includes "any information you share with a public audience," etc. In the same document, the platform makes clear that if a user shares information, i.e., "information and content you provide," then the user consents to Facebook's categories of data. However, research about ethics on digital media shows that users do not have a good understanding of public or private spaces online (Mukherjee 2017). In other words, Facebook, through a technological interpretation, contributes to shaping what online public spaces are, and consequently, redefine public information.

In the same vein, EU privacy laws do not use the category public data (or information) but use the type of infrastructure to identify the information shared with a public audience. The Directive on privacy and electronic communications (2002/58/EC) distinguishes electronic communication services from broadcasting services. In Article 2, the definition of communication excludes "any ***information conveyed as part of*** a ***broadcasting service to the public*** over an electronic communications network except to the extent that the information can be related to the identifiable subscriber or user receiving the information" (2002/58/EC). Nevertheless, as the Directive stated, the interpretations of the infrastructures of the Internet as being global is blurring distinctions between different types of electronic communication services. Thus, defining and categorizing data, like public data, contributes to redefining online public spaces, and *vice-versa*. However, defining data can be in conflict with other interpretations. From a human rights interpretation, public data is not a category that really works because it does not inform whether the individual is identifiable or not (Schwartz and Solove 2011).

To conclude, the definition of personal data depends on the technological interpretation of online services and the spaces they shape. Other key elements of the field application that have an impact on the redefinition of personal data are the general definition of data, and the uses of data, or data processing.

The Technological Interpretation

The technological interpretation concerns the general definition of data, and the definition of the uses of data, i.e., data processing, in privacy policies. Concerning the definition of data, almost all interviewees interpreted their definition from one or several interpretations, i.e., technological, economic, or human rights. Prior to discussing the different interpretations, a common trait among the responses (8 of the interviewees) was to define data as information, a collection of information, or electronic information. In privacy policies, there is no clear distinction either between data and information.

The technological interpretation of the definition of data is also found in the privacy policies of the GAFAM, and in some legal Acts of the EU concerning privacy. Location data and traffic data are defined in the Directive on privacy and electronic communications (2002/58/EC). Their definitions are purely technological. In a similar way, Amazon (2020), Apple (2019), Google (2020), Microsoft (2020) use the categories *location information, location data*, (Facebook 2018) uses *location-related information* and Microsoft (2020) refers to *traffic data*. Nevertheless, these categories of data are mentioned in technological *and* other contexts (e.g., economic). For example, Google (2020) refers to location data as "Information about things near your device, such as Wi-Fi access points, cell towers, and Bluetooth-enabled devices," which is one of the multiple ways to gain location information. Google (2020) states that it helps to offer features, i.e., technological purposes. Apple (2019) classifies location information directly as personal information, which the GDPR does as well when defining personal data in Article 4(1). Facebook (2018) states the purposes to collect location-related information as to "provide, personalize and improve our Products, including ads, for you and others." Although the definition of location information tends to be informed by a technological interpretation in laws, purposes are multiple in privacy policies. Given that different types of data can be used for several purposes, focusing on their uses is critical. Also, the uses of data determine epistemological specificities of the interpretation of the definition of data.

Categories and definitions of data depend on uses of data, i.e., data processing. In privacy policies, data processing tends to be defined technologically. The vocabulary in use does not refer to qualitative approaches like interpretation. For example, Google (2020) explains that it uses "algorithms to recognize patterns in data," and "automated systems that analyze your content to provide you with things customized search results, personalized ads..." In the same vein, Amazon (2020) has a category "automatic information," which it describes as follows: "we automatically collect and store certain types of information about your use of Amazon Services, including information about your interaction with content and services available through Amazon Services." Apple (2019) acknowledges the potential impact of these processes on the users, and it states: "Apple does not take any decisions involving the use of algorithms or profiling that significantly affect you." Although this sentence is vague, Apple recognizes the potential of automated means to affect the users through "decisions."

A corporate lobbyist (January 2018) adopts a technological interpretation likewise when discussing purposes as a legal basis[11] to process personal data: "it is not always possible to (...) specify the different things I would discover in the material." That is to say, defining purposes for processing personal data could impede potential discoveries. This interpretation is anchored in empiricism, which is based on exploration (Kitchin 2014, 257). In other words, the data collected will speak for themselves, and they bring objective answers (i.e., correlations or patterns). This interpretation suggests that technology overthrows scientific inquiries and methods (e.g., theories, models, hypotheses), i.e., the traditional approach to data.

In the same vein, the definitions of data processing in the GDPR and Microsoft offer an interpretation of data processing that overlooks data analysis and its biases. In the GDPR, the definition of data processing is:

> (...) any operation or set of operations which is performed on personal data or on sets of personal data, whether or not by automated means, such as collection, recording, organization, structuring, storage, adaptation or alteration, retrieval, consultation, use, disclosure by transmission, dissemination or otherwise making available, alignment or combination, restriction, erasure or destruction. (Article 4(2))

It resembles Griffith's definition of information science, which "is concerned with the generation, collection, organization, *interpretation*, storage, retrieval, dissemination, *transformation*, and use of information" (as cited in Capurro and Hjørland 2005, emphasis from the author). Both words highlighted in the second definition (*interpretation* and *transformation*) show the difference between a definition assumed as purely technological (in the GDPR), and one which includes elements from a qualitative approach (Griffith's). Capurro and Hjørland (2005) refer to Griffith's definition as the definition of information science *tools*. They highlight that the difference between information science and computer science is the object of study. IS includes a social sciences approach (e.g., "sociological patterns in knowledge production," philosophy of sciences, etc.)

As in the definition of data processing in the GDPR, the difference between the tools and the analysis vanishes in the privacy policy of Microsoft. Microsoft defines AI "as a set of technologies that enable computers to perceive, learn, reason, and assist in decision-making to solve problems in ways that are similar to what people do" (Microsoft 2020). This definition refers strongly to technological optimism, which strengthens the technological interpretation of Microsoft.

Although Microsoft acknowledges human interventions in some processing operations, it persists in using a technological interpretation of data processing. It "manually review[s] some of the predictions and inferences produced by the automated methods" (Microsoft 2020). The GDPR refers to automated and non-automated means likely concerning data processing. In both cases, although individuals might be involved in the process, there is no reference to interpretation. In other words, the use of data (i.e., data processing) is interpreted technologically in the privacy policies of the companies and in the GDPR.

In addition to the technological interpretation that defines data uses, an economic interpretation is to be found in the metaphor of data. It also defines key elements of the field of application, i.e., goals of using data.

The Economic Interpretation

The economic interpretation concerns mainly the goals of using data. The interviewees, the privacy policies of the GAFAM, and EU policies for privacy share an economic interpretation. Several interviewees described data embedded in an economic context. For example, a lobbyist (May 2018) described "what we do on data, on the use of data, we focus on the value of data for webshops." At the same time, the person had given a generic answer to define data, i.e., "data is something that is perceived by the brain of an individual, an information." This answer is rather qualitative. However, the interviewee referred to e-commerce to interpret data in context, and thus, adopted an economic interpretation.

In the GDPR, the economic interpretation frames partly the context of personal data protection with data flows. The title of the GDPR mentions the tools, i.e., the processing of personal data, and the economic context, i.e., the free movement of such data (within the European internal market). The regulation describes its economic goal together with a human rights goal:

> In order to ensure a consistent level of protection for natural persons throughout the Union and to prevent divergences hampering the free movement of personal data within the internal market, a Regulation is necessary to provide legal certainty and transparency for economic operators. (Recital 13)

This interpretation of data as having economic value resonates with privacy policies that emphasize the importance of data flows. In privacy policies, the economic interpretation stems from marketing mainly. It is sufficient to look at the revenues of Google or Facebook to understand why.[12] Apple does not depend on marketing for its revenue, and it states that it "does not sell personal information, and personal information will never be shared with third parties for their marketing purposes" (Apple 2019). Facebook (2018) also states: "We don't sell any of your information to anyone, and we never will." This statement points an important difference between selling and sharing, which corresponds respectively to transferring ownership and to providing access to data. Companies who provide analytics tools can implement the second option. In the case of Facebook, it shares information with third parties, and especially, through Facebook Business Tools (2018). It is not the only one to do so, and Google has marketing services as well, such as Google Analytics.

Whether their business models depend on marketing or not, the goals stated in the privacy policies of these companies are often similar, e.g., provision of services, improvement of services, performance, security, better experience, or marketing. These goals are mainly technological or economic. Aggregated data is the category of data mainly concerned by an economic interpretation. All the privacy policies of the companies explain that they aggregate data, directly or indirectly. For example, Facebook states that "Facebook and Instagram share infrastructure, systems and technology with other Facebook Companies (which include WhatsApp and Oculus) to provide an *innovative, relevant, consistent and safe experience* across all Facebook Company Products you use" (Facebook 2018, emphasis from the author). Microsoft provides a similar example with the smart speaker Cortana. Its privacy policy describes: "Cortana can process the demographic data (such as your age, address, and gender) associated with your Microsoft account and data collected through other Microsoft services to provide personalized suggestions" (Microsoft 2020). Apple's goals are not much different from other GAFAM, i.e., to "better understand customer behavior and improve [its] products, services, and advertising" (2019), which denotes technological and economic interpretations. The more data aggregated, the more personalization. Collecting personalized data for marketing purposes is a lucrative market, and the more fine-grained data, the more advertisers will pay (Schwartz and Solove 2011).

To conclude, it is clear that the human rights interpretation that defines personal data in the GDPR had had an influence on the redefinition of personal data itself in the privacy policies of the GAFAM. However, technological and economic interpretations are complementary to redefine spaces online, the uses of data, and the goals to use data. They are key elements that compose the field of application. In other words, both interpretations redefine the approach to the reality corresponding to online privacy through an essentialist approach, and which undermines the human rights interpretation, anchored in a traditional approach. To strengthen the human rights interpretation, it would be needed to include interpretations that can address the impacts and goals of data processing on society (e.g., imposing strong ethical requirements to prevent discriminatory biases in data processing).

4 Conclusion

Focusing on the definitions of data or information alone would have been insufficient to analyze changes in privacy policies. The metaphor denotes a change of meaning in a concept, and this change can be tracked with the analysis of the several interpretations the metaphor contains. The metaphor permits to conduct the analysis on a field of application, i.e., privacy policies. If a redefinition of a metaphor is ongoing in a field of application, the latter might be subjected to changes itself. In the analysis, key elements of the field of application analyzed in relation to the metaphor of data have suggested a change of the field of application.

Personal data are defined from a human rights interpretation in the GDPR, which has influenced the privacy policies of the GAFAM and the interviewees' definitions. For example, Microsoft (2020) has strengthened its privacy policy, partly based on the GDPR, and it offers the same level of protection regardless of the users' location.

Technological and economic interpretations define key elements of the field of application, that is, uses and goals of data processing. The definitions of data processing are mainly informed by an essentialist view of reality, which puts aside technological biases and limits ethical interpretations although the categorization of data cannot be objective or without purposes and decisions (Kitchin 2014). For example, the computed classification of individuals for marketing purposes involves risks regarding the protection of human rights, e.g., discrimination (Schwartz and Solove 2014).

Also, by defining the uses of data, the main platforms contribute to defining online spaces. As DeNardis and Hackl (2015) explained, platforms "have become vital components of the digital public sphere. How they design their platforms, how they allow content to flow, and how they agree to exchange information with competing platforms have direct implications for both communication rights and innovation" (2015, 769). Eventually, goals for processing data depend on the capacities and the needs of these platforms to play in the data market, and they are strongly defined from an economic interpretation.

The focus of this study is limited to economic, technological, and human rights interpretations and how they interplay together to influence the definitions of data in EU privacy policies. The goals of using personal data are subjected to governmental influences as well. For example, they have the capacities to strengthen the public interest against privacy to protect national security. Purposes linked to security create great frictions with human rights. These frictions are also a critical issue that deserves much attention.

Notes

1. Ricœur uses a different terminology, which informs a more complex theory. I adapted the theory and the terminology to fit this study.
2. Cheney-Lippold remarks that this is less true with unsupervised machine learning algorithms.
3. He lists four patterns, which should be covered by the right to communicate. The dissemination of information is protected by the freedom of expression, the consultation by access to information, and registration by the protection of privacy. However, the right to communication is not entirely covered because the fourth pattern is not protected by law, i.e., conversation or "transfer of messages." This right to communicate was defended in the 1970s and faded away in the 1990s.
4. Since data and information have been used interchangeably in privacy policies, I included in the metaphor of data definitions of information that

I found in privacy policies. In other words, I also consider both data and information as interchangeable concepts in the privacy policies I analyzed.

5. Directive 97/66/EC of the European Parliament and of the Council of 15 December 1997 concerning the processing of personal data and the protection of privacy in the telecommunications sector. This Directive is no longer in force and was replaced by Directive 2002/58/EC.
6. Directive 2002/58/EC of the European Parliament and of the Council of 12 July 2002 concerning the processing of personal data and the protection of privacy in the electronic communications sector (Directive on privacy and electronic communications). Also, a proposal for the ePrivacy Regulation was released on the 1st of October 2017 and the new Regulation will repeal Directive 2002/58/EC (Regulation on Privacy and Electronic Communications). For this study, the Proposal for the ePrivacy Regulation was left out of the data set.
7. Regulation (EU) 2016/679 of the European Parliament and of the Council of 27 April 2016 on the protection of natural persons with regard to the processing of personal data and on the free movement of such data, and repealing Directive 95/46/EC (General Data Protection Regulation) (Text with EEA relevance).
8. Global privacy policies were accessed from Sweden. They are general and there can be some adaptations to some regions. Although these privacy policies apply to some of the products and services of the companies, they state that some services and products have their own privacy policies, which are not included in the analysis.
9. These interviews are part of a larger set of interviews (18) conducted for a broader project. There were two interview campaigns, the first took place from December 2017 to July 2018 (nine interviews), and the second occurred from July 2019 to January 2020 (nine interviews). This study focuses and develops one element of analysis related to the broader project, i.e., the metaphor of data. The part of the interviews used in this study is the answers to the question: "How would you define data?".
10. To respect their anonymity, I did not assign individual identifiers, and I refer to them through one of the three categories. In addition, I do not use the day of the date of the interview to prevent identification.
11. Processing personal data is allowed if at least one of the six legal basis defined by the GDPR is applied (i.e., consent, contract, legal obligation, vital interest, public task, legitimate interest).
12. In 2019, out of 160.74 billion US dollars, Google earned 113.26 from advertising revenue. Facebook earned 69,655 million dollars with advertising out of 70.697 (Statista 2020). Apple, Amazon, and Microsoft do not depend financially on advertising.

Bibliography

Amazon. 2020. Privacy Notice. Amazon Privacy Notice, January 1. https://www.amazon.com/gp/help/customer/display.html?nodeId=201909010.

Apple. 2019. Privacy Policy. Legal—Privacy Policy—Apple, December 31. https://www.apple.com/legal/privacy/en-ww/.

boyd, danah, and Kate Crawford. 2012. Critical Questions for Big Data: Provocations for a Cultural, Technological, and Scholarly Phenomenon. *Information, Communication & Society* 15 (5): 662–79. https://doi.org/10.1080/1369118X.2012.678878.

Braman, Sandra. 1989. Defining Information. *Telecommunications Policy* 13 (3): 233–242. https://doi.org/10.1016/0308-5961(89)90006-2.

Capurro, Rafael, and Birger Hjørland. 2005. The Concept of Information. *Annual Review of Information Science and Technology* 37 (1): 343–411. https://doi.org/10.1002/aris.1440370109.

Cheney-Lippold, John. 2017. Categorization: Making Data Useful. In *We Are Data: Algorithms and the Making of Our Digital Selves*, 37–92. New York: New York University Press.

Couldry, Nick. 2017. The Myth of Big Data. In *The Datafied Society*, ed. Mirko Tobias Schäfer and Karin van Es, 235–239. Amsterdam University Press.

De Mauro, Andrea, Marco Greco, and Michele Grimaldi. 2014. What Is Big Data? A Consensual Definition and a Review of Key Research Topics. In *4th International Conference on Integrated Information*, 97–104. Madrid, Spain. https://doi.org/10.1063/1.4907823.

DeNardis, L., and A. M. Hackl. 2015. Internet Governance by Social Media Platforms. *Telecommunications Policy*, Special Issue on *The Governance of Social Media* 39 (9): 761–770. https://doi.org/10.1016/j.telpol.2015.04.003.

Facebook. 2018. Data Policy. Data Policy—Facebook, April 19. https://www.facebook.com/policy.php.

Google. 2020. Privacy Policy. Privacy & Terms—Google, March 31. https://policies.google.com/privacy?hl=en-US.

Google. n.d. Key Terms. Privacy & Terms—Google. Accessed 8 July 2020. https://policies.google.com/privacy/key-terms?hl=en-US.

Hamelink, Cees J. 2003. Human Rights for the Information Society. In *Communicating in the Information Society*, ed. Bruce Girard, Seán Ó Siochrú, and United Nations Research Institute for Social Development, 121–163. Geneva: United Nations Research Institute for Social Development.

Kitchin, Rob. 2014. *The Data Revolution: Big Data, Open Data, Data Infrastructures & Their Consequences*. Los Angeles, CA: Sage.

Lakoff, George, and Mark Johnson. 2003. *Metaphors We Live By*. Chicago: University of Chicago Press.

Markham, Annette N. 2018. Troubling the Concept of Data in Qualitative Digital Research. In *The SAGE Handbook of Qualitative Data Collection*, by

Uwe Flick, 511–523. 1 Oliver's Yard, 55 City Road, London EC1Y 1SP: Sage. https://doi.org/10.4135/9781526416070.n33.

Microsoft. 2020. Privacy Statement. Microsoft Privacy, June. https://privacy.microsoft.com/en-gb/privacystatement.

Mukherjee, Ishani. 2017. The Social Age of "It's Not a Private Problem," Case Study of Ethical and Privacy Concerns in a Digital Ethnography of South Asian Blogs against Intimate Partner Violence. In *Internet Research Ethics for the Social Age: New Challenges, Cases, and Contexts*, ed. Michael Zimmer and Katharina Kinder-Kurlanda, 203–212. Digital Formations, vol. 108. New York: Peter Lang.

Peek, Marcy E. 2006. Information Privacy and Corporate Power: Towards a Re-imagination of Information Privacy Law. *Seton Hall Law Review* 37 (1): 127.

Ricœur, Paul. 1972. La métaphore et le problème central de l'herméneutique. *Revue Philosophique De Louvain* 70 (5): 93–112. https://doi.org/10.3406/phlou.1972.5651.

Ricœur, Paul. 1975. *La métaphore vive*. L' ordre philosophique. Paris: Éd. du Seuil.

Schwartz, Paul M. 2004. Property, Privacy, and Personal Data. *Harvard Law Review* 117 (7): 2056. https://doi.org/10.2307/4093335.

Schwartz, Paul M., and Daniel J. Solove. 2011. The PII Problem: Privacy and a New Concept of Personally Identifiable Information. *New York University Law Review* 86: 1814.

Schwartz, Paul M., and Daniel J. Solove. 2014. Reconciling Personal Information in the United States and European Union. *California Law Review* 102 (4): 877. https://doi.org/10.15779/Z38Z814.

Statista. 2020. Google, Apple, Facebook, and Amazon (GAFA). https://www.statista.com/study/47704/google-apple-facebook-and-amazon-gafa/.

van Dijck, José. 2013. *The Culture of Connectivity: A Critical History of Social Media*. Oxford and New York: Oxford University Press.

Wodak, Ruth, and Martin Reisigl. 2016. Chapter 2: The Discourse-Historical Approach (DHA). In *Methods of Critical Discourse Studies*, ed. Ruth Wodak and Michael Meyer, 3rd ed., 1–22. London and Thousand Oaks, CA: Sage.

Legal Sources

Directive 97/66/EC of the European Parliament and of the Council of 15 December 1997 concerning the processing of personal data and the protection of privacy in the telecommunications sector. (1998). *Official Journal L 24*, 1–8.

Directive 2002/58/EC of the European Parliament and of the Council of 12 July 2002 concerning the processing of personal data and the protection of privacy in the electronic communications sector (Directive on privacy and electronic communications). (2002). *Official Journal L 201*, 37–47.

Regulation (EU) 2016/679 of the European Parliament and of the Council of 27 April 2016 on the protection of natural persons with regard to the processing of personal data and on the free movement of such data, and repealing Directive 95/46/EC (General Data Protection Regulation) (Text with EEA relevance). (2016). *Official Journal L 119*, 1–88.

Regulating Beyond Media to Protect Media Pluralism: The EU Media Policies as Seen Through the Lens of the Media Pluralism Monitor

Iva Nenadić and Marko Milosavljević

1 Introduction

In the European Union (EU) media pluralism has long been acknowledged as an indispensable condition for a robust democracy and as one of the core values upon which the Union is based. The 2000 Charter of Fundamental Rights of the EU, in its Article 11(2), mentions media pluralism as a crucial component of the right to freedom of expression, and requires that freedom and pluralism of the media are respected. The idea of media pluralism is, thus, at the core of European media policies. It is even more so in the recent years, which have been marked by the growing power of online platforms in shaping the information environments, and because of the perceived impact platforms have on informed

I. Nenadić
European University Institute, Florence, Italy

University of Zagreb, Zagreb, Croatia

M. Milosavljević (✉)
University of Ljubljana, Ljubljana, Slovenia
e-mail: Marko.Milosavljevic@fdv.uni-lj.si

S. A. Matei et al. (eds.), *Digital and Social Media Regulation*,
https://doi.org/10.1007/978-3-030-66759-7_5

citizenship and forming of the public opinion. However, it has never been as challenging for the Union as it is in recent years when it needs to face the issue of jurisdiction and exercising its influence over companies that operate globally and are mostly foreign-based (from USA and elsewhere), in order to protect its key values.

The European Commission (EC 2018b, c) has recognized the stream of illegal content online, virality of misinformation, coordinated disinformation campaigns, and the negative effects of micro-targeted political advertising as some of the major challenges for European democracies. In an attempt to respond to these challenges, and to protect and promote pluralism, the EC has introduced a set of legislative and other measures and has even led platforms to self-regulation. For example, EU rules on open internet access, or so-called net neutrality regulation, were adopted in 2015 and apply as of 30 April 2016; the General Data Protection Regulation (GDPR) was adopted in 2016 and became fully applicable across the EU in May 2018; in May 2016, the Commission agreed with Facebook, Microsoft, Twitter, and YouTube a Code of Conduct on Countering Illegal Hate Speech Online. In 2018, the EC adopted a Recommendation on measures to effectively tackle illegal content online, and a Communication on tackling online disinformation (EC 2018b), which resulted in self-regulatory Code of Practice on Disinformation signed by the leading online platforms—later that year. The revised Audiovisual Media Services Directive (AVMSD) was as well adopted, extending some of the rules governing TV broadcasting to video-sharing platforms. Most recently, after a heated debate, the Copyright Directive was approved in 2019, introducing the so-called press publishers' right (Art. 15), a ground for requesting platforms to remunerate press publishers for displaying previews of their content.

All these measures were adopted during the mandate of the Commission presided by Jean-Claude Juncker (2014–2019), which laid the foundation for taking a firmer stance toward the regulation of platforms. The new Commission, headed by Ursula von der Leyen, took office in 2019 for a five-year term and announced media pluralism as one of the priorities. In her mission letter to the Vice President for Values and Transparency—Věra Jourová—von der Leyen clearly stated that media pluralism is essential to democracy and that it needs to be protected (Von der Leyen 2019). One of the major projects of the current Commission is to modernize and update 20 years old e-Commerce Directive (EC 2000) into the Digital Services Act, an ex-ante regulatory instrument, which is expected to ensure transparency and accountability of online platforms.

This chapter aims to analyze both positives and challenges of the above-listed measures and instruments, which are going beyond media to protect media pluralism. The analysis uses the conceptual and operational framework of the Media Pluralism Monitor (MPM),[1] an independent research and monitoring project that understands media pluralism in a holistic way, and with both online and offline dimensions in mind. The MPM project has been run since 2012 by the Centre for Media Pluralism and Media Freedom at the European University Institute and is co-financed by the EU. This type of monitoring mechanism to assess the situation of media pluralism in the Member States is seen as a means to promptly react to possible threats and violations of fundamental rights (EP 2018). Even though the EU does not have a concrete competence to shape the national media policies, it is expected to intervene when fundamental rights, including media pluralism, are at stake (CMPF 2013). Furthermore, when facing the complex challenges brought about by the global players, having a common European approach is seen as more reasonable and effective than having fragmented national solutions.

2 Operationalization of Media Pluralism in the Media Pluralism Monitor

The MPM employs a broad definition of media pluralism, which encompasses legal, economic, and social-political dimension of the media pluralism, integrating the conceptual triangulation of plurality, diversity, and variety. It considers the factors of structural plurality or co-existence of a sufficient number of independent media in the media market (Klimkiewicz 2010); internal diversity of contents and views within a single media outlet; and exposure diversity manifested through the choices that users of information make (Napoli 2011). For the purpose of regular monitoring, the concept is operationalized through the four main areas: (i) *Basic protection*, that concerns with the fundamental conditions in a pluralistic and democratic society, such as the protection of freedom of expression and access to information, the status of journalists, the independence and effectiveness of the media authority, and the universal reach of traditional media and access to the internet; (ii) *Market plurality*, which evaluates market concentration, transparency of ownership, commercial influence over editorial content, and the media viability; (iii) *Political independence*, an assessment of media capture by political power through the distribution of the resources, ownership, appointment procedures and financing of the public service media, and manipulative practices in political advertising in the audiovisual media and on online platforms; and (iv) *Social inclusiveness*, which considers access to the media by various social and cultural groups, such as minorities, local/regional communities, people with disabilities, and women, as well as media literacy (Brogi et al. 2020).

Each of the topics addressed in the MPM is grounded in standards promoted by the EU, the Council of Europe (CoE), or by the European Court of Human Rights (ECtHR). For example, media pluralism cannot be achieved without ensuring security and economic aspects for doing journalism. According to the case-law of the ECtHR, countries have positive obligations to "create a favourable environment for participation in public debate by all persons concerned, enabling them to express their opinions and ideas without fear" (Dink v. Turkey, 2668/07, 6102/08, 30079/08, 7072/09, 7124/09). Furthermore, in the Declaration on the financial sustainability of quality journalism in the digital age (Decl(13/02/2019)2), adopted by the CoE's Committee of Ministers in February 2019, they call on the states and other stakeholders to acknowledge journalism committed to principles of "fairness, independence and transparency, public accountability and humanity" as a public good and support it through financial means.

The MPM is primarily designed to assess risks to media pluralism, which arise from a lack of available legal safeguards and frameworks, their poor implementation, or from the actual situation in practice. The Monitor stems from a comprehensive questionnaire to which the answers are provided by the local research teams in the countries covered (EU Member States and selected EU candidate countries). To a great extent, the monitoring is based on secondary data, but some primary data is collected as well through methods such as semi-structured in-depth interviews with experts on certain topics. For a number of questions require a qualitative measurement but which cannot be based on easily available or verifiable data, and the answers provided by the country teams need to include adequate additional references as well as undergo a peer review by a group of stakeholders and experts in the same respective country.

In 2019, the MPM questionnaire underwent a significant revision and update, introducing the set of new topics which have emerged as relevant for pluralism in the online environment and in the context of a broader digital transformation (CMPF, n.d.). While it is of utmost importance to closely follow the conditions in the online sphere, traditional sources of risk should not be neglected as they still hold many threats for media pluralism (Brogi et al. 2020). The MPM, therefore, seeks to maintain a holistic assessment of the state of play of pluralism considering both online and offline information environments but with a possibility to extract a digital specific risk score (Brogi et al. 2020).

In the last two decades, the news environment has experienced major changes reflected in news business models, modes of production, distribution, and consumption. The gatekeeping role of deciding on "what the public needs to know, as well as when and how such information should be provided" (Domingo et al. 2008, 326) has been shifting from the media to online platforms, which are increasingly serving as the first bearers of news, especially to younger demographics (EB92 2019; Newman et al. 2020). Despite online mediums not being media in a traditional sense (i.e., not producing content of their own), platforms perform certain media-like functions: acting as gatekeepers (Milosavljević and Broughton Micova 2016) or social editors (Helberger 2016) by prioritizing and personalizing the content on offer; and providing a public sphere, even if "the vision of a singular, integrated public sphere has faded in the face of the social realities" (Dahlgren 2005, 152).

This has prompted the MPM to introduce new variables that would allow for the assessment of media pluralism with regard to online platforms (Brogi et al. 2020). The focus of the MPM is extended beyond the media to include all relevant actors that offer news and contribute to the shaping of public debate (Brogi et al. 2020). Some of the new components in each of the four areas of the MPM are used in the sections below to examine the extent to which legislative and other EU interventions may improve the conditions for media pluralism at a Member State level. Several Member States have adopted national laws to tackle challenges related to platforms. These, too, are evaluated.

3 Basic Protection: Net Neutrality and Freedom of Expression

The basic protection area of the MPM concerns the fundamental conditions in a pluralistic and democratic society. The internet became "a catalyst for individuals to exercise their right to freedom of opinion and expression" (La Rue 2011, 22), which made access to the internet a necessary infrastructure which should be universal. It is, however, not sufficient to ensure only access to the infrastructure, but the access to online content should be guaranteed as well. Freedom of expression is only fully protected if there is no discrimination of internet traffic by ISPs and if arbitrary filtering, blocking, or removals of content by either ISPs, online platforms, or states are disabled.

Net Neutrality Regulation

With this in mind, the MPM assesses the implementation of European net neutrality rules (EU 2015), which have been applied throughout the EU as of 30th April, 2016, and establish common rules to safeguard equal and non-discriminatory treatment of data traffic by ISPs (Art. 1). The measures provided for in the regulation align with the principle of technological neutrality, that is, they do not support or discriminate the use of a particular type of technology. One of the main provisions enshrined is that end-users "shall have the right to access and distribute information and content, use and provide applications and services, and use terminal equipment of their choice, irrespective of the end-user's or provider's location or the location, origin or destination of the information, content, application or service, via their internet access service" (Art 3(1)). This right is granted as long as the content, applications and services are lawful. The lawfulness of the content is not a matter of this regulation that concerns primarily with safeguarding open internet access.

To contribute to the consistent application of the regulation by national regulators in Member States, the Body of European Regulators for Electronic Communication (BEREC 2016) has provided guidelines on the implementation and has clearly communicated that the providers of the infrastructure should be applications agnostic. The latest implementation of the MPM has, however, shown that net neutrality violations are still recorded or attempted in some Member States through differential pricing or zero-rate offers. It is possible, however, the risk stems from the lack of transparency on the regulation's implementation, more specifically when relevant authorities fail to report on their actions in an accessible and transparent way (Brogi et al. 2020).

Countering Illegal Hate Speech Online

With respect to the online content, the basic protection area of the MPM examines whether freedom of expression online is ensured the same way as it is offline. This is in line with the Council of Europe's standards (European Convention on Human Rights, Art. 10, para. 2), which require that the restrictions to freedom of expression are prescribed by law, legitimate, proportionate, and necessary in a democratic society. This said, the MPM, for example, assesses whether the legal rationale of the online content removal/filtering/blocking by platforms is clear, and whether platforms report about filtering and removals in a transparent and effective way (i.e., the full repository of the cases should be available).

Platforms' content moderation practices are largely based on their own terms of service to which the users need to consent in order to use the service. Furthermore, states and state authorities regularly require online platforms companies to remove illegal content outside of legal process and based on non-binding agreements (Kaye 2018). In the Communication on Tackling Illegal Content Online (EC 2017b), the European Commission acknowledged that the online platforms "are important drivers of innovation and growth in the digital economy. They have enabled an unprecedented access to information and exchanges as well as new market opportunities..." but the European Commission also warns that the "spread of illegal content that can be uploaded and therefore accessed online raises serious concerns that need forceful and effective replies."

The Commission's requirement to step up the fight against illegal content online is largely directed toward the online platforms. This is grounded in the e-Commerce Directive (EC 2000), which exempts platforms from liability for hosting illegal content, as long as they remove it "expeditiously" upon obtaining knowledge of it. This approach is known as notice-and-action, and the notice, as highlighted in the Commission's Communication, can come in the form of an administrative order, from competent authorities, trusted flaggers, users, and through platforms own investigations. The latter requires platforms to be proactive and use technology in detecting and removing illegal content (EC 2017b). This directive be seen as necessary given the volume of contents carried by platforms, but may also result in further risks stemming from the lack of transparency of platform's algorithms and operations. The Communication asks from platforms to disclose their content policies and to provide detailed reports on notices and actions taken. It further calls on platforms to put in place appeal mechanisms and safeguards against abuse of the system and over-removals. The requirements of this Communication are operationalized through the Code of Conduct on Countering Illegal Hate Speech Online (Code of Conduct 2016).

Code of Conduct

In May 2016, the EC agreed with Facebook, Microsoft, Twitter, and YouTube on the terms of a Code of Conduct—presented as a voluntary self-regulation of platforms, which includes a list of commitments to counter the spread of illegal hate speech online. The Code of Conduct defines illegal hate speech as "all conduct publicly inciting to violence or hatred directed against a group of persons or a member of such a group defined by reference to race, colour, religion, descent or national or ethnic origin." This definition derives from the Council of the EU's Framework Decision (2008) on combating certain forms and expressions of racism and xenophobia by means of criminal law and national laws transposing it. The key commitment of the Code signatories is to have in place clear and effective processes to review notifications for removal of illegal hate speech within 24 hours and remove or disable access to such content on their services, when necessary.

On 22 June 2020, the EC published the results of its fifth evaluation of the Code. The results are presented as overall positive, highlighting that the signatories are "assessing 90% of flagged content within 24 hours and removing 71% of the content deemed to be illegal hate speech." Nevertheless, the Commission used the occasion to call on the platforms to improve transparency and feedback to users, and the EC's Vice President for Values and Transparency, Vera Jourová, emphasized the need to ensure consistency in content evaluation and that all platforms have the same obligations (EC 2020a). While Instagram, Google+, Snapchat, and Dailymotion joined the Code of Conduct over the course of 2018, and Jeuxvideo.com in January 2019, the Code still does not include all platforms, it is not binding, and even among the signatories of the Code the approach to the removal of illegal content and reporting about actions is not harmonized and coherent. Harmonization here is difficult to achieve since the EU and Member States lack a common legal definition of hate speech (Alkiviadou 2017). Furthermore, each platform is having its own explanation of what the meaning of hate speech is (Alkiviadou 2019). The lack of common definition and increasing pressure toward the platforms to detect and remove illegal content as soon as possible may also result in removals of content that in some Member States is legal, which may negatively impact freedom of expression and media pluralism. To address these issues, the EU is funding a number of research projects that implement artificial intelligence to produce immediate notifications for removal of illegal hate speech as soon as it is detected by algorithms and software, while employing appropriate legal definitions by national legal systems (e.g., EMBEDDIA 2019).

Over the four years of its existence, the Code of Conduct has been seen as a positive development toward an online sphere with less hate speech (Alkiviadou 2019), but it was also regularly criticized for putting private companies in the position of deciding the legality of content without providing clarity on the standards and procedures (Bukovska 2019).

4 Social Inclusiveness: Protection Against Hate Speech

The self-regulation and legislation against hate speech online is a matter of consideration also within the MPM area of social inclusiveness, but from a slightly different perspective—the one that in the focus places the rights of various minorities to enjoy the freedom of expression and access to the public communication spaces. The European Parliament resolution of 13 November 2018 on minimum standards for minorities in the EU (2018/2036(INI)) warns that "persisting harassment, discrimination - including multiple and intersectional discrimination - and violence limit the ability of people to fully enjoy their fundamental rights and freedoms, and undermine their equal participation in society." Against this background, the resolution highlights the fact that the media play a central role with regard to minorities rights to access, receive, and publish information, and that the states should enable them to share their views, language, and culture with the majority (43). Furthermore, the EP called on the Commission and the Member States "to ensure by appropriate means that audiovisual media services do not contain any incitement to violence or hatred directed against people belonging to minorities" (46). In the MPM, the same standard is expected from online platforms as they increasingly serve as the main media platform for a growing number of users (e.g., Newman et al. 2020), and because the Commission's Communication on tackling illegal content online suggests the same approach by noting that "what is illegal offline is also illegal online."

The issue of hate speech against vulnerable social groups online, as included in the MPM, assesses whether there is a (self)regulatory framework to counter hate speech online and whether it has been efficient in removing hate speech while not presenting any risk to the freedom of expression. The most recent MPM results (2020a) show that the issue is underinvestigated and inadequately handled. As per the MPM2020 results, efforts to counter this type of illegal content from social media, especially when directed toward ethnic or religious minorities, or toward women, have largely been perceived as not effective in the current form. Only four countries (Belgium, Germany, Luxembourg, and Sweden) have regulatory frameworks perceived as effective in countering hate speech against vulnerable groups online. In Germany, hate speech has been addressed by the Network Enforcement Act since 2017. At the moment, it does not explicitly refer to the protection of ethnic and religious minorities, but a legislative amendment of the Act might require platforms not only to remove such illegal content rapidly and provide information on the extent to which groups of people are particularly frequently affected by hate speech (Roßmann 2020; Holznagel and Kalbhenn 2020).

The protection against hate speech online is in the MPM social inclusiveness area paired with the media literacy indicator as it is deemed that the more media literate people are, the more resilient they should be to hate speech, and they should also resist spreading it online by understanding the potential consequences (including legal) (Brogi et al. 2020).

5 Political Independence: Ensuring Political Pluralism, Tackling Disinformation

In its policies and communication, the EU marks a difference between illegal content and the one that is legal but can be harmful, such as the large scale and strategic spread of disinformation. The Commission (2020a) is also aware of blurred boundaries between the various forms of false or misleading content, and different motivations to spread it, ranging from targeted influence operations of foreign actors to purely economic motives. While it concerns also with misinformation, which can be unintentional, the focus is on disinformation, which is defined as "verifiably false or misleading information that is created, presented and disseminated for economic gain or to intentionally deceive the public, and may cause public harm" (EC 2018b). Disinformation is seen as particularly problematic in the context of elections (EC 2018b), when it appears in the form of both organic content or paid-for advertising, and can undermine the legitimacy of the process dependent on informed citizenship and plural political debate (Nenadić 2019).

Further to disinformation, in the context of elections, and in the aftermath of the Cambridge Analytica scandal (Cadwalladr and Graham-Harrison 2018) the EC has also raised concerns about the opaque practices of political marketing that exploit technological and social affordances of online platforms and make use of personal data on individuals, sometimes in an unlawful way (EC 2018c). Theoretical concepts assume that in offering personalized content tailored to users' individual interests, platforms propel users into filter bubbles (Pariser 2011) and echo chambers (Sunstein 2001), limiting their exposure to diverse news (Dwyer and Martin 2017).

There is a lack of comprehensive evidence as to whether today people are exposed to more or less diverse political information and what indeed are the effects of exposure to disinformation and micro-targeted political messages to people's position on issues and trust in the media and politics, as well as on political participation (Tucker et al. 2018). Even for the legacy media there is no conclusive evidence about the effects that editorial policies and reporting may have on political attitudes and voters behavior (see, e.g., Reeves et al. 2016). Yet, the perceived effects of audiovisual media on voters (Schoenbach and Lauf 2002) and the fact that television channels benefit from the public and limited resource of the radio frequency spectrum (Venice Commission 2009, paras. 24–28, 58), resulted in audiovisual media facing stronger regulation during elections. As online platforms are increasingly serving as the key intermediaries between parties and citizens, it has been argued that regulating legacy media but leaving the online platforms free from regulatory oversight and transparency requirements creates distortions in the political information and news environment and cannot provide for a sufficient protection of media pluralism. Moreover, as the platforms enable new conditions and techniques for political communication, adequate safeguards need to be reflective of the specific environment. The key principles of media regulation during the electoral period are non-discrimination and equal treatment of candidates in their access to the media and the public (Venice

Commission 2010, para. 148), and in the online environment additional emphasis needs to be on transparency.

In an attempt to assess the risks to political pluralism online, the MPM has introduced a set of variables that aim to assess: (i) the existence of legal safeguards to prevent certain political actors from capturing online political communication by buying and targeting online political advertising in a non-transparent manner; (ii) the availability of rules for political parties to disclose campaign spending on online platforms in a transparent way; (iii) the effectiveness of the Code of Practice on Disinformation in a specific national context; and (iv) the activities of the data protection authority in monitoring the use of personal data by political parties for electoral campaign purposes (Brogi et al. 2020, 79). These variables are elaborated in line with the standards promoted by the "European approach" to tackling online disinformation (EC 2018b). The approach was introduced in April 2018 through the Communication from the Commission to the European Parliament, the Council, the European Economic and Social Committee, and the Committee of the Regions. The Communication reflects the process of consultations with experts and stakeholders, including the recommendations of the High-Level Expert Group on Fake News and Online Disinformation (HLEG 2018), and answers to the concerns expressed by EU citizens' on the spread of online disinformation and the risks it poses for democracy (Eurobarometer 2018). The key principles contained in the Communication are: transparency, ensuring diversity and credibility of information, and cooperation between different stakeholders and authorities (EC 2018b; Nenadić 2019), and the key output is a Code of Practice on Disinformation (Code of Practice), another instrument presented as self-regulatory but initiated by the EC.

Code of Practice on Disinformation

The EU Code of Practice is a globally unique example of voluntary actions by online platforms to respond to the problems of disinformation and political manipulation online. The Code has been signed and presented in fall 2018 by Facebook, Google, Twitter, and Mozilla, and by advertisers and advertising industry (EC 2018a). In May 2019, Microsoft joined the signatories (EC 2019), and in June 2020, TikTok signed up to the Code as well (EDiMA 2020). The Code begins with a reference to the Commission's Communication on tackling online disinformation

(EC 2018b) and further contains commitments with which the platforms aim at achieving the objectives set out by the Communication. There are five main commitments: (1) *scrutiny of ad placement* to disrupt monetization incentives of the accounts that consistently misrepresent themselves and spread disinformation; (2) increased transparency of *political and issue-based advertising* by labeling it, indicating sponsors, and the amounts spent; (3) *integrity of services* by clearly indicating bots (automated accounts), and removing fake accounts; (4) *empowering consumers* by improving the findability of trustworthy content; (5) *empowering the research community* to conduct research into disinformation and political advertising on platforms or by obtaining access to platforms' data.

The signatories of the Code of Practice are asked by the EC to regularly report on their actions (EC 2019) and the implementation of the commitments is monitored with the support of the European Regulators Group for Audio-visual Media Services (ERGA) (EC 2018d), a platform of representatives of national regulatory bodies in the field of audiovisual media, whose main task is to advise the Commission on the implementation of the EU's Audiovisual Media Services Directive (AVMSD). Based on the monitoring conducted by audiovisual regulators in the Member States during 2019, ERGA published an Assessment of the implementation of the Code of Practice (2020: 3) acknowledging the Code "as an important step in the process of building a new relationship between its signatories, the EU and National AV Regulators," but also highlighting its "significant weaknesses." These weaknesses include lack of transparency and details provided by the platforms on how they are actually implementing the Code, considering that commitments are very general and the procedures, including the definitions of the key concepts, differ significantly between the platforms. In the report, ERGA also reminds that the number of platforms that have so far signed to the Code is still limited, and, therefore, suggests co-regulation or "more conventional regulation" as a potentially more effective way to tackle the problem. The findings of the MPM2020 are in line with the criticism expressed by ERGA, showing that in the majority of EU Member States issues were noted in relation to the implementation of the Code of Practice with regard to the clear labeling and registering of political and issue-based advertising, and in terms of indicating who paid for it (Brogi et al. 2020).

General Data Protection Regulation

In an attempt to combat the unlawful application of micro-targeted political advertising on online platforms, the EC is also relying on the hard law—General Data Protection Regulation (GDPR) that started to apply across the EU as of May 2018, one year before the European Parliament elections. In September 2018, the Commission issued another Communication, focused on securing free and fair European elections (EC 2018e), in which it stated that the principles set out in the European approach for tackling online disinformation (EC 2018b) should be seen as complementary to the GDPR.

To harmonize the interpretations and to further emphasize that any data processing should comply with the GDPR principles, the Commission also prepared specific guidance on the application of GDPR in the electoral context (EC 2018g). Under the GDPR (Art. 5), individuals must be informed of the existence of the processing operation and its purposes. Particular attention is given to the processing of sensitive data, such as political opinions, which GDPR generally prohibits unless the individual has given explicit, specific, fully informed consent; such information is manifestly made public by him/her; when they are a current or former members of the organization or in a regular contact; and when processing is needed for reasons of "substantial public interest" (GDPR, Art. 9, para. 2). The Commission's guidance on the application of GDPR in the electoral context particularly emphasizes the strengthened monitoring and sanctioning powers of relevant regulators. Whether the data protection authorities indeed take this more proactive stance in the specific context of elections has been assessed in the MPM2020. Especially considering that European data protection authorities, in general, do not have a tradition of dealing with political parties for fear of not interfering too much with political speech. The MPM 2020 results show that in the majority of EU Member States the data protection authorities do not proactively monitor the use of personal data by political parties for election campaigning purposes, therefore, still not using fully the powers and responsibility given by the GDPR.

6 Market Plurality: Digital Tax in Support of Media Viability

The news media business model has suffered tremendously from the online platforms ability to provide more effective advertising and, thus, to claim the major share of the online advertising market. Among the indicators of market plurality in the MPM2020 are: online platforms concentration and competition enforcement; and media viability, or the conditions that make it possible for the media to operate in a sustainable way while maintaining professional standards and independence. The results of the most recent round of monitoring (Brogi et al. 2020) show that the sustainability of traditional media is at risk, and the most vulnerable are newspapers and local media industries. No sector in the news media industry registered positive trends in the past two years, only audiovisual and digital native media seem to perform slightly better than the newspapers.

At the same time, Facebook's annual revenues in 2019 amounted to 69.65 billion US dollars (Facebook 2020), which is higher than the Gross Domestic Product of some EU Member States, and the majority of this revenue was generated through advertising. In the same fiscal period, Google advertising generated 134.81 billion dollars (Alphabet 2020). The MPM2020 findings indicate risk in all the countries monitored related to the dominance of a few players in the online advertising market and the online audience concentration around the same platforms.

There have been a number of cases where the EC has applied its competition law to the large tech companies (EC, n.d.). In March 2019, the Commission fined Google 1.49 billion euros for breaking the EU antitrust rules by abusing its dominant position in brokering advertising space on other websites (including on news media). In 2017, Facebook was fined 110 million euros for providing misleading information during the Commission's inquiry on the WhatsApp takeover (EC 2017a). However, further to the use of the existing competition tools and regulations, the Commission and the Member States are increasingly considering their updates and the new mechanisms to cope with the increasingly complex competition problems. During the summer 2020, the EC was running consultations with stakeholders on a possible new competition rule, including in the form of ex-ante regulation of online platforms (EC 2020b). Germany was again a frontrunner in the reform to further strengthen the control of abusive behavior in the digital sphere by drafting the 10th Amendment to the Act against Restraints on Competition (Gesetzgegen Wettbewerbsbeschränkungen). This act seeks to adapt competition law to the increasing digitization of the market so as to improve the effectiveness of the competition enforcement in regulating the platform economy (Holznagel and Kalbhenn 2020).

As regards media viability in such an environment, it comes as no surprise that media companies struggle to ensure sustainability. In an attempt to detect potential responses to this troubling situation, the MPM also explores whether there are good practice examples of alternative business models to finance news production in the Member State, and it considers the potential role of regulatory incentives, such as direct public support and fiscal provisions in the form of the digital service tax. In the MPM2020, the tax on selected turnover of large digital companies is viewed as a way to help develop a level playing field in the market, and the results show it has been introduced in six EU Member States (Austria, Czech Republic, France, Italy, Slovenia, Spain), in the UK (former EU MS), and Turkey (EU candidate country). In most cases it is too early to assess the effectiveness of such a regime. Nonetheless, one of the final remarks in the MPM2020 states that "a form of 'digital service tax' (hopefully, harmonized at a supranational level) could help media pluralism in two ways: by reducing the disparity in the fiscal burden between industries which are players in the same market; and by earmarking a part of the DST's revenue to support media pluralism" (Brogi et al. 2020, 157).

After a heated debate and a fierce opposition, especially to Articles 15 and 17, the new EU Directive on copyright and related rights in the Digital Single Market (Directive (EU) 2019/790) was approved in 2019 and needs to be transposed into the Member States national laws by mid-2021. Article 15, known as press publishers' right or "link tax," grants publishers of journalistic publications the right to require remuneration from major online platforms for displaying previews of their content, excluding hyperlinks and "very short extracts." The latter are free to share. The directive further calls on the Member States to ensure that the appropriate share of the revenues that press publishers receive from platforms for the use of their press publications reaches also the authors of those contents, namely journalists (Art. 15(5)).

7 National Laws in Member States

In Germany, as of the beginning of 2018, hate speech is addressed by the Network Enforcement Act (Netzwerkdurchsetzungsgesetz). The Act obliges online platforms to remove or block illegal content within a legally defined time (content that is manifestly unlawful within 24 hours of receiving the complaint). What is considered unlawful content in the country is defined by the Criminal Code (Bundesamt für Justiz 2019), and, under the Network Enforcement Act, platforms are expected to publish regular transparency reports on the mechanisms for submitting complaints, handling of complaints, and the criteria applied in deciding whether to delete or block unlawful content. The law was criticized and opposed invoking the risks of entrusting platforms with deciding on the legality of the content, which may lead to over-blocking to avoid fines. These negative effects for free speech seem yet unproven (Holznagel and Kalbhenn 2020). However, due to other issues noted in the past two years, the law is now being amended (Heldt 2020).

Different case was in France where in May 2020 the parliament passed the Law on Countering Online Hatred, so-called Avia Law. The French law was also requiring platforms to determine whether the content is manifestly unlawful within 24 hours of receiving the complaint, but was strongly criticized "for being overly broad in terms of the scope of the platforms affected and the content that they are expected to remove" (Article 19 2020). This was confirmed by the country's Constitutional Court, which rejected the core of the law on the ground that it "undermines freedom of expression and communication in a way that is not appropriate, necessary and proportionate to the aim pursued" (Conseil Constitutionnel 2020).

Smaller states are setting the ground for an additional legislation as well, including additional taxes on "big tech" or "GAFAM" (Google, Amazon, Facebook, Apple, Microsoft) companies and advertising revenue streams (e.g., Austria, Slovenia, Czech Republic). Similar plans were announced in August 2019 by France, with plans to tax both digital platforms and online advertising (Gouvernement 2019).

The UK, as European country but not an EU member, has also imposed similar levy of 2% on British revenues of global technology companies (so-called Facebook Tax).

In the Summer of 2020, the finance ministers of France, Italy, Spain, and UK, have sent a joint letter to the US Treasury Secretary, stating that these technological companies had benefited from the COVID-19 pandemic and had become "more powerful and more profitable" and needed to "to pay their fair share of tax." Further, "The current Covid-19 crisis has confirmed the need to deliver a fair and consistent allocation of profit made by multinationals operating without – or with little – physical taxable presence," the letter said (Neate 2020), signaling an even more active stance of EU countries toward GAFAM companies due to the economic consequences of COVID-19 crisis.

In addition, the UK also floated the idea of imposing criminal penalties. This idea came as part of a sweeping proposal in April 2019 to make all companies that carry user-generated content and communications responsible for everything on their sites.

Several EU Member States are extending the requirements for fair treatment and transparency of political advertising during electoral campaigns also to the online environment (Belgium, Bulgaria, Denmark, Finland, Germany, Italy, Lithuania, Portugal, and Sweden).

This proactive role of the European Union and of some European countries in the attempts to regulate digital environment and (among other aims) to establish conditions for sustaining media plurality within its borders has been identified recently also by key digital stakeholders. In an op-ed in March 2019, Mark Zuckerberg (Facebook) actually praised regulation which "could set baselines for what 's prohibited"; he also offered strong praise of the EU's privacy standard, the GDPR (Zuckerberg 2019).

All these regulatory activities of different EU countries as well as EU as a whole mark a different attitude of Europe toward digital aspects of contemporary economic and media systems. New York Times summarized this new politics: "The fracture of the internet into different spheres of influence would be bad for his business, and to that end, the company would much rather impose European sensibilities on the American internet than deal with multiple standards." And: "The French, the Germans and the Irish will set their own bar for online speech. In the future, American speech – at least online – may be governed by Europe" (Jeong 2019).

8 Final Remarks

Media pluralism is a multifaceted concept that can only be protected with a set of complementary measures, combining legal and other instruments, that can ensure protection of fundamental rights and relevant institutions in the media sphere, market plurality, political pluralism, and socially inclusive media environment. This was never an easy task and one that grows more difficult today when the media environment is increasingly shaped and dominated by online platforms. In an attempt to protect pluralism, the European Union faces at least two challenges: internally, the disparities between national legislative, regulatory, and other capacities to tackle the problem and the distribution of competencies between the Union and the Member States; and externally, the fact that it is dealing with powerful technological companies that operate globally and are mostly foreign-based.

Our analysis shows a combination of approaches and measures as particularly relevant and popular:

- A stronger national role with national legislation and national regulators is combined with stronger networking of regulators (such as European Regulators Group for Audiovisual Media Services—ERGA) and EU regulatory directions covering not just media or social media, but many shapes and forms of content production, editing, and distribution.
- EU regulations and directives form a wider regulatory framework for new digital media landscape, opening the gates also to more direct interventions on national levels.

As a consequence, a stronger national role and bolder EU approach toward regulating digital platforms has evolved and established a general approach of new digital regulation as not just possible, but needed and necessary to protect both national media pluralism and media industry.

Apart from the competition policy, in which the EU holds exclusive competence in respect of Member States, there is in general a lack of concrete competence of the EC with regard to holistic media pluralism (CMPF 2013). Nonetheless, the EC is expected to exercise a proactive role in supporting, coordinating, and supplementing the actions of the individual countries, especially as the challenges to media pluralism presented in this chapter are brought about by the online platforms whose operations transcend national boundaries. Some Member States, such as Germany and France, have initiated legislative changes at the national level, but to avoid regulatory fragmentation and the problem of jurisdiction, the Commission is strongly advocating for a joint EU action. So far, and compared to other parts of the world, the EU is taking a more assertive stance toward the regulation of platforms in an attempt to, on the one hand, combat the risks associated with the platforms' affordances and practices, and, on the other, to protect media pluralism.

In practice, the Commission's responses to tackling the problems of hate speech and disinformation are still largely dependent upon the voluntary actions of a limited number of online platforms. While the signatories of such self-regulation are trying to improve transparency of various activities carried out by different actors on their infrastructures (e.g., political advertising), they are, at the same time, lacking transparency about their own policies and operations. This makes it difficult for public authorities, academia, and civil society to oversee and evaluate their efficacy. This is the main criticism of the current state of play and something that the future (legal) instruments seek to address. At the time of writing this chapter, the Commission was carrying out consultations on future regulation for digital platforms. The Digital Services Act package is reviewing the liability regime of various digital services set out by the 2000 e-Commerce Directive. It is also considering additional horizontal rules that would "enable collection of information from large online platforms acting as gatekeepers by a dedicated regulatory body at the EU level" (EC 2020a: 3, Inception impact assessment). It is still not fully clear whether this would mean the formation of a new EU regulator dedicated to platforms, nor would it then imply the establishment of such a regulator in all the Member States or the task could be carried out by the existing authorities. The GDPR has increased monitoring and sanctioning powers of data protection authorities and the Audiovisual Media Service Directive (2018), by extending its scope to the regulation of video-sharing platforms, has opened a space for media authorities to engage further in the regulation of platforms. Through ERGA, national regulatory authorities are already participating in the oversight and the assessment of the platforms' self-regulation on tackling disinformation. However, as indicated by ERGA itself (2019) and the MPM2020 report, the competencies and capacities of national media authorities to act on matters related to platforms differ significantly, which makes it difficult to harmonize their actions across the EU.

The revised AVMSD is the first EU-level legislation that has addressed specific content regulation on any kind of digital platform (Kuklis 2019). Video-sharing platforms services are subject to the AVMSD regulation in four areas of content: commercial communication (Art. 9(1) and 28b); protection of minors (Art. 28b in relation to the Art. 6a(1)); criminal offense (Art. 28b); and hate speech (Art. 28b). This shifts the EU approach to tackling hate speech online from self-regulation of platforms (Code of Conduct) to more conventional regulation based on law. As the revised AVMSD was adopted in late 2018, it still remains to be seen how it will be transposed into the national laws of Member States and, ultimately, implemented. The same goes for the new EU Copyright Directive, adopted in 2019 after a heated debate on its provisions that require special types of online platforms to conclude the licensing agreements with right holders for the use of their works (Art. 17). If such an agreement is not concluded, platforms must make "best efforts to ensure the unavailability of specific works" or act "expeditiously, upon receiving a sufficiently substantiated notice from the right holders, to disable access to, or to remove from their websites, the notified works or other subject matter, and made best efforts to prevent their future uploads" (Art. 17(3)(b) and (c)). This has been interpreted by scholars and civil society as the request for the adoption of automated upload filters to prevent copyright infringements, which may result in serious risks for freedom of expression as, again, the decisions that would otherwise be made by the courts are placed in the hands of platforms and their algorithms.

The evolving risks related to platforms, as well as regulatory interventions in the field, are carefully considered by the Media Pluralism Monitor, and the definition of media pluralism is regularly rethought to reflect current realities. Methodologically, it is a challenging task, especially as there is a lack of sound cross-country comparable data for the assessment of many digital-related phenomena. It will be the task of the future MPMs to evaluate whether the more interventionist EU approach will provide more transparency of platform operations and whether it will improve the conditions for media pluralism in the Member States.

Note

1. Both authors are affiliated with the project: Nenadić as a member of the central CMPF team and Milosavljević as a lead correspondent for Slovenia.

References

Alkiviadou, Natalie. 2017. Regulating Hate Speech in the EU. In *Online Hate Speech in the European Union: A Discourse-Analytic Perspective*, ed. Stavros Assimakopoulos, Fabienne H. Baider, and Sharon Millar, 6–10. Cham: Springer.

Alkiviadou, Natalie. 2019. Hate Speech on Social Media Networks: Towards a Regulatory Framework? *Information & Communications Technology Law* 28 (1): 19–23. https://doi.org/10.1080/13600834.2018.1494417.

Alphabet. 2020. Alphabet Announces Fourth Quarter and Fiscal Year 2019 Results. Last modified February 3, 2020. https://abc.xyz/investor/static/pdf/2019Q4_alphabet_earnings_release.pdf.

Article 19. 2020. France: Avia Law Is Threat to Online Speech. Last modified May 13, 2020. https://www.article19.org/resources/france-avia-law-is-threat-to-online-speech/.

(AVMSD) Audiovisual Media Services Directive. 2018. *Consolidated text: Directive 2010/13/EU of the European Parliament and of the Council of 10 March 2010 on the Coordination of Certain Provisions Laid Down by Law, Regulation or Administrative Action in Member States Concerning the Provision of Audiovisual Media Services*. 02010L0013-20181218. https://eur-lex.europa.eu/legal-content/EN/TXT/?uri=CELEX:02010L0013-20181218.

(BEREC) Body of European Regulators for Electronic Communication. 2016. *Guidelines on the Implementation by National Regulators of European Net Neutrality Rules*. BoR (16) 127. https://berec.europa.eu/eng/document_register/subject_matter/berec/regulatory_best_practices/guidelines/6160-berec-guidelines-on-the-implementation-by-national-regulators-of-european-net-neutrality-rules.

Brogi, Elda, Roberta Carlini, Iva Nenadic, Pier Luigi Parcu, and Mario Viola de Azevedo Cunha. 2020. *Monitoring Media Pluralism in the Digital Era: Application of the Media Pluralism Monitor in the European Union, Albania and Turkey in the Years 2018–2019*. ISBN: 978-92-9084-887-5. Florence, Italy: European University Institute. https://cadmus.eui.eu/bitstream/handle/1814/67828/MPM2020-PolicyReport.pdf.

Bukovska, Barbora. 2019. *The European Commission's Code of Conduct for Countering Illegal Hate Speech Online: An Analysis of Freedom of Expression Implications*. Transatlantic High Level Working Group on Content Moderation Online and Freedom of Expression (TWG) project. https://www.ivir.nl/publicaties/download/Bukovska.pdf.

Bundesamt für Justiz. 2019. German Criminal Code. June 19. https://www.gesetze-im-internet.de/englisch_stgb/index.html.

Cadwalladr, Carol, and Emma Graham-Harrison. 2018. Revealed: 50 Million Facebook Profiles Harvested for Cambridge Analytica in Major Data Breach.

The Guardian, March 17. https://www.theguardian.com/news/2018/mar/17/cambridge-analytica-facebook-influence-us-election.

(CMPF) Centre for Media Pluralism and Media Freedom. n.d. MPM2020. Accessed August 10, 2020. https://cmpf.eui.eu/media-pluralism-monitor/mpm-2020/.

(CMPF) Centre for Media Pluralism and Media Freedom. 2013. *European Union Competencies in Respect of Media Pluralism and Media Freedom*. EUI RSCAS PP; 2013/01. https://cadmus.eui.eu/handle/1814/26056.

Conseil Constitutionnel. 2020. Decision n 20020-801 DC du 18 juin 2020—Communique de presse. June 18. https://www.conseil-constitutionnel.fr/actualites/communique/decision-n-2020-801-dc-du-18-juin-2020-communique-de-presse.

Copyright Directive. 2019. *Directive (EU) 2019/790 of the European Parliament and of the Council of 17 April 2019 on Copyright and Related Rights in the Digital Single Market and Amending Directives 96/9/EC and 2001/29/EC*. 32019L0790. https://eur-lex.europa.eu/eli/dir/2019/790/oj.

Council of Europe. 2019. *Declaration by the Committee of Ministers on the Financial Sustainability of Quality Journalism in the Digital Age*. Decl(13/02/2019)2. https://search.coe.int/cm/pages/result_details.aspx?objectid=090000168092dd4d.

Council of the European Union. 2008. *Framework Decision 2008/913/JHA of 28 November 2008 on Combating Certain Forms and Expressions of Racism and Xenophobia by Means of Criminal Law*. 32008F0913. https://eur-lex.europa.eu/legal-content/en/ALL/?uri=CELEX%3A32008F0913.

Dahlgren, Peter. 2005. The Internet, Public Spheres, and Political Communication: Dispersion and Deliberation. *Political Communication* 22 (2): 147–162. https://doi.org/10.1080/10584600590933160.

Domingo, David, Thorsten Quandt, Ari Heinonen, Steve Paulussen, Jane B. Singer, and Marina Vujnovic. 2008. Participatory Journalism Practices in the Media and Beyond. *Journalism Practice* 2 (3): 326–342. https://doi.org/10.1080/17512780802281065.

Dwyer, Tim, and Fiona Martin. 2017. Sharing News Online. *Digital Journalism* 5 (8): 1080–1100. https://doi.org/10.1080/21670811.2017.1338527.

(EB92) Standard Eurobarometer 92. 2019. Media Use in the European Union. December. https://ec.europa.eu/commfrontoffice/publicopinionmobile/index.cfm/Survey/getSurveyDetail/surveyKy/2255.

EDiMA. 2020. TikTok Signs Up to EU Initiative to Fight Disinformation. *DOT Europe*, June 22. https://doteurope.eu/news/tiktok-signs-up-to-eu-initiative-to-fight-disinformation/.

EMBEDDIA. 2019. Horizon 2020 project, ID 825153. https://embeddia.eu/.

(EC) European Commission. n.d. Antitrust Cases. Accessed October 5, 2020. https://ec.europa.eu/competition/antitrust/cases/.

(EC) European Commission. 2000. *Directive 2000/31/EC of the European Parliament and of the Council of 8 June 2000 on Certain Legal Aspects of Information Society Services, in Particular Electronic Commerce, in the Internal Market (Directive on electronic commerce—E-Commerce Directive)*. 32000L0031. https://eur-lex.europa.eu/legal-content/EN/ALL/?uri=CELEX%3A32000L0031.

(EC) European Commission. 2016. *Code of Conduct on Countering Illegal Hate Speech Online*. https://ec.europa.eu/info/policies/justice-and-fundamental-rights/combatting-discrimination/racism-and-xenophobia/eu-code-conduct-countering-illegal-hate-speech-online_en.

(EC) European Commission. 2017a. Mergers: Commission fines Facebook €110 Million for Providing Misleading Information About WhatsApp Takeover. May 18. https://ec.europa.eu/commission/presscorner/detail/en/IP_17_1369.

(EC) European Commission. 2017b. *Communication from the Commission to the European Parliament, the Council, the European Economic and Social Committee and the Committee of the Regions, Tackling Illegal Content Online: Towards an Enhanced Responsibility of Online Platforms*. COM/2017/555 final. https://eur-lex.europa.eu/legal-content/EN/TXT/?uri=CELEX%3A52017DC0555.

(EC) European Commission. 2018a. Code of Practice on Disinformation. September 26. https://ec.europa.eu/digital-single-market/en/news/code-practice-disinformation.

(EC) European Commission. 2018b. *Communication from the Commission to the European Parliament, the Council, the European Economic and Social Committee and the Committee of the Regions: Tackling Online Disinformation: A European Approach*. COM(2018) 236 final. https://eur-lex.europa.eu/legal-content/EN/TXT/PDF/?uri=CELEX:52018DC0236&from=EN.

(EC) European Commission. 2018c. State of the Union 2018: European Commission Proposes Measures for Securing Free and Fair European Elections. September 12. https://ec.europa.eu/commission/presscorner/detail/en/IP_18_5681.

(EC) European Commission. 2018d. Action Plan on Disinformation: Commission Contribution to the European Council. December 5. https://ec.europa.eu/commission/publications/action-plan-disinformation-commission-contribution-european-council-13-14-december-2018_en.

(EC) European Commission. 2018e. *Communication from the Commission to the European Parliament, the Council, the European Economic and Social Committee and the Committee of the Regions: Securing Free and Fair European Elections*. COM(2018)637 final. https://ec.europa.eu/commission/sites/beta-political/files/soteu2018-free-fair-elections-communication-637_en.pdf.

(EC) European Commission. 2018f. *Commission Recommendation on Measures to Effectively Tackle Illegal Content Online*. C(2018) 1177 final. https://ec.europa.eu/digital-single-market/en/news/commission-recommendation-measures-effectively-tackle-illegal-content-online.

(EC) European Commission. 2018g. *Commission Guidance on the Application of Union Data Protection Law in the Electoral Context*. COM(2018)638 final. https://ec.europa.eu/commission/sites/beta-political/files/soteu2018-data-protection-law-electoral-guidance-638_en.pdf.

(EC) European Commission. 2019. Code of Practice on Disinformation One Year On: Online Platforms Submit Self-Assessment Reports. October 29, 2019. https://ec.europa.eu/commission/presscorner/detail/en/statement_19_6166.

(EC) European Commission. 2020a. Commission Publishes EU Code of Conduct on Countering Illegal Hate Speech Online Continues to Deliver Results. June 22. https://ec.europa.eu/commission/presscorner/detail/en/IP_20_1134.

(EC) European Commission. 2020b. Antitrust: Commission Consults Stakeholders on a Possible New Competition Tool. June 2. https://ec.europa.eu/commission/presscorner/detail/en/ip_20_977.

(EP) European Parliament. 2018. *Resolution of 3 May 2018 on Media Pluralism and Media Freedom in the European Union*. 2017/2209(INI). https://www.europarl.europa.eu/doceo/document/TA-8-2018-0204_EN.html.

(ERGA) European Regulators Group for Audio-Visual Media Services. 2020. *Report on Disinformation: Assessment of the Implementation of the Code of Practice*. https://erga-online.eu/wp-content/uploads/2020/05/ERGA-2019-report-published-2020-LQ.pdf.

Eurobarometer. 2018. Flash 464: Fake News and Disinformation Online. March. https://ec.europa.eu/commfrontoffice/publicopinion/index.cfm/survey/getsurveydetail/instruments/flash/surveyky/2183.

(EU) European Union. 2015. *Regulation (EU) 2015/2120 of the European Parliament and of the Council of 25 November 2015 Laying Down Measures Concerning Open Internet Access and Amending Directive 2002/22/EC on Universal Service and Users' Rights Relating to Electronic Communications Networks and Services and Regulation (EU) No 531/2012 on Roaming on Public Mobile Communications Networks Within the Union*. 32015R2120. https://eur-lex.europa.eu/legal-content/EN/TXT/?uri=CELEX%3A32015R2120.

Facebook. 2020. Facebook Reports Fourth Quarter and Full Year 2019 Results. January 29. https://investor.fb.com/investor-news/press-release-details/2020/Facebook-Reports-Fourth-Quarter-and-Full-Year-2019-Results/default.aspx.

(GDPR) General Data Protection Regulation. 2016. *Regulation (EU) 2016/679 of the European Parliament and of the Council of 27 April 2016 on the Protection of Natural Persons with Regard to the Processing of Personal Data and on the Free Movement of Such Data, and Repealing Directive 95/46/EC*. 32016R0679. https://eur-lex.europa.eu/eli/reg/2016/679/oj.

Gouvernement. 2019. Taxation: The Outlines of the GAFA Tax Revealed. March 6. https://www.gouvernement.fr/en/taxation-the-outlines-of-the-gafa-tax-revealed.

Helberger, Natali. 2016. Facebook Is a New Breed of Editor: A Social Editor. *Media Policy* (blog), September 15. https://eprints.lse.ac.uk/81436/.

Heldt, Amelie. 2020. Germany Is Amending Its Online Speech Act NetzDG... but Not Only That. *Internet Policy Review*, April 6. https://policyreview.info/articles/news/germany-amending-its-online-speech-act-netzdg-not-only/1464.

(HLEG) High Level Expert Group on Fake News and Online Disinformation. 2018. *A Multi-dimensional Approach to Disinformation: Report of the Independent High Level Group on Fake News and Online Disinformation*. KK-01-18-221-EN-C. https://ec.europa.eu/digital-single-market/en/news/final-report-high-level-expert-group-fake-news-and-online-disinformation.

Holznagel, Bernd, and Jan Kalbhenn. 2020. *Monitoring Media Pluralism in the Digital Era: Application of the Media Pluralism Monitor in the European Union, Albania and Turkey in the years 2018–2019, Country Report: Germany*. QM-01-20-149-EN-N. https://cadmus.eui.eu/bitstream/handle/1814/67803/germany_results_mpm_2020_cmpf.pdf.

Jeong, Sarah. 2019. Facebook Wants a Faux Regulator for Internet Speech. It Won't Happen. *The New York Times*, April 7. https://www.nytimes.com/2019/04/07/opinion/facebook-content-moderation.html.

Kaye, David. 2018. *Report of the Special Rapporteur on the Promotion and Protection of the Right to Freedom of Opinion and Expression*. A/HRC/38/35. https://documents-dds-ny.un.org/doc/UNDOC/GEN/G18/096/72/PDF/G1809672.pdf.

Klimkiewicz, Beata. 2010. Structural Media Pluralism. *International Journal of Communication* 4: 906–913.

Kuklis, Lubos. 2019. Video-Sharing Platforms in AVMSD—A New Kind of Content Regulation. *SSRN* (November 26). https://doi.org/10.2139/ssrn.3527512.

La Rue, Frank. 2011. *Report of the Special Rapporteur on the Promotion and Protection of the Right to Freedom of Opinion and Expression*. A/HRC/17/27. https://www2.ohchr.org/english/bodies/hrcouncil/docs/17session/A.HRC.17.27_en.pdf.

Milosavljević, Marko, and Sally Broughton Micova. 2016. Banning, Blocking and Boosting: Twitter's Solo-Regulation of Expression. *Medijske studije* 7 (13): 43–57. https://doi.org/10.20901/ms.7.13.3.

Napoli, Philip M. 2011. Exposure Diversity Reconsidered. *Journal of Information Policy* 1: 246–259.

Neate, Rupert. 2020. Treasury Denies It Plans to Drop "Facebook tax" in Favour of Trade Deal. *The Guardian*, August 23. https://www.theguardian.com/business/2020/aug/23/uk-to-drop-facebook-tax-covid-in-favour-of-post-brexit-trade-deal.

Nenadić, Iva. 2019. Unpacking the "European Approach" to Tackling Challenges of Disinformation and Political Manipulation. *Internet Policy Review* 8 (4). https://doi.org/10.14763/2019.4.1436.

Newman, Nic, Richard Fletcher, Anne Schulz, Simge Andı, and Rasmus Kleis Nielsen. 2020. *Reuters Institute Digital News Report 2020*. https://reutersinstitute.politics.ox.ac.uk/sites/default/files/2020-06/DNR_2020_FINAL.pdf.

Pariser, Eli. 2011. *The Filter Bubble: What the Internet Is Hiding from You*. New York: Penguin.

Reeves, Aaron, Martin McKee, and David Stuckler. 2016. It's The Sun Wot Won It': Evidence of Media Influence on Political Attitudes and Voting from a UK Quasi-Natural Experiment. *Social Science Research* 56: 44–57. https://doi.org/10.1016/j.ssresearch.2015.11.002.

Roßmann, Robert. 2020. Justizministerin will NetzDG nachbessern. *Süddeutsche Zeitung*, January 16. https://www.sueddeutsche.de/digital/netzdg-lambrecht-zensur-straftaten-1.4758635.

Schoenbach, Klaus, and Edmund Lauf. 2002. The "Trap" Effect of Television and Its Competitors. *Political Communication* 29 (5): 564–583. https://doi.org/10.1177/009365002236195.

Sunstein, Cass. 2001. *Republic.Com*. Princeton, NJ: Princeton University Press.

Tucker, Joshua Aaron, Andrew Guess, Pablo Barbera, Cristian Vaccari, Alexandra Siegel, Sergey Sanovich, Denis Stukal, and Brendan Nyhan. 2018. Social Media, Political Polarization, and Political Disinformation: A Review of the Scientific Literature. *SSRN Electronic Journal* (March 19). https://doi.org/10.2139/ssrn.3144139.

Venice Commission. 2009. *Guidelines on Media Analysis During Election Observation Missions, by the OSCE Office for Democratic Institutions and Human Rights (OSCE/ODIHR) and the Venice Commission*. CDL-AD(2009)031. https://www.venice.coe.int/webforms/documents/default.aspx?pdffile=CDL-AD(2009)031-e.

Venice Commission. 2010. *Guidelines on Political Party Regulation, by the OSCE/ODIHR and the Venice Commission*. CDL-AD(2010)024.

https://www.venice.coe.int/webforms/documents/default.aspx?pdffile=CDL-AD(2010)024-e.
Von der Leyen, Ursula. 2019. *Mission Letter: Vice-President-Designate for Values and Transparency*. https://ec.europa.eu/commission/sites/beta-political/files/mission-letter-vera-jourova-2019_en.pdf.
Zuckerberg, Mark. 2019. Mark Zuckerberg: The Internet Needs New Rules. Let's Start in These Four Areas. *The Washington Post*, March 30. https://www.washingtonpost.com/opinions/mark-zuckerberg-the-internet-needs-new-rules-lets-start-in-these-four-areas/2019/03/29/9e6f0504-521a-11e9-a3f7-78b7525a8d5f_story.html.
(ERGA) European Regulators Group for Audiovisual Media Services. 2019. *Internal Media Plurality in Audiovisual Media Services in the EU: Rules & Practices*. https://erga-online.eu/wp-content/uploads/2019/01/ERGA-2018-07-SG1-Report-on-internal-plurality-LQ.pdf

From News Diversity to News Quality: New Media Regulation Theoretical Issues

Inna Lyubareva and Fabrice Rochelandet

1 Introduction

Online platforms and services have challenged the press industry for more than twenty years. Internet media made possible the proliferation of news from a wide variety of sources, including non-professional sources, on different supports (tablet, smartphone, computer), and with high diversity of alternative viewpoints and opinions. In light of concentration in the media industry and lack of media independence, now is an ideal opportunity to give way to alternative media models, to social minorities, to heterogeneous political interests—that is to say to media pluralism.

However, one may notice: Diversity is not so much the problem in the digital context with the dramatic increase in the amount and variety

The original version of this chapter was revised: The chapter has been changed from non-open access to open access and the copyright holder has been updated. The correction to this chapter is available at
https://doi.org/10.1007/978-3-030-66759-7_11

I. Lyubareva
École Nationale Supérieure Mines-Télécom Atlantique, Paris, France
e-mail: inna.lyubareva@imt-atlantique.fr

F. Rochelandet (✉)
Université Sorbonne Nouvelle, Paris, France
e-mail: fabrice.rochelandet@sorbonne-nouvelle.fr

S. A. Matei et al. (eds.), *Digital and Social Media Regulation*,
https://doi.org/10.1007/978-3-030-66759-7_6

of news available online. Information pluralism, in its normative sense of what journalism must be to accomplish its democratic role (Karppinen 2018; Rebillard and Loicq 2013; Merrill 1968), is far from achieved. Indeed, diversity and abundance are no longer synonymous with more quality, open debates, and equality. There are many obstacles in the way: circulation of fake news, hate speech and illicit content, social and political polarization, extremism in content and in users' opinions, cultural and ideological confinement of readers because of platforms' recommendation systems, large-scale diffusion of poor and meaningless information.

These phenomena clearly contrast with the widespread idea—notably among mainstream economists—that competition goes hand in hand with efficient outcomes. This diversity-pluralism discussion clearly necessitates an introduction of a third component, information quality, and a set of rules—regulation—to guarantee some minimal quality of the information in circulation.

Potential regulation tools may target various parts of the production value chain: economic models of news providers and middlemen (incentive regulation), media concentration (antitrust), actual conditions to access and impart news, media literacy, rights to information. One aspect rests crucial: Without any clear definition and measure of quality, media regulation will be difficult to build.

More precisely, we propose fundamental difficulties in regulation reside in three main factors: (1) multidimensional nature of the concept of information quality, widely discussed in the literature (*are there some prior dimensions to be respected or all of them are of the same importance?*); (2) multiplicity of agents' wishes and needs in respect of the information quality (*whose needs should be covered by the regulation taking into account that different consumers may diverge significantly in their preferences?*); and (3) lack of empirical evidence about the impact of different value chain modalities (*economic models, property rights, or how we access information*)—i.e., potential targets of regulation—on the quality of the circulated information.

This scholarly article discusses these three elements and proposes an original framework for the analysis of the information quality with new dimensions and with respect to the heterogeneity of consumers' preferences. This framework may be also used to get a legible presentation of the link between the existent media strategies regarding produced information and their economic models, property owners, or any other available media characteristics. Such comprehensible representation makes possible implementation of specific regulation tools in order to promote information pluralism and democracy.

In the next sections, we, first, propose a short overview of the impact of digital platforms on media industry, in general, and information characteristics, in particular. Second, we make a literature review on how the quality concept is approached in different works and some inherent limits of the proposed definitions. On this basis, we formulate, in the third section, an original approach on how to analyze news quality. The final section proposes a short empirical example of implementation of our approach to real market data, based on the French media industry.

2 The Platformization of the Media Industry

Digital platforms such as Twitter, Facebook, Instagram, or TikTok have become information gatekeepers, prompting a new set of concerns impacting the production, diffusion, and consumption of information. They encourage new kinds of 'alternative' actors—readers, politicians, activists, etc.—which produce their own content in the information marketplace. This mixes up with established media and their newsrooms, which removes newsrooms as lone gatekeepers of the news selection and delivery process. As a consequence an unprecedented plethora of heterogeneous information, from professional news to info-tainment and user-generated content, now competes for readers' attention.

Foremost, by providing direct access to news articles and new practices of 'picking,' digital platforms enable readers to bypass the front-page of online outlets. In so doing, they challenge the editorial line of the outlet and their traditional revenue models. This is doubly adverse for media increasingly dependent on advertising revenue. Symmetrically, online intermediaries ('infomediaries') have become essential and control direct relationship with readers, enabling the intermediaries to collect vast amounts of personal user data. Since access to news by individuals passes often through social media, producers of information are subject to disadvantageous pricing conditions imposed by platforms when sharing advertising revenue. Consequently, one may observe that the audiences' capture—based on Google Trends, 'likes,' Google Analytics, and so forth—is the main criteria of performance. Or, that in-depth, costly, staff-written articles make way for wire service copy and the plagiarism associated with (almost) zero production costs. This pressure adds to that felt from investors, who tend to focus on short-term economic results and require newspaper managers to cut back on resources to increase profitability (already threatened by reduction in advertising revenues).

Then, media industry has become extremely dependent upon audience/web metrics. Journalistic and professional practices are polarized around data produced by the algorithms of digital platforms. The press, newsrooms, and journalists share the same data that is publicly available or produced by the same algorithms. *Speed-driven journalism* illustrates the impact of such a generalized behavior where, on the one hand, the selection and treatment of news topics are determined according to their online popularity, and on the other hand, articles only survive in the light of their own popularity on the internet. Such behaviors impact the quality and diversity of information, whether in terms of the reduced variety of subjects addressed, or in focusing the attention of online readers on a small number of 'star' topics.

Finally, another important transformation element is situated alongside both the users' side and the practices associated with news consumption. Importance of digital platforms as main support induces not only the availability of free offerings (and therefore the problem of profitability for producers), but also new constraints on the content format, information deepening, and complexity. Circulation of short, easy-to-read-and-share news (not necessarily fakes) attracts larger public and stimulates network effects based on interactions among platforms' users' on news. This permits the massive collection of users' data by the digital giants reinforcing their market power as essential intermediaries in access to online news. As a result, today consumers often have strong preferences for short and descriptive 'snack content.' More generally, networking tools such as 'likes' or 'retweets' expand mimic behavior through which individuals select and share the same kinds of information, whatever the intrinsic quality of veracity, originality, or richness of that information. In addition, the well-known fact that the content selection procedures are often determined by the platform's algorithms and user's previous choices then reduces the user's feasible search space. This could lead to filter bubble (Pariser 2011), where users get less exposure to diverse, conflicting viewpoints and prove to be isolated in their own informational bubble.

To summarize, these transformations lead to a higher variety of sources of information (blogs, social networks, alternative media, and more) and of conditions stipulating the production and consumption of news (end of the monopoly of traditional media, data-driven journalism, etc.). The widespread and often free provision of digital tools and services on these platforms has undeniably lowered the barriers to entry in the production and distribution of news: less capital requirements to create and sustain an outlet; decentralization of production sources; sharp reduction in distribution costs; and more yet unlisted. In this context of information abundance, the problem of news quality has become crucial in this changing environment. It is not surprising that one may observe today flourishing organizations and initiatives aimed at developing new standards in journalism, supposed to sustain and to improve information quality, and consequently, media pluralism. Among them are The Fourth Estate, The Independent Press Standards Organisation, The Organization of News Ombudsmen and Standards Editors, The Media Pluralism Monitor—this list is far from exhaustive. While being mainly focused on the supply side and the characteristics of the produced content, these initiatives create more questions than answers (Karppinen 2018; Carpentier and Cammaerts 2006; McLennan 1995).

To shed some light on these questions, we need first to clarify the concept of quality.

3 Defining News Quality

Beyond some differences between USA and European traditions, the concepts of pluralism and diversity are quite established in media studies literature. Whereas pluralism refers to a normative orientation and democratic role of journalism, diversity is understood as its measure, i.e., the heterogeneity at the level of various production elements (Karppinen 2018; Rebillard and Loicq 2013). The dimensions of diversity vary depending on the levels of analysis ranging from the media ownership to the content characteristics. Among the most well-known classifications of information diversity, Napoli (1999, 2003) proposes to distinguish between sources diversity, content diversity, and exposure diversity (both vertical and horizontal). Source diversity refers to ownership and nature of outlets; content diversity concerns formats and viewpoints; and exposure diversity addresses either the variety of information provided by different outlets available to consumers (horizontal diversity) or the variety of information provided by an individual outlet (vertical diversity). For McQuail (2005) the main dimensions of diversity are ‘genre, style of format in culture or entertainment; news and information topics covered; political viewpoints; and so on.’ Rebillard (2012) proposes a definition based on topics’ diversity, topics’ equilibrium, and their disparity of treatment.

In the aforementioned approaches, diversity is used as synonym to news quality: The presence of this characteristic in the journalistic information supply available on the market is supposed to be associated with higher quality and further, the necessary and sufficient condition for normative media pluralism. However, especially in the digital context, diversity does not necessarily imply any quality (e.g., circulation of poor or wrong information, content promoting illicit activities, etc.). Moreover, the problem arises when one tries to deconstruct the value of pluralism: Are there some limits to diversity and whether at some point 'healthy diversity' may turn into 'unhealthy dissonance'? Are all interests equal in defining the quality attributes or some issues are of higher priority? How to connect individual-level criteria to social-level outcomes which are more than just a summing of individual utilities? In Karppinen (2018) one can find a detailed discussion on this matter. The author argues that in the context of growth of digital media, characterized more by abundance than scarcity, the conceptual ambiguity and divergence of definitions of normative and political frameworks are stronger than ever, making difficult their measures and promotion of some quality standards.

To tackle this problem, some authors elaborate on the idea of the quality of the journalistic information, *complementary* to diversity. According to Meyer and Kim (2003), quality definition comprises two levels—organizational and content ones. The former level focuses on the media or press outlet as unit of analysis, whereas the latter one is inherent to the produced information. Often these levels are somehow mixed up in media studies literature.

At the organizational level, quality indicators can correspond to the reputation of the media (Stone et al. 1981) or its organization characteristics such as integrity, staff enterprise, community leadership, editorial independence, staff professionalism, editorial courage, decency, influence, and impartiality (Gladney 1990). Among other features, Merrill (1968) proposes such criteria as (1) financial stability; integrity; social concern; good writing and editing; (2) strong opinion and interpretive emphasis; world consciousness; nonsensationalism in articles and makeup; (3) emphasis on politics, international relations, economics, social welfare, cultural endeavors, education, and science; (4) concern with getting, developing and keeping a large, intelligent, well educated, articulate and technically proficient staff; (5) determination to serve and help expand a well- educated, intellectual readership at home and abroad; desire to appeal to, and influence, opinion leaders everywhere.

Bogart (1989) conducted a large survey asking newspaper editors how they rate different attributes of newspaper quality[1]: accuracy, impartiality in reporting, investigative enterprise, specialized staff skill, individuality of character, civic-mindedness, and literary style. Bogart justifies for the choice of such subjective criteria because they are allegedly commonly shared by newspaper editors themselves when assessing the quality of their own outlets.[2]

Rather in line with the content level, abundant literature proposes originality, diversity of topics and comprehensive coverage, comprehensive coverage, accuracy of reporting and expert judgment, timeliness, and novelty as indicators to characterize news quality. Picard (2000) considers quality as related to the amount of journalistic work in terms of investigation, verification, and sourcing that have been carried out before writing the news.[3] Abdenour and Riffe (2019) note that, in general, academics tend to focus on strong investigative reporting to infer news quality indicators. McQuail (2005) holds honesty and checkability as the characteristics of journalism products. In addition, quality can be defined by negative indicators like shallowness, incompleteness, inaccuracy, bias, or misinformation (Craig 2011; Urban and Shweiger 2014). For instance, Magin (2019) shows that tabloidization generates lots of news of lower quality and associated with a large share of 'politically irrelevant topics, a focus on episodic framing and a visual, emotionalised, opinion-driven style.' In addition, some researches put in light the value of audience engagement and digital interactivity on the news as quality dimensions (see, for instance, Bogart 2004; Blanchett Neheli 2018; Belair-Gagnon 2019).

Finally, some authors argue that, in addition to the supply-oriented approaches presented above, quality definition must take into account the type of actors who define it, i.e., academics and journalists, politicians, judges and lawyers, or final users (Meier 2019; Lacy and Rosenstiel 2015). For example, the focus on the consumers' and recipients' perceptions (Lacy 2000; Urban and Schweiger 2014; Rosenstiel et al. 2015; Lacy and Rosenstiel 2015) is in line with the Federal Communications Commission's proposition: 'As an alternative to measuring the "supply" of content to assess viewpoint diversity, should we take a "demand side" approach and utilize measures of audience satisfaction and media consumption as proxies for viewpoint diversity.' In this demand approach, any news is considered as a bundle, and '[its] quality aggregates individual consumer's perceptions of how well journalism serves their needs and wants' (Lacy and Rosenstiel 2015).

Some quality elements (e.g., news accuracy or fairness) are quite the same as the supply approach that surveys media managers and journalists. However, demand approach implies that, contrary to the supply approach where the concerned economic actors share the same concept of quality, 'two different news consumers would evaluate the quality as being different because of their differences in information wants and needs' (ibid.). Depending on the types of individual media uses and motives (e.g., feel connected to community, decide places to go, stay healthy, etc.), which differ from one consumer to another, the news consumer evaluates quality of the content, i.e., how well it meets individual information needs and wants.

The definitions of news quality raise a set of problems.

As demonstrated in Urban and Schweiger (2014), 'the level of analysis in these studies is quite broad. Most of them ask for recipients' evaluations of whole media brands like the New York Times or whole media genres like newspapers or news websites. Hence, the results cannot say much about recipients' concrete evaluations of different news items. They rather express an aggregate opinion over a variety of articles, sections and editions. It remains unclear which part of the coverage was judged.' Then, often in different studies, the set of criteria chosen to evaluate information quality is the result of a specific filtering through the lens of academic expertise and not directly derived by surveying recipients' expertise. Therefore, sometimes it is unclear whether media users or journalists taking part in surveys and experiments are able or understand—at least, in the same way as researchers—the indicators they have to rate in order to evaluate quality of news (Urban and Schweiger 2014). Such research biases can negatively impact overall results.

The organization-level criteria of news quality, presented in the literature, may be called into question. To our knowledge, there is no empirical evidence in the area of causes and consequences, or more generally relationships, between different production context and organization and the characteristics of the produced news. For instance, we cannot say, without an in-depth study, when news are staff-written the characteristics of honesty or checkability of information produced by journalists are always present; or that there is a link between media's sources of revenue (e.g., advertising) and accuracy; or again that media ownership has always a direct impact on the spectrum of the subjects that covered by this media or that actually interest the public, and so on.

At the content level, particular sets of news characteristics as quality standards puts the problem of perspective. For instance, investigative reporting may be one of the dimensions of quality from the supply-side, professional perspective. However, from the demand-side perspective, it may be of no importance for some users' information. In the same manner, in some contexts readers may appreciate shallowness (for instance, if one wants to have a short review of current affairs) or opinion-driven style in news (for instance, if one wants to know the viewpoint of a political party or an interest group on a given situation). For the same reasons, focusing exclusively on the demand-side may also be insufficient to define the news' quality, taking into account heterogeneity of information users and their needs and wishes in respect of the news consumption. Finally, quality criteria do not necessarily meet unanimity among both journalists and readers: 'legitimate' journalists will be able to put forward some criteria that otherwise are not considered as important (or even evaluated negatively) by certain categories of readers (geeks in a hurry, compulsive information sharers, and so forth) or journalists (gonzo, alternative, or others entirely).[4]

Facing these problems we suggest that some consensus can be found due to the introduction to the analysis of the information as example of economic goods. In example: a product that 'satisfies human wants' and is 'exchanged on the market' (Milgate et al. 1987). In this economic sense, goods are not 'just physical objects, but the qualities with which they are endowed' (ibid.); their value is the combination of 'objective conditions of production' and 'subjective conditions of their consumption' (ibid.).

When considered this way, the definition of the news quality may be reformulated as follows. First, journalistic information is produced to satisfy concrete users' needs and wishes. Users may be final consumers, regulators, industrial actors, etc.; their needs may be of various natures (to be informed of the news, to share an opinion, to sustain political diversity or polarization, etc.). In this sense, different characteristics of journalistic information (rates of staff-written content, checkability, covered subjects, etc.) and their combinations are supposed to satisfy various wishes and needs. Second, among various users' wishes, as for any other economic good, one can find those unanimously assumed by all actors (e.g., preference for being informed by truth information at the consumers' side, preference to be considered as reliable media for producers) and those for which users' (and other actors) may differ a lot. For the former needs, the associated information characteristics refer to a sort of 'objective' goal and underlying condition for information pluralism. The latter range of users' needs implies the presence on the news market of diverse information characteristics attracting heterogeneous users.

The quality of information exchanged on the market (or its value) resides in the existence of sustainable economic models which lead to the availability of the market of journalistic information capable to satisfy the both criteria: unanimous features and diversity criteria.

We propose to consider this condition, which, contrary to previous definitions goes beyond the characteristics of the content or its production conditions, and which makes a bridge between supply-side and demand-side perspectives, as necessary requirement for information pluralism. Our next section develops in detail this approach.

4 A Theoretical Framework

Product Quality and News' Characteristics

The notion of quality exists in some creative and cultural industries as both established social convention and the main criteria which help professionals, users, and regulators rank and compare the goods. This kind of collective consensus prevails, for instance, in the arts market, where originality and uniqueness as criteria of quality (and the prices) of works distinguishes originals from fakes (Lazzaro 2006; Benhamou and Ginsburgh 2002; De Marchi and Van Miegroet 1996). On the one hand, the case of news and journalistic information in general is quite different as there is little chance that all readers will weight equally different characteristics of the content (e.g., some information users prefer subjective journalism and others appreciate impartiality and the use of illustrations). In this sense, contrary to artworks, there is no established social convention that would help to range any journalistic information according to its quality. On the other hand, taking into account the crucial role of information in democracy and the scope of problems coming from platformization and digital context (cf. here above), some conventions emerge today to rule on the quality of journalistic information. Some of them are of legal nature (e.g., misinformation laws, legal definition, and control of the content promoting illicit activities, etc.). Other emerging norms are less clearly defined and identifiable.[5] For example, lack of originality (plagiarism) among press outlets in the digital context, demonstrated by previous research (Cagé et al. 2017), may be negatively perceived by the majority (if not all) of the news' users, who are trying to choose a particular outlet to satisfy their information needs.

We suggest that the Kevin Lancaster's theory (Lancaster 1966) is particularly useful to analyze the specific case of journalistic information as an economic good. According to this approach, for any kind of goods and services, quality is defined as a relationship between product characteristics and the preferences and needs of consumers. In the case of news, each 'service' corresponds to a unique combination of features providing for different levels of utility for readers by satisfying their needs. Figure 1 illustrates this idea. 'Service 1,' for instance, combines different features to provide for the need, in our example, 'stay informed.'

Different features of both news and media may be of varied values for different information users: If someone only wants to stay informed, she may have higher preferences for 'accuracy,' 'originality,' or 'interviews' than to 'impartiality' and 'authenticity,' even if all these components must be brought together to make information valuable for them. This way we obtain a range of consumers' needs and wishes of the news consumption and particular content features permitting their satisfaction. At the intersection of this data, we then measured the weights associated with each feature, representing its importance for the satisfaction of consumers. Figure 2 gives such example. Note that our illustrations are purely arbitrary and only (large-scale) surveys and experimentations could permit to fill this kind of table by asking or testing people about their needs in terms of journalistic information.

Such a representation permits this essay to grapple with the multidimensionality of the news quality and its evaluation. All the combinations of 'need-information features' characterized by high divergence in the weights' ordering among information users, make reference to news and media characteristics for which no social convention is applicable (and, if exists, may be harmful for the diversity). At the same time, the combinations evaluated similarly by different information consumers constitute the ground for the development and support of collective norms and conventions. In terms of information quality—the first combination's higher quality is associated with the diversity of information features available on the market. On the contrary, for the second set of combinations, higher information quality means obligatory presence of particular features in the journalistic information. These considerations situate the question of

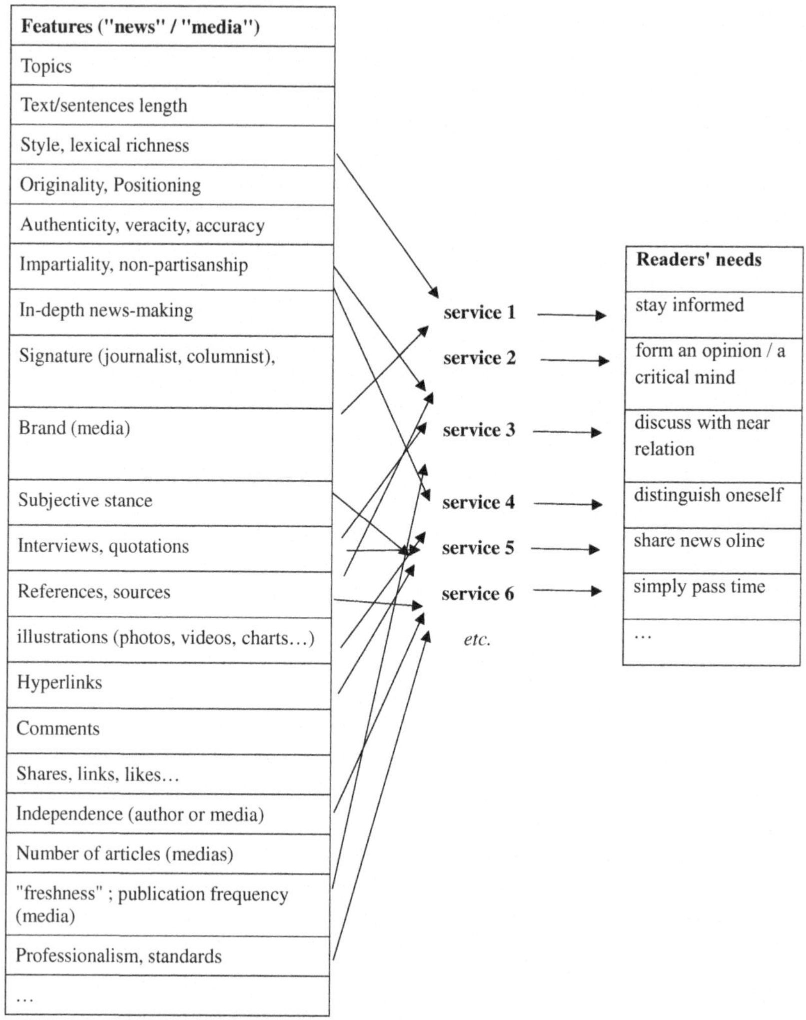

Fig. 1 News' quality (1/2)

Needs / Features	Stay informed	Discuss	Distinguish oneself	Form an opinion	Share online	...
Specific news topics	---	+++	+++			
Accuracy	+++	+++	++	+		
Independence				+++		
Text/sentences length	-			+++	---	
Style, lexical richness						
Originality	+++	+++	+++	+++	++	
Impartiality, non-partisanship	+			+++		
....	+++	+++	+	+++		
Online sharing tools		+++	+++		+++	

Fig. 2 News' quality (2/2)

information quality definition and measurement in the framework of the economic theory of differentiation.

Horizontal and Vertical Differentiation

This approach defines 'quality' of news by envisaging it in an economic theoretical framework and analysis grid associated with the horizontal and vertical differentiation (Gabszewicz and Thisse 1979; Lyubareva et al. 2020).[6] As mentioned above, different news features correspond to different levels of 'quality' according to readers' needs. Combinations of product features produce 'services' that consumers use to satisfy their needs and wishes.

In the case of *horizontal differentiation*, the same features will give rise to different 'qualities' according to the tastes and expectations of readers (*de gustibus non est disputandum*). Here, goods are considered as different in their characteristics, proving impossible to order them according to unanimous criteria. In other words, there is no social consensus because consumers' tastes are heterogeneous regarding certain attributes of news. Applied to the journalistic information, a short article, an in-depth analysis or a subjective standpoint (e.g., 'gonzo' journalism) will not be appraised in the same way when the reader is a highbrow individual, a journalist, or a social media addict. The 'qualities' of news (thematic, formats, points of view ...) correspond to the various opinions in place each reader choosing a specific quality.

By contrast, in the case of *vertical differentiation*, some features could correspond to socially unanimous criteria of quality. At identical prices, each consumer will rank a vertically differentiated good in the same order. Quality refers to vertical differentiation, where the weight of some information features can be classified on a unanimous basis and therefore considered as being of higher quality (this basis may be established by the users themselves or come from some socially desirable or legal objectives established by regulators for example). For instance, in the automotive industry, all buyers agree on the highest efficient brake systems (at a given price). In the press industry, (almost) all actors consider fake news as being undesirable whereas they will prefer a true story that is verified. Readers will always choose news with the second attribute (truth and authentication) against the first ones (misleading fabrication). The same prevails regarding originality and plagiarism, as is the case in the art market.

This horizontal/vertical differentiation theoretical approach enables to envisage many aspects of the news ecosystem from the social practices and economic models to the regulation tools of media pluralism.

At the level of social practices, it can help to better identify the differences in the readers' perceptions, needs, and consumption according to news quality. At the level of news providers' strategies, firms can choose to differentiate the goods they produce in order to increase their profits or to reduce the competition by insulating their own market according to some degree (goods are imperfect substitutes). It clearly depends upon their skills, reputation (brand), initial market position, and competitors' (potential) reaction. In the same way, from consumers perspective, differentiation, in particular vertical differentiation, can create inequalities. For low-income people, the price to be paid to get vertically differentiated goods (luxury goods, for example) can be too high. In addition, news production and consumption can be analyzed altogether using this approach. For instance, frequent releasing of fresh news can prevent a media from verifying systematically their authenticity but such low-cost information can suit readers not very demanding and/or with low willingness-to-pay. More generally, a media is supposed to produce news compliant with the expectations and preferences of its particular audience (*horizontally differentiated news*), but not necessarily in terms of the unanimous qualitative criteria, e.g., plagiarism or copy-paste of news vs. original content (*vertically differentiated news*).

At a more holistic level—the news industry and more generally the media ecosystem (including social media, independent news producers)—this approach makes it possible to assess the actual degree of media pluralism associated with the production and circulation of news. We can consider that one major goal of media regulation is to favor the extension of such 'horizontality,' i.e., that media industry and news providers supply readers and communities with the largest range of news (socially and legally acceptable) in terms of topics, political viewpoint, gender and ethnic representation, and so on in order for individuals to make their sovereign choices with all kinds of accessible information.

Another major objective of media regulation is to promote economic models or consumers' interest that favor the most the production and circulation of news of the best possible *vertical* quality in order for people to make non-biased sovereign choices with the highest-quality information and to stimulate the 'good practices' from both production and consumption sides. This requires the definition of *unanimous* quality standards corresponding to the viewpoints of all stakeholders (readers, journalists, politicians, civil society). This condition is, indeed, crucial, in oder to avoid transforming news into 'merit goods,' i.e., to favor the production and release of the kinds of information that politicians or regulators would favor according to their sole criteria and interests.

An Analysis Grid: Crossing Vertical and Horizontal Quality

By crossing the two dimensions of news quality, we can conjure an analysis grid to determine whether or not pluralism is achieved in its multiple aspects. Gabszewicz and Resende (2012) and Gabszewicz and Wauthy (2012) suggested such a theoretical framework to study the market strategies of media competitors in terms of differentiated pricing. Figure 3 illustrates this theoretical framework with a simplified representation.

In this graph, we distinguish four possible cases: (A) and (B) correspond to the provision of news of high vertical quality—original news—but correspond to two distinct tastes or judgments from readers, journalists, etc. For instance, A-type news can be objective information with argumentation and many references whereas B-type corresponds to news

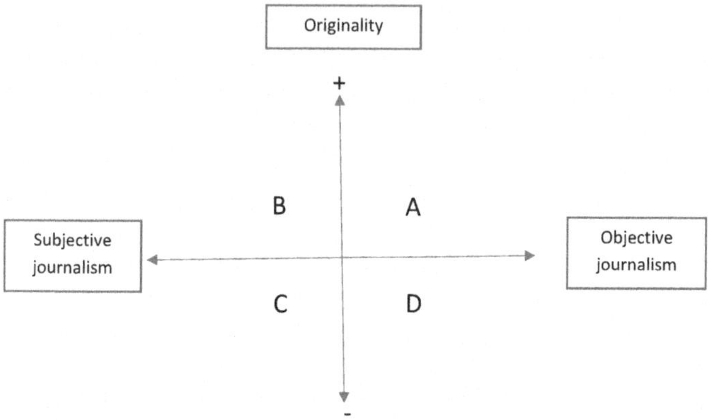

Fig. 3 A simplified example with two dimensions

based on first-person narrative and interviews. (C) and (D) cases refer to news of low vertical quality—information and news providers of copy-paste content of breaking news—that can be horizontally differentiated in the same manner as (A) and (B) cases.

By definition, A-type and B-type news are costlier to produce and, therefore, might be behind a paywall, whereas the other types can be cheaper or free to access (with or without ads). In the first case, higher costs incurred by media outlets and independent journalists can be explained by different expensive operations and resources, i.e., getting exclusivity of news, interviewing specialists, sending reporters in the field, and making undercover journalism. To exist, (A) and (B) media supposes that the number of readers and readership communities willing to pay for such news is sufficient to make their production profitable. By contrast, C-type and D-type news are cheaper to produce and then could correspond to undemanding readers that prefer short, concise, fresh news. Even though such news could be unoriginal, they can be easily shared and discussed with friends and family. Digital platforms contribute to the production and proliferation of those information goods. In this context, *speed-driven journalism* and *snack contents* are representative and widespread practices.

5 An illustration: Editorial strategies, news quality, and media pluralism[7]

We applied our conceptual framework to make an empirical study on the news quality produced by French news producers. Using a linguistic discourse analysis method on 31 striking events and 93,648 articles published over the 2015–2019 period in France, we characterized their editorial choices of 55 representative media outlets. This study shows that media strategies nowadays make it possible to produce journalistic information that is sufficiently differentiated horizontally to meet distinct consumer needs, albeit with significant disparities in vertical quality.

Our sample is made of traditional press media, all online digital media players (e.g., Yahoo News!), and 'alternative' or 'partisan' left- and right-wing media. Each selected event meets two main criteria: is singularized without ambiguity as well as containing associated key words in our publishing window. To measure the two types of news quality available in the market, we used the following dimensions as criterion. On the one hand, the *originality* of the information was used to assess the vertically differentiated quality. We assumed that to avoid copy-and-paste of wires or plagiarism is commonly accepted among readers. The doc2vec method (Le and Mikolov 2014) was applied to measure the semantic distance between press articles and all previous AFP wires on the same news topic. On the other hand, *argumentation* or *analysis*, as an added value proposed by journalists in the articles, was used to assess horizontal differentiation. A rhetorical analysis of documents (Roze 2013) quantifies the relationships between sentences and the presence of morphosyntactic indicators referenced in the literature. We calculated an argumentative index that makes it possible to distinguish between articles containing an analysis, consensual content or a discussion of a current subject, articles based on facts or precise positions leaving less room for analysis. This index is implicitly associated with heterogeneous tastes and preferences of news recipients.

Crossing the vertical dimension (*originality*) and the horizontal dimension (*analysis*) makes it possible to visualize the variety of editorial strategies for media outlets. On the following graph, the horizontal axis intersects the vertical axis at the median value of the maximum distance between press articles and AFP wires for the same topics. The AFP is logically located at the bottom of the southwest square associated with no significant analysis and no originality. This mapping of news providers presented above is based for each title on the aggregate values of originality and analysis for several events treated during the period 2015–2019. Depending on the nature of the event as well as the political, thematic, and geographical orientation or the level of their own resources, media may cover news topics in very different ways (Fig. 4).

Each quadrant corresponds to a type of news providers—two categories are rather specialized and then located mainly in one isolated zone. Magazine presses (monthly or weekly/paid-for publications) are mostly present in the North-East quadrant where high vertical quality (*argumentation*) is associated with high production costs that require important funding. The alternative media ('partisan' news) are also specialized but prevail in the North-East quadrant: They are characterized by the originality of information they produce but not the treatment of all viewpoints and aspects of the topics they cover (*analyze*). Their readers belong to well-identified and stable communities sharing similar opinions so that those media do not systemically try to set out arguments to convince their readership by discussing the opposite stakes, points of view, etc. By contrast, national daily press is present in all quadrants in a quite

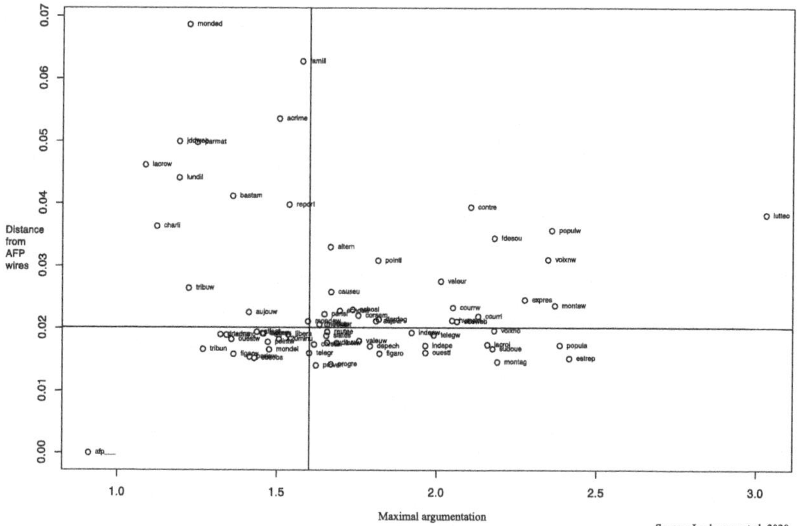

Source: Lyubareva et al. 2020.

Fig. 4 Mapping of editorial strategies of French media

balanced way with some of the newspaper opting for two different strategies. Publishing strategy can also lead national newspapers to replicate agency wires (low originality) and after to significantly enrich some articles according to the importance of the topics, sometimes to differentiate from rivals. As for regional newspapers, they are slightly more present in the South-West quadrant. While they publish news close to the AFP wires, those media outlets differentiate horizontally in terms of argumentation. This result can be explained by the fact that our survey covers only national and international events less treated by regional newspapers which allocate more human resources to local events and topics.

This analysis highlights the editorial strategies of French news producers. There is a relation between those strategies and news quality. We also show that variety and viability of editorial choices of media can be closely linked to their economic models. These media have expanded in the market during two decades of digital transformation. For example, national and regional media, in order to foster their position as leaders, systematically explore diversified editorial strategies to generate new kinds (and streams) of revenues. Their strategies, despite their substantial resources, are concentrated in areas with higher demand (and therefore profitability) and not necessarily with higher added value (as suggested by the overrepresentation of these players in the north-eastern quadrant in our graph). For alternative media, the only way to survive this competition is to position itself in highly targeted niche markets. These actors must unite loyal and stable communities of readers to finance their production so as not to disappear or be bought by bigger media groups. But an excessive dependence upon a readers' community might lead them to an overproduction of news consistent with the opinions of the target readership. For more generalist new media creators, which were largely free when they emerged in the media landscape, a choice is currently being made between adopting a pay-for model or remaining free on condition of producing low added value information. Advertising revenues, which drive this decision, prove insufficient to profitably finance production in the press sector. The problem with these choices is that the financial success of the pay-for strategy is not guaranteed if the number of actors adopting it increases significantly.

Finally, our study suggests that the criterion of horizontal quality (*diversity*) of the information provided by the French media is satisfied because the large supply of vendors is likely to meet the readers' tastes and needs for different types of information. Readers can thus find any type of information by focusing on one type of media or by combining several media according to their preference. There are also all types of media in terms of vertical quality. However, a low willingness to pay of readers might lead them to select a (too) low vertical quality, raising a crucial issue for liberal democracies and therefore for regulation: How can media be encouraged to improve the quality of their supply or readers to increase their willingness to pay for higher vertical quality? For instance, regulation could aim to increase the readers' willingness to pay for higher vertical quality news without restraining their access to horizontally differentiated information. This could consist in influencing their individual preferences—training young and easily influenced people to better identify fakes or misleading news—or increasing their real income by awarding virtuous news producers (reduced taxation) and overtaxing those providing recipients with excessive amounts of copy-paste from wires or proven fakes. Implementing such a cross-taxation might be possible precisely by being able to identify and target outlets according to the nature of news quality they provide in the media market. The range of such tools then may cover a large area of instruments from education, promotion campaigns, taxation, and subsidies to sanctions and rewards.

6 Further Research

In this chapter, we discussed the issue of news quality as a key aspect of media pluralism. We elaborated upon a theoretical framework that permits to evaluate the news quality in an economic perspective. Depending on the definition of quality (veracity, independence, etc.) and the stakeholders' expectations, the criteria used for the analysis can be classified according to the vertical and horizontal axes. As a tool, the resulting media mapping helps identify editorial areas with high media concentration against underdeveloped areas. This approach can serve to explore different phenomena in the media ecosystem and, from a regulation perspective, to correct new and traditional market failures. Once we agree on the description of the news by means of needs and features (i.e., as an economic good), understanding of the factors determining users' preferences and producers editorial choices opens the discussion on potential regulation tools.

On the side of readership preference: Cultural capital, the social influence by peers (the media and type of news that social neighbors look up), the social media used by readers, and more generally their demographics play a key role in forming their preferences. Thus, these factors are among the main factors that could impact the quality expectations of the news' consumers. For instance, a reader with a high cultural capital is likely to be more demanding on certain characteristics of news (i.e., in-depth news making, references…) and will discredit the media producing unverified or tabloid information that does not meet their expectations. This factor may also determine how other actors like academics, journalists, politicians, and legal experts appraise the quality of news.

In dealing with supply: Media competition, ownership, and business models are capable of determining which characteristics of news will be produced by the media. For instance, the business models[8] choice implies particular market positioning, customer segments serving by the media, the customer relationships established and maintained with each customer segment, the revenue and pricing model, the cost structure and financing, and the partnership network (in-house production vs. outsourcing). All these elements may be determinant for the editorial choice—as in, the set of information features produced by the media to satisfy demand, expectations, and needs.

Finally, the perception of quality by different actors can be impacted by more general factors—i.e., the institutional framework, actions of civil society such as NGOs, (medi)activist groups, trade unions, and political parties—whose actions and decisions could influence some news features to the detriment of others (veracity against sensationalism) (Fig. 5).

A general mapping of media, according to horizontal and vertical axes of different news features, crossed with the factors underlying producers' (e.g. economic models) and consumers' (e.g. number of subscribers) editorial choices substantiate potential efficiency of various regulation

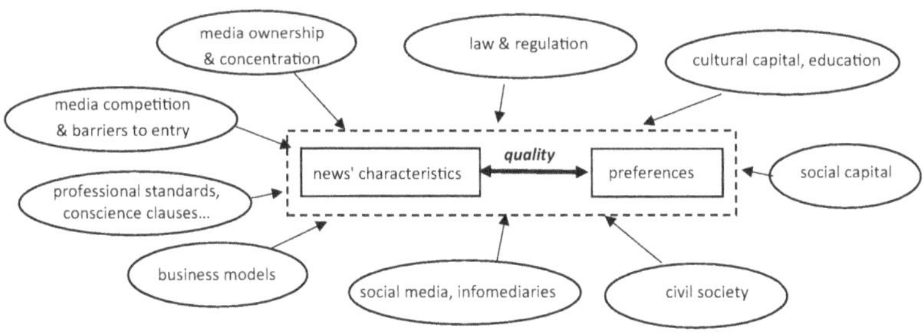

Fig. 5 The determinants of quality

tools. Distinguishing news according to their quality—horizontal or vertical—by using transparent and measurable criteria could permit to finely design and advice for regulation instruments (media education and prevention campaigns, taxation and subsidies, rewards, sanctions, and prohibitions…) to preserve and promote media pluralism.

Notes

1. In addition, Bogart (1989) proposes the following three measures for quality in outlets: (1) high ratio of staff-written articles to wire service copy, (2) high amount of editorial (non-advertising) content, and (3) high ratio of interpretation.
2. In the same way, many studies use the same selection method based on what previous researches have done. Meyer and Kim (2003) select 15 quality indicators they identify in the literature to ask newspaper editors to rate them. In her survey on the impact of audience metrics on news quality, Fürst (2020) also uses literature-based indicators to evaluate news quality according to the journalistic production processes in newsrooms.
3. Picard (2000) suggests that the journalistic quality is directly correlated to journalistic activity that can be measured by interviews; telephone gathering of information, arranging interviews; attending events about which stories are written; attending staff meetings, discussions, and training; reading to obtain background material and knowledge; thinking, organizing material, and waiting for information and materials; traveling to and from locations where information is gathered.
4. Cf. Debates between authors like Kunelius, Jacobsson & Jacobsson, Usher, Shapiro, Bogart Kovach et Rosenstiel. Some of them think that only journalists are able to evaluate the quality of journalistic information—the social role of journalism is to permit citizens to form opinions—while others suggest that individuals are able to know what they want by their own (snack news or investigative journalism).
5. Information is a type of "credence good," which real qualities are often difficult to observe by consumers even after purchasing. This creates information asymmetries between information producers and users and makes sometimes impossible objective evaluation of these qualities (Gabszewicz and Resende 2012). For example, readers have limited capabilities to evaluate the accuracy with which some media outlets select and dispatch their news.
6. We elaborate this theoretical framework as part of a general research project on the question of pluralism and social media in France: Pluralism of online news (http://www.anr-pil.org).

7. This section summarizes the main results of a study published elsewhere (Lyubareva et al. 2020). It was conducted in a research project (*Pluralisme de l'Information en Ligne*, www.anr-pil.org/) supported by the French National Agency of Research.
8. Some studies examine the relationship between business models and performance/profitability—do media spending resources in higher quality (i.e., by providing more investigative news) make more profits? (Udell 1978; Meyer and Kim 2003; Abdenour and Riffe 2019)—but not the relationship between quality choice and business models: Are there some combinations in terms of customer segments, cost structure, revenue streams... matching with quality choice?

References

Abdenour, J., and D. Riffe. 2019. Digging for (ratings) Gold: The Connection Between Investigative Journalism And Audiences. *Journalism Studies* 20 (16): 2386–2403.

Belair-Gagnon, V. 2019. News on the Fly: Journalist- Audience Online Engagement Success as a Cultural Matching Process. *Media, Culture and Society* 41 (6): 757–773.

Benhamou, F., and V. Ginsburgh. 2002. Is There a Market for Copies? *Journal of Art, Management, Law and Society* 32 (1): 37–56.

Blanchett Neheli, N. 2018. News by Numbers. *Digital Journalism* 6 (8): 1041–1051.

Bogart, L. 1989. *Press and the Public: Who Reads What, When, Where and Why in American Newspapers*. Hillsdale, NJ: Lawrence Erlbaum Associates.

Bogart, L. 2004. Reflections on Content Quality in Newspapers. *Newspaper Research Journal* 25 (1): 40–53.

Cagé, J., N. Hervé, and M.-L. Viaud. 2017. *L'information à tout prix*. Bry-sur-Marne, France: INA.

Carpentier, N., and B. Cammaerts. 2006. Hegemony, Democracy, Agonism and Journalism: An Interview with Chantal Mouffe. *Journalism Studies* 7 (6): 964–975.

Craig, D. 2011. *Excellence in Online Journalism: Exploring Current Practices in an Evolving Environment*. Thousand Oaks, CA: Sage.

De Marchi, N., and H.J. Van Miegroet. 1996. Pricing Invention: 'Originals', 'Copies', and Their Relative Value in Seventeenth Century Nederlandish Art Markets (pp. 27–70). In *Economics of the Arts: Selected Essays*, ed. V.A. Ginsburgh and P.-M. Menger. North Holland, Amsterdam: Elsevier Science.

Fürst, S. 2020. In the Service of Good Journalism and Audience Interests? How Audience Metrics Affect News Quality. *Media and Communication* 8 (3): 270–280.

Gabszewicz, J., and J. Resende. 2012. Differentiated Credence Goods and Price Competition. *Information Economics and Policy* 24 (3–4): 277–287.

Gabszewicz, J., and J.F. Thisse. 1979. Price Competition, Quality and Income Disparities. *Journal of Economic Theory* 20 (3): 340–359.

Gabszewicz, J., and X.Y. Wauthy. 2012. Nesting Horizontal and Vertical Differentiation. *Regional Science and Urban Economics* 42 (6): 998–1002.

Gladney, G.A. 1990. Newspaper Excellence: How Editors of Small and Large Papers Judge Quality. *Newspaper Research Journal* 11 (2): 58–71.

Karppinen, K. 2018. Journalism, Pluralism and Diversity. In *Journalism*, ed. T.P. Vos, 493–510. De Gruyter.

Lacy, S. 2000. Commitment of Financial Resources as a Measure of Quality. In *Measuring Media Content, Quality and Diversity: Approaches and Issues in Content Research*, ed. R.G. Picard, 25–50. Turku, Finland: The Media Group, Business and Research Development Centre, Turku School of Economics and Business Administration.

Lacy, S., and T. Rosenstiel. 2015. *Defining and Measuring Quality Journalism.* Rutgers School of Communication and Information.

Lancaster, K.J. 1966. A New Approach to Consumer Theory. *Journal of Political Economy* 74 (2): 132–157.

Lazzaro, E. 2006. Assessing Quality in Cultural Goods: The Hedonic Value of Originality in Rembrandt's Prints. *Journal of Cultural Economics* 30 (1): 15–40.

Le, Q., and T. Mikolov. 2014. Distributed Representations of Sentences and Documents, *International Conference on Machine Learning*, 1188–1196.

Lyubareva, I., F. Rochelandet, and Y. Haralambous. 2020. Qualité et différenciation des biens informationnels. Une étude exploratoire sur l'information d'actualité. [*Quality and differentiation of information goods. An exploratory study on news information*]. Revue d'Economie Industrielle. 172: 133–177.

Magin, M. 2019. Attention, Please! Structural Influences on Tabloidization of Campaign Coverage in German and Austrian Elite Newspapers (1949–2009). *Journalism* 20 (12): 1704–1724.

McLennan, G. 1995. *Pluralism.* Buckingham: Open University Press.

McQuail, D. 2005. *McQuail's Mass Communication Theory*, 5th ed. London: Sage.

Meier, K. 2019. Quality in Journalism. In *The International Encyclopedia of Journalism Studies*, ed. T.P. Vos and F. Hanusch. Hoboken, NJ: Wiley.

Merrill, J.C. 1968. *The Elite Press: Great Newspapers of the World.* New York: Pitman Publishing Corp.

Meyer, P., and K.H. Kim. 2003. Quantifying Newspaper Quality: "I Know It When I See It". Unpublished paper.

Milgate, M., J. Eatwell, and P.K. Newman. 1987. *The New Palgrave: A Dictionary of Economics*. London, New York, Tokyo: Macmillan Stockton Press Maruzen.

Napoli, P.M. 1999. Deconstructing the Diversity Principle. *Journal of Communication* 49 (4): 7–34.

Napoli, P.M. 2003. *Audience Economics: Media Institution and the Audience Marketplace*. New York: Columbia University Press.

Pariser, E. 2011. *The Filter Bubble: What the Internet Is Hiding from You*. New York: Penguin.

Picard, R.G. 2000. Measuring Quality by Journalistic Activity. In *Measuring Media Content, Quality and Diversity: Approaches and Issues in Content Research*, ed. R.G. Picard, 97–104. Turku, Finland: The Media Group, Business and Research Development Centre, Turku School of Economics and Business Administration.

Rebillard, F. (Ed.) (2012). Internet et pluralisme de l'information. *Réseaux*, n° 176.

Rebillard, F., and M. Loicq. 2013. *Pluralisme de l'information et media diversity. Un état des lieux international*. Louvain-la-Neuve, Belgique: De Boeck Supérieur.

Rosenstiel, T., J. Sonderman, T. Thompson, J. Benz, J. Sonderman, E. Swanson. 2015. How Millennials Get News: Inside the Habits of America's First Digital Generation, Media Insight Project.

Roze, C. 2013. *Vers une algèbre des relations de discours*. Thèse de doctorat. Paris: Université Paris- Diderot.

Stone, G.C., D.B. Stone, and E.P. Trotter. 1981. Newspaper Quality's Relation to Circulation. *Newspaper Research Journal* 2 (3): 16–24.

Udell, J.G. 1978. *The Economics of the American Newspaper*. New York: Hastings House.

Urban, J., and W. Schweiger. 2014. News Quality From the Recipients' Perspective. *Journalism Studies* 15 (6): 821–840.

The Stakes and Threats of the Convergence Between Media and Telecommunication Industries

Françoise Benhamou

1 Introduction

In many countries, especially the USA, a twofold movement is developing: Media industry consolidation on the one side, and on the other, cross-ownership of electronic media platforms built on convergence of broadcast and broadband media. Telecom operators provide content and, conversely, broadcasters are buying broadband operators. At the same time, traditional TV channels are increasingly delivered via broadband. Giant companies (Alphabet, Facebook, Amazon, Netflix) enter these markets by buying or developing their own channels, or investing in infrastructure (fiber networks, satellites) and content creation. Those changes imply a disruption in standard economic models and a looming shift in economic power. Ownership of property rights on content in order to capture the attention of users is more important than ever. Yet, these same economic models are based on the exploitation of personal

The original version of this chapter was revised: The chapter has been changed from non-open access to open access and the copyright holder has been updated. The correction to this chapter is available at
https://doi.org/10.1007/978-3-030-66759-7_11

F. Benhamou (✉)
University Sorbonne-Paris Nord, Villetaneuse, France

S. A. Matei et al. (eds.), *Digital and Social Media Regulation*,
https://doi.org/10.1007/978-3-030-66759-7_7

data. Monetizing consumers' data allows companies to dominate markets. When this careful arithmetic is played to its conclusion, the market power held by corporate giants strongly incentivizes consolidation and convergence among these corporate giants. This potential market condition requires a strong regulation, which should be updated in order to ensure diversity and independence of content. Further, to assert accessibility to Internet, avoiding the risk of abuse of power of operators acting as gatekeepers (Jensen 2016).

This paper gives examples of convergence between telecom carriers and media content providers (2). It stresses this hypothesis in order to better understand the wave of mergers and contracts between telecoms and content industries; the essay encapsulates the synergies between telecom carriers and media content providers (3). The wave of convergence raises the question of independency of media, considering independency as a necessary condition for diversity (in opinions, in journalists' profiles, etc.). This paper demands regulators question the relevance of the existing regulatory framework considering new variables, including investment, competition, and Net Neutrality (4).

2 Some Examples of Convergence Between Telecom Carriers and Media Content Providers

Indeed, the cases of convergence between online media and telecommunications are numerous. Some of them failed.

At the beginning of the 2010s, the French media giant company Vivendi specialized in video game publishing, music distribution, satellite distribution, and telecoms. Vivendi then decided to concentrate on contents and to sell its shares in telecom operators (Maroc Telecom in 2013, SFR in 2014, and the Brazilian company GVT in 2015), putting an end to its strategy previously based on convergence. In 2014, Vivendi bought the French national pay-TV channel Canal+, focused on cinema and sport. In 2019, Vivendi bought the French publisher Editis from Spanish owner Planeta in a €900 million deal. This purchase pattern confirms Vivendi's wish to focus on content industries and to put an end to investment in telecoms.

Similar cases exist. During the 2010s, the French telecom operator Orange decided to develop a strategy for contents and services by creating subsidiary companies: Orange Sport, cinema channels, etc. But Orange gave up those investments in order to favor partnerships with Deezer (music) and Dailymotion (videos), which have been more or less abandoned since their cooperative endeavors. Orange still holds

Orange Cinéma Séries (OCS), a collective of French television channels devoted to series and cinema, available on satellite, cable, and IPTV. In the former case, convergence was an too-early-too-costly strategy; for Orange, convergence was not abandoned but reshaped more modestly and cautiously. In both situations, companies failed to capitalize on a sustainable industrial strategy.

In a US context, the merger of AOL-Time Warner failed, considered a deep strategic error for both companies. Jeffrey Bewkes, chief executive of Time Warner, describes his company's failure to merge with AOL: "You had a lot of people saying you should've combined a donkey with a rabbit and gotten a flying unicorn" (*New York Times*, October 23, 2016).

However, other cases were more promising. One such case includes Time Warner-AT&T, or countless smaller mergers with less global, monopolistic ramifications between numerous co-operations in the press industry and telecom companies. In the case of the press in France, the three of the four largest telecom operators are integrating into their mobile packages a virtual kiosk, bringing together many titles of press and magazines. SFR (owned by Altice) includes in most of its offers access to more than 80 newspapers and magazines, at a price of €19.99 per month. Bouygues Telecom provides an unlimited press bouquet with more than 1,000 press titles (called "The Kiosk") accessible in a few clicks and even offline on smartphone, tablet, or computer. Orange provides two services: ePresse (more than 300 newspapers and magazines) and Izneo by Fnac (more than 3000 comics), at € 9.99 per month. Contents are accessible via computer, tablet, or smartphone with or without a connection.

3 Synergies Between Telecom Carriers and Media Content Providers. Some Cases

Over the last decade, telecom companies and media content providers have found synergies between their respective markets. In the case of TV, cinema, and telecom, one notably impressive case is the $85 billion deal between Time Warner and AT&T (Table 1) in December 2016, recently approved by the antitrust authority. After a first trial, the judge ruled that the government had failed to prove that the deal violates antitrust law. Then, in February 2019, the federal government lost its second court challenge to AT&T's merger with Time Warner, allowing the merger to proceed. The objective of the merger was to allow the combined company to leverage more viewer data, to permit CNN to benefit from

Table 1 AT&T and Time Warner at the time of the merger, February 2019

AT&T	*Time Warner*
- First American provider of pay TV (following its acquisition of DirectTV for $50 billion in 2015) - Second-largest wireless company (142 M wireless customers) - Third-largest broadband provider in the country	- One of the largest American media content companies, owns: - HBO, Warner Bros, Studios - Cable networks including CNN and TNT - Numerous other entertainment and news offerings

Table 2 French National daily press, million copies sold

Years	*2000*	*2005*	*2010*	*2015*	*2016*
Copies	7.024	7.022	5.970	3.943	3.634

Source https://www.senat.fr/rap/a19-145-42/a19-145-420.html#toc16

AT&T's know-how in data and targeting. Therefore, it would be possible to monetize the time spent by millions of viewers on their mobile devices and better customize the content for CNN's followers. In short, to sell more targeted ads. Moreover, according to both companies, this source of efficiency can help diminish prices for consumers.

The other impressive case of convergence concerns Sky (the leading pay-TV platform in the UK) and the US cable operator Comcast in September 2018. Comcast bought NBCUniversal in 2009, and, by taking control of the leading European satellite television broadcaster Sky (23 million subscribers in Europe, 29 million customers in the USA), Comcast generated more revenue in Europe, accelerated online video consumption, and expanded its geographic coverage. By growing in size and becoming stronger, Comcast invests in content control and resists competition from Netflix (125 million subscribers) or Amazon.

For media, different factors are at play.

First, the search for new readers and viewers plays a central role. This is double important considering the crisis of the newspaper industry (see Tables 2 and 3) and of a decrease in traditional pay-TV revenues—raising the number of subscribers/readers/viewers brings more ads and therefore higher revenue. According to Digital TV Research, global pay-TV

Table 3 Sales trends for the main daily newspaper in eight countries since 2000

Country	*Newspaper*	*2000*	*2005*	*2010*	*2015*	*2016*	*2017*
Germany	Bild	4,390,000	3,829,000	2,900,000	2,220,000	1,791,000	1,687,717
UK	The Sun		3,263,000	2,929,000	1,800,000	1,712,000	1,565,945
France	Ouest France	785,000	781,000	781,000	713,000	694,000	685,000
Japan	Yomiuri Shimbun	14,407, 000	13,982,000	9,951,000	9,101,000	8,926,000	8,676,000
USA	The Wall Street Journal/USA Today	1,763,000	2,084,000	2,118,000	4,139,000	3,600,000	2,900,000

Source *id*

revenues for 138 countries peaked in 2016 at US$202 billion and will fall to US$150 billion in 2025 in spite of the fact that the number of pay-TV subscribers will actually increase by 35 million between 2019-25. Moreover, the report notes that revenues will decline in 61 countries, with the USA providing the most dramatic fall of US$31 billion.[1]

Second, as the economic model of media is based on two-sided markets (Rochet and Tirole 2003), mergers are supposed to help companies optimize advertising thanks to the better knowledge of consumer tastes and habits. Media (press and TV) are mainly supported by advertising revenue. Competition for viewers is very strong, and the more people who read a newspaper or watch a TV program, the more other people wish to read or watch the same items. Therefore, convergence allows an increase in the number of subscribers and a better accuracy of advertisements. Moreover, by selling connection and content in one package, convergence takes into account the new forms of consumption which rely on the illusion that a part of the offer is free of charge or «all included».

Future growth for telecoms depends from an increase in supply and new services in an era of strong demand for media content and digitized entertainment. Consumers buy full packages including TV programs, press, movies, and other media. For telecoms, content becomes the new field of competition, and convergence with media content providers allows telecom carriers to offer connectivity and premium content simultaneously.

Telecom companies face a threefold challenge with convergence. First, they try to reinforce their position in a context of heightened economic concentration. For example, in the USA the merger between T-Mobile and Sprint led the country to decrease from 4 to 3 national mobile network operators. In France, there remain 4 main operators, who compete for more concentration.

The second challenge concerns revenues: Depending on their situation, services can enable operators to generate additional ARPU (Average Revenue Per User). Diversifying services and content attract new subscribers and generate more revenue. To boot, it secures customer loyalty. New subscribers and operators try to increase switching costs in such a way that churn declines.

For example, Altice bought football rights in order to "capture" several hundred thousand subscribers. Similarly, in Spain, Telefonica obtained the rights to broadcast the Champions League and Europa League.

Other expected benefits are in force. In France, the Value Added Tax (VAT) rate is 20%. One of the more important indirect subsidies for press consists in a reduced rate of 2.1%. By introducing press offers in their packages, French operators used to apply a reduced rate to the "press" part of the package. The cost for the budget of the State was €400 million for SFR, and €260 million for Bouygues. Both operators benefited for almost two years from this fiscal "trick" around services imposed on their customers, but had to face a VAT reform introduced in the finance bill for 2018 that put an end to the possibility to apply a reduced VAT rate to a part of the price of subscriptions (Table 4).

4 Regulation and Convergence

Regulation covers four concerns: investment, competition, net neutrality, and diversity in opinions.

No operator can afford not to have a content strategy, but deals between contents and telecoms deserve a close look from regulators. First, such deals can create barriers to new entrants in both industries. Second, convergence may imply a loss in independency for press and TV, because their economic future relies on the distribution of their content by operators. Moreover, there exists a threat for quality of the service: a lower level of competition may lead to a decrease in investment and innovation and a drop in quality. For video (streamed or downloaded video), operators should avoid excess latency and delays in service through technological innovation. Users expect omnichannel experience: content delivery in multiple formats, across multiple channels to roaming users on

Table 4 Summary of the objectives of convergence

Objectives	*Case*
Tax optimization	Savings in VAT in France, until 2019
Increasing ad revenues	Integrated companies offer integrated packages for viewers that cover all kind of Internet access Advertisers target consumers whether they are on phones, TV, computers, etc.
Increasing the number of subscribers	Bundles: Subscription to the *New York Times* sold with free access to Spotify: for \$5 a week, readers had access to all the articles and the streaming music platform. Subscribers pay \$260 a year to access all the publications of the daily and Spotify without advertising, instead of \$370 previously for both services. The newspaper hopes to reach its target of 10 million subscribers (compared to 5 million in 2020, of which 1.85 million web-only) British Telecom succeeded in buying the rights of the English Premier League
Lock-in of users	Long-term commitments for subscribers Decreasing the churn because of higher switching costs
Vertical integration and diversification	Diversification of activities and revenues, in the case of Comcast- NBCUniversal or AT&T-TW deals: vertical integration by purchasing a supplier of TV and film content

any device. Concentration may reduce quality for customers. Therefore, regulators should pay attention to the possibility to change their Internet provider.

The playing field is complicated further by the power of platforms like Netflix. For example, in 2018, Comcast tried to bid for part of 21st Century Fox.[2] Disney acquired the company in 2019. With Fox, Disney wanted to counter Netflix. Regulation must take into account this dimension: media concentration becomes unavoidable facing network effects that mean that most powerful platforms may grow without any limit.

The Existing Regulatory Framework

Regulation combines multiple dimensions. In France, three independent agencies are respectively specialized in competition and telecom regulation: Autorité de la concurrence, Autorité de régulation des communications électroniques et des Postes (ARCEP), CSA (Conseil Supérieur de l'Audiovisuel). In the USA, two agencies are in charge: the Federal Communications Commission (FCC) regulates interstate and international communications by radio, television, wire, satellite, and cable in all 50 states, the District of Columbia, and US territories. Also, the FTC's Bureau of Competition enforces the USA's antitrust laws. In the UK, both regulators work in the same agency, OFCOM, which regulates communications services (broadband, home phone and mobile services, TV, radio, and video-on-demand sectors, universal postal service, and airwaves over which wireless devices operate).

Which Tools? Are Existing Regulations Relevant?

When disruptive innovation occurs in regulated industries, there is a need for new tools. Cortez (2014, p. 176) emphasizes a need to disrupt regulation:

> The innovation might puncture prevailing regulatory orthodoxies, forcing regulators to reorient their postures or even rethink their underlying statutory authority. The quintessential example is the Internet, which rumpled not just one, but several regulatory frameworks, including those of the Federal Communications Commission ("FCC"), the Federal Trade Commission ("FTC"), and the Food and Drug Administration ("FDA").

Antitrust in the age of telecommunication and media convergence have twofold dimensions: discrimination against rival networks and discriminatory behaviors against users, which conflicts with net neutrality principles.

Discrimination Against Rival Networks

In the case of Comcast-NBC, the FCC imposed a series of conditions on the merger in order to prevent Comcast/NBCUniversal from using its power in order to squeeze out cable channels or video services that competed with NBC's channels or Comcast's own video streaming service. But the conditions didn't work. There were complaints about unfair treatment of rival services and channels. For example, Bloomberg complained that Comcast violated a condition requiring that it group news channels together in "neighborhoods" on its channel grid. Further, complaints about unfair treatment by Comcast of online video distributors such as Netflix and Amazon Prime were submitted to arbitration.

Discriminatory Behavior

In the case of AT&T-Time Warner, the government alleged that a combined AT&T-Time Warner would have too much leverage in negotiations with television distributors. This market power would hurt competitors, harm innovation, and could lead to increased cable prices for consumers. AT&T would be in a situation where the company could favor its own users. Moreover, it would be possible to restrict choice through different means: access to studio content (especially HBO), network providers control access to the pricing of broadband facilities, or incentive to favor network-owned content thereby placing unaffiliated content providers at a competitive disadvantage.

This possibility raises the question of net neutrality. Net neutrality implies that Internet service providers (ISPs) should treat all data that travel over their networks fairly, without discrimination in favor of particular apps, sites, or services. Net neutrality was very controversial in the USA, yet enforced in Europe. Zero-rating, however, is problematic for fairly-applied Net Neutrality. Zero-rating designates the behavior of Internet service providers who apply a zero price to the data traffic associated with a particular application. For example, when an Internet access service does not charge a user for the data used to access a specific music streaming application. Zero-rating opens an avenue for discrimination.

Data, Diversity, and the Future of Press: A Failure of Regulation?

If access to press relies on contracts with telecom operators, then, for consumers, access to content may depend on subscriptions to an Internet provider. This situation raises two inquiries. First, on the supply side, will innovators be marginalized while press companies lose direct access to data on audiences? Second, how gravely is opinion diversity threatened when a deal gives a huge corporation the opportunity to influence news reporting? ISPs then control the valve of information, meaning they may favor news linked to their own interest. Then, adding a no-price package of newspapers or TV access generates a kind of depreciation of the value of cultural goods and services. Finally, this low price or free of charge access to culture and information raises the question of covering the production costs of culture, which risks a decrease in quality and in the diversity of opinions.

5 Concluding Remarks

The questions surrounding the drop in value of content sit atop of the agenda of media companies. Thus, a fork in the road emerges—the digital business environment may evolve toward an open or closed system. In an open system, networks are interconnected. Platforms and devices are characterized by interoperability and common standards. Convergence does not prevent the existence of a constellation of media players. Instead, a regulatory environment supports openness. Conversely, in proprietary networks, platforms and devices are characterized by closed system. Interoperability is limited within silos. It is especially the case when there is a strong level of vertical integration between content, services, and amenities. Convergence reinforces closed systems in which customers are captured and diversity of content is at risk.

The spread of the new coronavirus (COVID-19) in early 2020 increases uncertainty for media, leading to higher customer dependency on the quality of their Internet access. This has led to an increase in media consumption, but, as Gerard Pogorel and Augusto Prera underline (2020), with lower for-free TV and pay TV (less ads because of the stopping of the economic activity and sport activity), and an increase in video streaming revenues, especially for magnates such as Netflix and Disney+. Some sectors of economic activity and education continue in spite of the pandemic, thanks to fixed and wireless access to Internet. But the monetization of the access is difficult and mergers with media give market power to integrated companies. This is a key element in order to understand battles where the right to buy catalogues and an overabundance of content is at stake.

Notes

1. For more details, see https://www.digitaltveurope.com/2020/05/28/pay-tv-revenues-to-fall-to-us150-billion-by-2025/.

2. 21st Century Fox, owned by Rupert Murdoch, included the 20th Century Fox, Fox Searchlight, Fox 2000, Blue Sky Animation film studios, The Fox News, Fox Sports Stations, FX Cable Stations, and National Geographic TV holdings and a 30% share of Hulu streaming (and other international holdings).

References

Cortez, Nathan. 2014. Regulating Disruptive Innovation. *Berkeley Technology Law Journal* 29: 175–228. http://ssrn.com/abstract=2436065.

Jensen, Mike. 2016. Global Trends in Broadband and Broadcast Media Concentration. Digital Convergence. https://www.observacom.org/digital-convergence-global-trends-in-broadband-and-broadcast-media-concentration/.

Pogorel, Gérard, and Augusto Prera. 2020. *Streaming Media and Telecommunication: The Turning Point?* Webinar. Robert Schuman Foundation. https://www.telecom-paris.fr/agenda/streaming-media-telecommunication-turning-point.

Rochet, Jean-Charles, and Jean Tirole. 2003. Platform Competition in Two Sided Markets. *Journal of the European Economic Association* 1 (4): 990–1029.

Linking Theory and Pedagogy in the Comparative Study of US–French Media Regulatory Regimes

Sorin Adam Matei and Larry Kilman

As international telecommunications have become more intertwined, the actors, the rules they can use, and their actual power for governing global media have turned into a confusing amalgam of voices, claims, and needs. One of the most ambiguous problems is how to regulate Internet and new media. If "regulation" referred only to the basic Internet communication protocols, such as those that direct traffic or define addresses, there would be no problem. We have, in fact, a satisfactory technical governance and interconnection regulatory system supervised by bodies such as IANA (Internet Assigned Numbers Authority), ICANN (Internet Corporation of Assigned Names and Numbers), or IETF (Internet Engineering

---

The original version of this chapter was revised: The spelling of the author name has been changed from "Fabienne Graff" to "Fabienne Graf". The correction to this chapter is available at https://doi.org/10.1007/978-3-030-66759-7_10

S. A. Matei (✉)
Purdue University, West Lafayette, IN, USA
e-mail: smatei@purdue.edu

L. Kilman
American Graduate School in Paris, Paris, France

S. A. Matei et al. (eds.), *Digital and Social Media Regulation*,
https://doi.org/10.1007/978-3-030-66759-7_8

Task Force)/Internet Society that have successfully navigated the development of a global communication infrastructure. From an engineering standpoint, the Internet is a triumph of flexibility and interconnectivity. Yet many governance domains and necessary rules not related to technical matters, such as those dealing with privacy, intellectual property, or freedom of expression, suffer from ambiguity and conflict. While each nation-state has created its own rules and defined powers and institutions to rule over these matters—at least for the people living on their territories—their authority over transborder actors and production models that bring together people from many nations remains in a state of continuous negotiation and, at times, disputation.

This chapter will look at the fundamental ambiguity and state of flux that affects intellectual property, privacy, and freedom of expression, with respect to trans-Atlantic, and specifically US–French, relationships. We will compare and contrast the French and the North American approaches to privacy, copyright, and freedom of expression regulation, highlighting the main points of contention. We will examine these emerging differences, as well as possible strategies for rapprochement, from both a theoretical and pedagogical perspective. We are not only communication scholars, but also educators, and we have learned from our teaching experience that the basic ambiguities in these three domains matter the most when it comes to educating a future generation of media leaders to design convergent strategies for producing, using, or regulating transborder media transported by the Internet. Our chapter will start with an overview of the philosophical and legal differences between the US and France regulatory regimes and will end with the pedagogical dimension of teaching about them.

Theoretically, using Curien's perspective (elaborated in the first chapter of this volume), we will use his metaphor of the fishbowls suffused in an ocean, that is, of the national regulatory regimes existing in a much vaster, all-encompassing space of under- and non-regulation, to highlight how the two regimes might meet but probably not half-way. Furthermore, we can expect that the global "ocean" of interactions and communication that keeps the "fishbowls" together to either merge them, or to make them leakier and leakier. Of course, there is the possibility of vigorous political action, to counter the process of amalgamation. This, however, speaks about a future of isolationism, protectionism, and potential conflict that would change everything—and not for the better. Given the uncertainties of this future (which are in fact explored in the last chapter of this volume), we will limit our investigation to what is immediately possible and demanded by the constraints of the day.

In view of this, for the near future (and also following Curien), we will propose a "co-regulation" perspective that would cross not only the business-regulator barrier, but also national boundaries.

Once the theoretical framework is established, we will examine the differences between the two regulatory regimes from the points of view of several groups of American and French communication professionals engaged in an experiential learning experience in France created by the authors. The participants were interviewed after two courses that engaged French and American regulators and academics, and will provide an understanding of the most problematic ambiguity points and most promising spaces of co-construction of new collaborative French-American regulatory practices.

1 Theoretical Overview

Social media does not adhere to national borders. Frontiers are elusive realities in cyberspace. Yet regulation does exist, although it remains largely local and regional. This sets up a natural tension among non-compatible regimes in various national and civilizational context, which may very well be transitory and will move toward convergence. Furthermore, the domain boundaries between local and global governance regimes are elusive. Curien, in the first chapter of this volume, likens each national regulatory regime to fishbowl at the bottom of the global media ocean. Both the ocean and the fishbowls share the same water. The owners of each of the fishbowls think they have a sovereign right to choose which fish should live in the bowls, what they should eat, and how large they should get. But they have no control over the water that comes in and goes out. Neither can they completely control the flow of the fish from the ocean to the fishbowl and back. While some control can be imposed, by preventing some unwanted tentacles of some predators to enter the fishbowl, there is little that can be done to prevent the fish from leaving the fishbowl to find nutrients in the ocean. Furthermore, once outside the fishbowl, many of the fish might grow too big to return. Or might not want to return.

This conversion of the local into global and vice versa forces regulators to take new paths and consider new ways to act in the world. Some of the new paths involve more stringent rules that apply to global and local actors equally and without preference. With the issuance of the General Directive of Privacy Regulation by the European Union, followed by the suspensions of the Safe Harbor Policy in 2015 and the Privacy Shield Framework in 2020, all major US and global companies have been forced to change their data collection, holding, processing, and exploitation, for all regions, in the way desired by the EU. At the same time, such attempts to regulate the world by regulating one's own fishbowl could backfire. These measures depend on the vagaries of international relations and politics and could lead to trade and economic conflict of various degrees of intensity. Furthermore, conflicts between the leading open economies and polities of the world can create favorable conditions for the emergence of actors protected by strong economic power with less than desirable content protection policies, such as China or Russia.

In this context, compromise and new, creative methods of regulation and co-regulation are needed, which should bring together the leaders in producing intellectual property—knowledge, opinion, and data—to create the grounds for innovation and growth while protecting fundamental individual rights focused on autonomy, creativity, and freedom of expression and thought. Within this new framework, as suggested by Curien in the first chapter, one of the most urgent needs is to consider allowing for a certain degree of regulatory ambiguity and actor-level leeway, which could protect both group and individual rights. The novel idea of co-regulation, or regulating with the regulated, proposed by Curien could also be embraced.

Given this array of challenges, what are the domain-specific issues that have emerged across the Atlantic, specifically, in the United States and France, over the last couple of decades? What impact did the regulatory regimes have on the world of content production and intellectual property, privacy, or freedom of expression? In the following section we will explore comparatively these main challenges, setting the scene for the final conversation about the ways in which advanced graduate students encounter and tackle these issues. Within this conversation we will focus not only on the student questions, but also on ways in which the conundrums they flag can be tackled pedagogically.

2 Main Issues

Copyright

Is the concept of copyright—the exclusive legal right to reproduce, publish, sell, or distribute the matter and form of something (such as a literary, musical, or artistic work)—obsolete in the Internet age? It depends on who you ask. A digital native would say copyright no longer serves its purpose because "information wants to be free." The large social media platforms argue that a strict rendering of copyright would break the Internet. But artists, musicians, journalists, authors, filmmakers and many other individuals and companies would say copyright is an essential component of the creative ecosystem and should continue to be respected, both online and off.

For more than 300 years, copyright has been an engine of creativity, rewarding content creators with remuneration for their unique ideas and products. It provided a way for creators to protect the ownership of their intellectual property, allowing them to decide who can use it and when in the same way property owners have use of their land.

In the digital age, the search engines and social platforms, with their enormous aggregation machines, removed all barriers to the sharing of content and, in fact, encourage such sharing. One could argue those massive companies exist because of, and for, this social sharing. It is the central reason for their existence.

Social media regulation today is an attempt to balance these two competing concepts—remuneration for, and encouragement of, cultural creativity, versus the very human desire to share everything and anything of interest.

For today's generation of students, it is easy to take this sharing environment for granted. Through licensing agreements worked out between copyright holders and companies like Netflix, Amazon Prime, Spotify, and many others, they have access to an enormous online database of music, films, books, news media and other copyrighted materials at very little cost.

With the plethora of content available online, the value of each discrete piece of content has been significantly reduced. A musician might earn a fraction of a cent each time his or her music is accessed on Spotify, far lower than would be received from recorded music in pre-digital days. But at least there is remuneration and the deal—whether one believes it fair or not—continues to respect the musician's copyright. But the free sharing of material—both legal and illegal, when somebody uploads something to the Internet, or otherwise makes it available for sharing in the digital, space—provides them even less return, or nothing at all. People post copyrighted videos on YouTube all the time. The movies can be removed, only to be posted again, like a giant game of Whack-a-Mole (Peeler 1999). To this one can add the possibility that songs, images, or creative work could be used in support of various causes or to harm certain individuals or groups, even if the content is licensed. Should the authors and holders of the copyright have a "moral right" that supersedes the narrow understanding of copyright laws? This is a new development, especially in Europe, where the concept of moral rights has been on the books for some time and is used in practice more and more.

Copyright has contributed in a fundamental way to economic development and to the wide variety of artistic and cultural materials we so freely enjoy today. But the system has been disrupted by the giant content distribution platforms. Even if they have negotiated licenses to use copyrighted content, the amounts they pay are far lower than previously gained by the content creators, and have had a severe impact on all sectors of the content economy. News media—an essential provider of the news and information citizens need to make choices in democratic society—are failing, even as their content has wider distribution than ever before. Big musical groups may continue to thrive, but it has become much harder for new acts to make the same kind of living—again, even as access to their music has become greater than before (Neilstein 2016). And the film industry, while not dying, is certainly evolving from big screen theaters to small screens fueled by Netflix et al. and their influence on original content.

As with privacy, cultural, political, and business differences between the United States and Europe have led to different approaches to copyright in the digital sphere, with greater state intervention in Europe than in the laissez-faire United States.

In the United States, the constitutional provision of Article 1, section eight, and elaborated in the Copyright Law of 1976—*Copyright Act, U.S. Code* 17 (1976)—remain the core regulatory documents. The intention of both documents is clear and expansive. Intellectual property belongs to the creator as an inalienable and limited in time right. Copyright starts as soon as intellectually property is recorded on tangible medium and it does not need to be registered. Furthermore, intellectual property is separate from the medium that carries it. Owning a book does not mean that you own the copyright to the book. Although you can sell the book, for a residual price, you merely sell a copy, with no claim regarding intellectual property.

However, the shift from analog (print or recorded) media to digital products that can travel and be distributed through networks raised the question if the copies of, let us say, mp3 songs that one acquired, can be resold or reshared the way one would reshare a book. Digital media brought to the fore the less known fact that copyright gives the authors the sovereign right to license, that is, to limit the ways and amounts of copies used by the individuals he or she allows to use the intellectual property.

In this respect, all songs one listens on their own phone, streamed or downloaded, come with strings attached, including strict limits on where and how the content can be shared. The same applies to Kindle books. Although it would be possible and easy for publishers and music producers to allow the users to resell the songs, the new Internet regulatory regime took a step back, in terms of accessibility, from the old world of printed books and vinyl records. The reasons are multiple. First, there was the crisis of the 1990s and early 2000s when illegal copying and sharing of musical products was rife. Second, there was the realization that a digital world of production and consumption relies on digital copies only in part, with live performances and ancillary products supporting the industry in another, major way. Due to these factors, intellectual property is seen less as a way to sell discrete objects (books, records, etc.) and more as the fuel, the "intellectual capital" of the entire business model. As this intellectual capital become more and more integrated on platforms, such as iTunes or Spotify, the license-only (vs. ownership of ancillary products) has become the norm.

However, the current strong defense of intellectual property in the US legislation is limited to the national borders and to some friendly nations, such as those of the European Union, who share the same interest and respect for copyright as the United States. Major international operations, including multiple forms of intellectual property, from scientific papers to movies and patents, are infringed everyday by organized crime, countercultural organizations, and foreign governments. Recent estimates put the losses due to intellectual property theft in the United States alone within a range spanning from 225 to 600 billion dollars a year (Blair and Huntsman 2017; United States Intellectual Property Enforcement Coordinator 2019; Oh 2018). The challenge that needs to be tackled is, thus, regulating not the fishbowls, but the ocean in which they are suffused. This is still a desideratum, despite support for expansive definitions of copyright and intellectual property coming from Europe, where the discussion has moved from fiduciary to moral rights. The most tangible effort was to push back against some of the most egregious international violators, mainly by taxes and tariffs, as was the case for the trade war between the United States and China. However, these measures only deal with the broadest framework of the agreement, leaving a lot of leaks in the enforcement process.

In France, and more generally in the European Union, the intellectual property regime has become in the last decades more stringent, similarly impelled by the digital crisis of copyright. The core copyright laws and the European Union Copyright directive (EU Commission 2015) strongly and directly continue to protect intellectual property. Furthermore, protection has become increasingly punitive in nature, from the establishment of HADOPI ("LOI N° 2009-669 Du 12 Juin 2009 Favorisant La Diffusion et La Protection de La Création Sur Internet" 2009) in France to new "copyright taxes" imposed on social media platforms that redistribute, even if inadvertently, copyrighted content without the explicit permission and material compensation to the original copyright holders. This is particularly true to news and user-generated content aggregators, such as Google News, Facebook, and YouTube.

In France, the law HADOPI is one of the more interesting experiments. The High Authority for the Dissemination of Works and Protection of Copyrights, known by its French acronym HADOPI, was created in 2009 to protect intellectual property owners on the Internet. HADOPI took aim at Internet accounts that had been used to share copyrighted material illegally; it could remove the Internet account holder's right to Internet access if the subscriber failed to secure their account and prevent use of their access to download or share files illegally.

The law worked on a three-strikes system: the holder of an account used for illegal file sharing was first warned to secure the account. A second infringement within six months led to a warning letter by registered post. If there is another offense within a year, the case was referred to criminal court, with penalties of up to a €1500 fine and a cut of Internet service for up to one year.

But the Internet disconnection penalty was removed from the law in 2013 as it was deemed a threat to freedom of communication, leaving the three-strike policy with fines only. In 2020, the French Constitutional Council found the entire law anticonstitutional because the tools used to identify Internet users did not guarantee sufficient protection of privacy. Even before the decision, the law was on the way out; the government was working on a new audio/visual law that would have abolished HADOPI and transfer its tasks to the Conseil Supérieur de l'Audiovisuel (CSA), the media regulation agency (Leloup 2020)

But during its lifetime, was HADOPI effective? It did not begin auspiciously: between October 2010 and February 2013, there were only 1,600 first warnings, and only 29 cases referred to prosecution, with 1 Internet suspension for 15 days. By 2018, there were 1.3 million warnings, with 1,045 referrals to court, leading to 83 convictions and fines ranging from €500 to €1500 (Perotti 2019).

The HADOPI experiment is not the only approach to protecting copyrighted materials in Europe. On April 17, 2019, the European Directive on Copyright in the Digital Single Market came into force with the goal of improving cross-border access to content, creating a better functioning copyright marketplace, and providing copyright exceptions for using materials in education, research, and cultural heritage (Giorello 2016).

The EC's copyright directive took a different approach from the HADOPI law to protect intellectual property rights. Its Article 17 requires Online Content Sharing Service Providers (OCSSP)—Facebook, YouTube and the like—that makes use of works uploaded by users *for profit making purposes,* to do their "best efforts to obtain an authorization" from the copyright holder. If they don't get permission, they must make "best efforts" to ensure unavailability, which means filtering and blocking any work for which they don't have authorization, and to maintain systems to take down unlicensed contact and ensure it stays down (Perotti 2019).

The law intends to encourage content owners to contact OCSSP to negotiate licensing agreements or, in the absence of agreement, to provide relevant information that will allow OCSSP to block uploading and use.

The copyright directive also creates a "European publisher right," which gives the publishers the exclusive right to authorize reproduction of their content by any means and in any form, with regard to the online use of their materials. This gives publishers legal standing to prosecute violations in their own right, gives them a stronger negotiating position with the online platforms for use of their content, levels the playing field for smaller publishers, who tended to be overlooked by the big platforms, and provides more legal certainty over their rights. These are the same rights provided to broadcasters, and music and film producers, whose works are protected in their entirety (Perotti 2019).

But two previous European efforts to provide a publisher's right, in Germany and Spain, failed. In Germany, courts ruled the publisher's right was unenforceable because the government failed to notify the European

Commission about it. In Spain, which required Google to provide mandatory fair compensation for using publishers content in Google News, Google simply withdrew from the market.

These European initiatives to protect intellectual property differ substantial from the US approach, where a "fair use doctrine" allows limited use of copyrighted materials without seeking permission of the owner, in an effort to balance the interests of copyright holders with the public interest of wider distribution. But the law precedes the Internet, and courts have now applied the statute to new technologies such as Internet search, making enforcement of true violations difficult (Perotti 2019).

Again, as national borders are irrelevant in the digital world, US-based organizations representing copyright holders have been looking to the European examples for a way forward to protect intellectual property, and several initiatives have resulted in new and proposed legislation, including 2019's Journalism Competition and Preservation Act, which allows publishers to band together to negotiate with online platforms.

Privacy

In any comparative study of social media policies and regulations, a good starting point for discussion is the larger societal and cultural differences, to help students better understand the underlying factors that help explain the wide variety of national and regional regulatory activity. This is particularly important for understanding privacy regimes.

For American students, whose exposure to European culture and history may be superficial, or who may be ambivalent toward it, exposure to the cultural and political context of French and European social media regulation is an essential component before embarking on the regulations themselves. As William Faulkner once said, "The past is never dead. It's not even the past" (Faulkner 2011).

General societal differences often come as a surprise, and discovering them help inform students' understanding of the culture. For example, the broad differences between French and Americans in attitudes toward many aspects of life: communal versus individual responsibilities and rights; moderation in all things versus abundance; work versus *joie de vivre* (Rozin et al. 2011). There are historic and cultural elements that lead directly to today's regulatory environment, and influence French and American attitudes toward the digital challenges for privacy, copyright, and freedom of expression. For instance, those ubiquitous shutters on French houses are more than decorative; they have roots in a time when the king's taxmen used to peer inside people's houses to see what's inside for tax assessment. The shutters are a symbol of the French desire for privacy (Nadeau and Barlow 2003). It is no surprise to find this attitude extended into the digital realm.

Even among liberal western democracies, there is a great deal of difference in regulatory approaches, born out of the differences in the societies themselves.

Though both American and French people have concerns about an erosion of privacy, there are differences in the levels of concerns, and even what privacy means (Pelet and Taieb 2017).

As mentioned earlier, avoidance of the tax assessor's glare helped shape French attitudes to personal privacy. And this has since been amplified by the European experience in World War II, when the Nazi conquerors used private data to identify Jews and other minority groups (Waxman 2018).

"For Europeans, privacy is a human right, while for Americans, privacy tends to be about liberty," wrote J. Trevor Hughes, President and CEO of the International Association of Privacy Professionals. "It's often thought that the Holocaust and the rise of totalitarianism in 20th-century Europe have been the catalysts behind the region's strong privacy and data protection regimes" (Hughes 2013).

Attitudes toward business and government also contribute to these positions. Europeans, and the French in particular, are more open to interventionist governments and more reliant on state policies of income redistribution, accepting a level of government in their daily lives that would be anathema in the United States. Government regulation is more often seen as the solution in Europe, and a hindrance in the United States (Alesina and Glaeser 2006).

These different outlooks clash in the digital world, which has no respect for borders. National and regional regulations can have global impact, with the regulation effectively applying far from where it was conceived. This is the case with the European General Data Protection Regulation, which not only gives individual control over their personal data but addresses the transfer of personal data outside of the EU. No matter where a digital company is based, it has to comply with the GDPR if its products and services are available in Europe.

No such federal regulation exists in the United States, though California passed the GDPR-like California Consumer Privacy Act in 2018, which applies to companies that hold data on more than 50,000 people and do business in California.

Regulation without enforcement is toothless, and European countries have data privacy authorities that enforce the GDPR. Companies found guilty of discarding the key principles of GDPR, or suffering data breaches due to poor security, face fines of up to 4% of annual global turnover or €20 million, whichever is greater.

Even if the United States had a similar federal regulation, there doesn't exist an agency in enforce it. The Federal Trade Commission, which is tasked with enforcing US privacy policy, does not have authority over a wide range of businesses, including airlines, universities, non-profit organizations, and banks (Hawkins 2018).

Clearly, the irrelevancy of national borders in the digital realm, and the reach of regulation across those borders, has enormous implications for the concept of self-governance. If Americans and American companies are bound by regulations imposed from outside, without a representative voice, the US form of representational government is inadequate for the digital environment.

This is a key area for academic discussion: Is the present social media regulatory framework transitory and unsuited for the digital realm, and is a more global approach the solution? And how might this come about? If we are to look at the issue from Curien's perspective presented in this volume, the challenge here is not that we need to create a global regulatory regime, that is to tame the ocean, but to find the way to connect the fishbowls to each other while keeping the waters of the ocean transparent. One way would be to push for a global treaty on data protection, similar to the international copyright agreements.

The difficulty is, however, that the cultural, political, and economic assumptions will get in the way. Yet, again, these issues have been around for a long time, which did not prevent the creation of many international regulatory regimes. If we take the example of telecommunications and frequency allocations, then the challenge is how to cast data as a common good.

The Napoli and Graf chapter in this volume offers a possible solution, although it might be an over-expansive one for libertarian regimes. Regardless of immediate solutions, the question is how the current and emerging leaders perceive the problem, an issue that we will explore below when examining the student reactions to the challenges they encountered in learning about the differences between the US and French privacy regulatory regimes.

Freedom of Expression

In the United States, you can say almost anything without fear of being punished by the government for it. In Europe, with the possible but not absolute exception of the United Kingdom, there are some things you simply cannot say or do. In essence, we have two traditions, one libertarian, inspired by British parliamentarian tradition (Bogen 1983), and the other communitarian-statist, inspired by Rousseau and the idea of the state as an intangible common good that cannot be criticized without unravelling the social fabric (Kelly 1997).

The 1st Amendment to the US Constitution and subsequent case law provides wide protections for freedom of speech. Short of yelling fire in a crowded theater, anything goes, and it is almost impossible to libel or defame public figures. Even the more stringent regulations imposed on broadcast media in the name of scarcity, public service, and intrusiveness have been loosened in the last decades.

Western Europe has similar protections, but with more exceptions. Because of self-evident historical reasons, Holocaust denial and some hate speech is criminalized in Germany. In France, the balance between privacy and freedom of expression sometimes tips in favor of privacy—public figures including politicians are granted private lives and reporting on certain elements can lead to substantial fines for invasion of privacy. Defamation lawsuits, even when brought by public figures, can more easily succeed than in the United States.

This difference can be seen in the statutes that protect freedom of expression.

The 1st Amendment states: "Congress shall make no law respecting an establishment of religion, or prohibiting the free exercise thereof; or abridging the freedom of speech, or of the press; or the right of the people peaceably to assemble, and to petition the Government for a redress of grievances" (U.S. Const., amend. I).

The French constitution also protects freedom of expression, but with a difference. It rests on the Declaration of Human and Civil Rights issued in 1789 ("Déclaration Des Droits de l'Homme et Du Citoyen de 1789" 1789), which in Article 10 states: "No one may be disturbed on account of his opinions, even religious ones, as long as the manifestation of such opinions does not interfere with the established Law and Order." Article 11 says: "The free communication of ideas and of opinions is one of the most precious rights of man. Any citizen may therefore speak, write and publish freely, except what is tantamount to the abuse of this liberty in the cases determined by Law."

So, while recognizing the importance of freedom of expression, the French Constitution also allows legislation to limit it. That legislation is not abstract; it has been used to balance freedom of expression against other rights. To protect the presumption of innocence of defendants, the media is barred from publishing pictures of defendants in handcuffs, something that is not prohibited in the United States, and in fact is an iconic news image—the so-called perp walk, with defendants in handcuffs after arrest.

Hate speech is banned in France; a 1972 amendment to the 1881 press law prohibits speech that is intended to "provoke discrimination, hate, or violence towards a person or a group of people because of their origin or because they belong or do not belong to a certain ethnic group, nation, race, or religion" ("Loi N° 72-546 Du 1 Juillet 1972 Relative à La Lutte Contre Le Racisme - Légifrance" 1972). This was later expanded to include hate speech based on gender, sexual orientation or identity, and disability. Denial of crimes against humanity, or advocating or justifying terrorism, is also proscribed (Weber 2015).

In the United States, there are some who believe the 1st Amendment goes too far, and restrictions like those in France are reasonable. There is also pressure on freedom of expression from those who believe people have a right not to be offended. This has led, particularly among students and on university campuses, to cases of well-known speakers being blocked from speaking, and for attacks on unpopular viewpoints (Hudson 2018).

But in both the United States and Europe, freedom of speech is considered a basic human right. Article 19 of the United Nations' Declaration of Human Rights states: "Everyone has the right to freedom of opinion and expression; this right includes freedom to hold opinions without interference and to seek, receive and impart information and ideas through any media and regardless of frontiers" (UN General Assembly 1948).

So even though differences exist between the United States and Europe concerning freedom of expression, government regulation that impacts this basic freedom is approached with caution. The ocean that separates the regulatory regimes of France and the United States, for example, is not as vast as it seems, despite procedural differences.

Even if such legislation is well-meaning and is used to balance respect for other rights like privacy, restrictions on freedom of expression in democratic countries are often used by dictators and despots to justify their own acts of repression. “When progressive thinkers agree that offensive words should be censored, it helps authoritarian regimes to justify their own much harsher restrictions and intolerant religious groups their violence” (*The Economist* 2016).

In the digital world, the pressure to restrict free expression is even greater than in the physical world, due to the multiplication effect of social media. It is one thing to stand on a street corner and spew hatred and falsehoods, and another to do so online, where such comments spread virally to millions. While social media has many positive attributes, the insidious and dangerous spread of falsehoods is clearly having a deleterious impact on our societies (Deb et al. 2017).

Balancing freedom of expression against other rights becomes even more difficult on platforms that can be misused to spread falsehoods that can manipulate elections, weaken open debate and even spark riots and murder.

Because governments are reluctant to regulate, the big platforms themselves are being dragged into policing their own platforms, also reluctantly, raising the question of who gets to be the arbiter of what constitutes protected speech, and when it crosses the line.

The big online platforms are not media companies in the traditional sense. There are no editors-in-chiefs vetting their content. Yet they effectively serve as media disseminators due to their widespread reach. Though they are not subject to media regulations, there are some who argue they should be defined and regulated as public utilities, “essential for social and political participation in the twenty-first century and accessible to all” (Jørgensen and Zuleta 2020).

The political implications of these debates are immense. US President Donald Trump, in an Executive Order issued on May 28, 2020, criticized the online platforms for policing content and sought to remove liability protections granted to them. The Order framed the debate this way: “Online platforms are engaging in selective censorship that is harming our national discourse. Tens of thousands of Americans have reported, among other troubling behaviors, online platforms ‘flagging’ content as inappropriate, even though it does not violate any stated terms of service; making unannounced and unexplained changes to company policies that have the effect of disfavoring certain viewpoints; and deleting content and entire accounts with no warning, no rationale, and no recourse" (The President of the United States 2020).

The order called for fundamental changes to Section 230 of the Communication Decency Act 947 U.S.C. § 230, which affords liability protection for online platforms, since they are not held legally responsible for content produced by others but posted on their sites. According to the order, the platforms are using that protection to stifle differing viewpoints. It argues that the platforms should "be exposed to liability like any traditional editor and publisher that is not an online provider" (The President of the United States 2020).

Whether such action would be successful—or could even be implemented—remains to be seen. According to the US Congressional Research Service, "Federal law does not offer much recourse for social media users who seek to challenge a social media provider's decision about whether and how to present a user's content. Lawsuits predicated on these sites' decisions to host or remove content have been largely unsuccessful, facing at least two significant barriers under existing federal law. First, while individuals have sometimes alleged that these companies violated their free speech rights by discriminating against users' content, courts have held that the First Amendment, which provides protection against state action, is not implicated by the actions of these private companies." It cited Section 230 the Communication Decency Act as the second reason (Brannon 2019).

In Europe as well, the online platforms have mostly been treated as intermediaries, described in the Directive of Electronic Commerce as being a "mere conduit" for content created elsewhere and therefore not liable for it. But that too is changing, with more proactive measures to make the platforms responsible for user-generated content (Jørgensen and Zuleta 2020).

The European Commission and Facebook, Microsoft, Twitter, and YouTube agreed in 2016 to a code of conduct on countering illegal hate speech online that included development of internal procedures for the rapid removal of it, and for partnerships with civil society organizations who would help flag content. The code defines hate speech as "publicly inciting to violence or hatred directed against a group of persons or a member of such a group defined by reference to race, colour, religion, descent, or national or ethnic origin," the same definition contained in the European Commission's Framework Decision on combatting certain forms and expressions of racism and xenophobia. But the Framework has been criticized for not complying with international standards of freedom of expression, again highlighting the difficult of regulating speech online (Jørgensen and Zuleta 2020).

Social media remain, however, a source of much anxiety and mistrust in Europe. The unexpected results of the British exit from the European Union referendum in June 2016, and the amplified discussion about the role of social media in electing Donald Trump in the United States in November 2016, both surrounded by claims of information manipulation, fake news campaigns, and mass behavior, has led to stern and restrictive measures throughout the entire European Union, including and especially in France. Between 2016 and 2020, several laws seeking to respond to these issues have been passed in France, Germany, Italy, the Netherlands, Spain, and Great Britain, as well as the European Union as a whole. These laws vary widely in coverage and scope, but all aim to control and hem in the flow of unverifiable information (Fig. 1).

It is clear from these actions that the problems of hate speech, misinformation, and manipulation are well recognized and measures are taken,

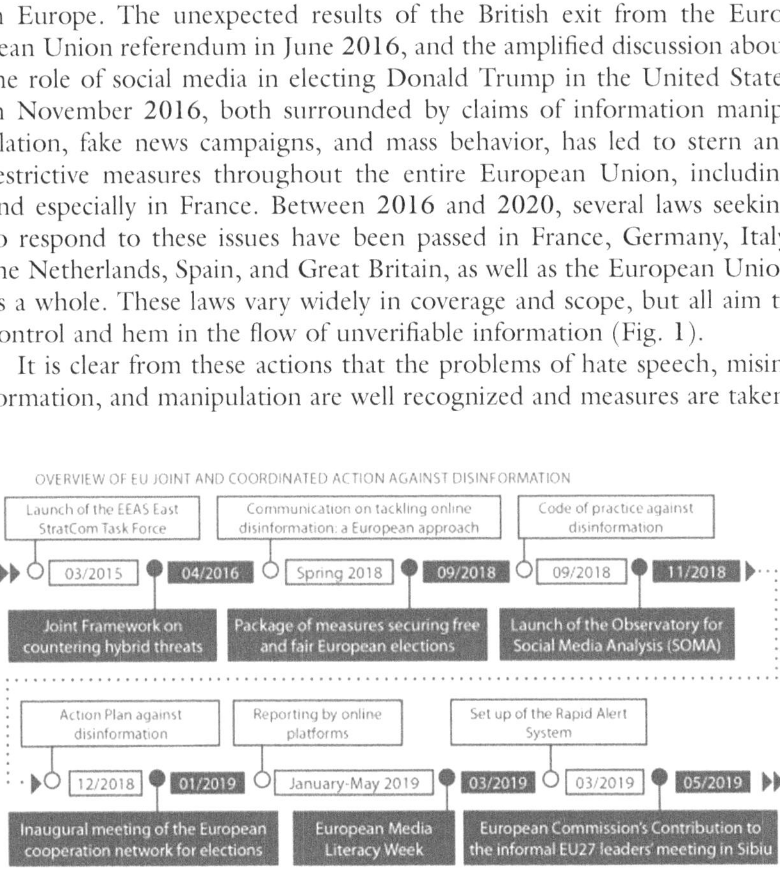

Fig. 1 Overview of EU activities against misinformation. From https://ec.europa.eu/digital-single-market/en/tackling-online-disinformation. Creative Commons Attribution 4.0 International (CC BY 4.0) license by the European Union Commission

even if the definition of those problems is not. Social media regulation is evolving, and protecting freedom of expression is one of the more complex and difficult areas. As we will see in the next section from the insights collected from the students we introduced to media regulation in a trans-Atlantic context, the answers seen by the students and the pedagogical means to address them include a variety of possible approaches.

3 Pedagogical Application and Insight

Over the past four years, the Global Communication Program launched by Purdue University has brought groups of students to Paris to study communication practices and regulatory affairs in a "living laboratory" context. The program was created in collaboration with the Purdue Online MA program in Strategic Communication, the Laboratory of Excellence in the Study of the Cultural and Artistic-Creative Industries at University of Paris, the Department of Communication at Sorbonne Nouvelle University (Paris 3), and the American Graduate School in Paris. The program has organized once-yearly experiential courses in Paris, enrolling American graduate students and including activities organized in collaboration with French students. The core course, titled Global Communication: Social, Political and Business Perspectives, has offered the students the opportunity to interact and learn from leading Labex ICCA academic experts, regulators (The Superior Council for Audio Visual Media, The National Commission of Informatics and Liberties, the Regulatory authority of electronic communication, postal services, and press distribution), companies (Google France, Daily Motion, Media Part), politicians (National Assembly), or consultant and experts in communication and public relations.

The goal of the program was to educate the students, the majority of whom are mid-career professionals working for corporate communication departments or media, to the main regulatory, political, and economic differences between the United States and France/European Union. The students were enrolled in an 8-week course, a majority of which they spent studying with instructors supported by a rich literature via online learning. They met as a group for a week in Paris, spending each day for 6–8 hours with the representatives of the organizations mentioned above. One of the course expectations was that the students would ask questions during the meetings and write reflections on the meetings and the conversations they had with the hosts and with the instructors. The authors of the present chapter were the instructors of the class, organizing the meetings, assigning the readings, directing the conversations, and grading the assignments.

The core assignment of the course, on which we drew the insights listed below upon IRB approval, asked the students to choose and reflect on a major political, regulatory, and media issue of the day. The students were invited to:

> Write a research paper about a topic you have encountered at one of our meetings or in one of the readings. The topic should be directly related to France and its media /Internet landscape. It can be about a technology or medium or about a political or legal issue. (e.g., Can social media change the political process in France? Will Google leave Europe? Can France become a new media powerhouse? Is privacy better protected in France than in the US?) The paper should be formulated as one long, factual, and argued answer to the question providing at least 3 reasons. [and implications]

While the paper explicitly asked for choosing a French media/Internet topic, implicitly the students were invited to discuss the matter in a comparative perspective. We collected 27 papers, produced by two cohorts of the class, one taught in 2018 (10 papers) and the other in 2019 (17 papers). The papers are identified by a numeric code, randomly assigned.

Given the framework discussed above, we reanalyzed the papers with an eye toward detecting to what degree the students focused on core regulatory issues that speak about the emergence of differences or similarities across the Atlantic within the three domains: intellectual property, privacy, and freedom of expression. In other words, how similar or different did the students see the regulatory regimes? What were the flashpoints, in specific terms? Finally, what common arguments emerged throughout the papers?

Analysis was performed by qualitative examination of the papers and their categorization in terms of perceived distance between regimes, flashpoints (problematic areas), and general assessment of the virtues or downsides of the two regulatory regimes. The two authors independently coded the paper for main focal point (IP, freedom of expression, privacy, other concerns), active use of a comparative perspective, perceived level of difference, and main areas of concern or overlap between the regulatory regimes.

The analysis provided some immediately intuitive results, while highlighting some interesting insights. The latter speak well about the intellectual distance that separates the French–US regulatory regimes, both in terms of how they are perceived and how they really operated.

Given the nature of the class and its reading list and meetings, the papers were distributed across the three focal areas, with a strong preference for privacy (16 or 59% of the papers). Interestingly, intellectual property stirred the least amount of interest, only one paper (4% of total) fully addressing it. Two papers addressed business processes in a broad sense (Fig. 2).

While the assignment asked the students to compare and contrast the US–French (European) regulatory and business processes, it did not demand that differences should be found. The students had the choice to indicate if significant differences exist or not, their magnitude, and, if they exist, their nature and impact. Although the course discussions and readings emphasized that the United States and France, along with many other Western European nations, share a common legal and regulatory background, and that there are reasons to believe they are slowly drifting toward each other, 80% (21) of the students decided that the two regimes

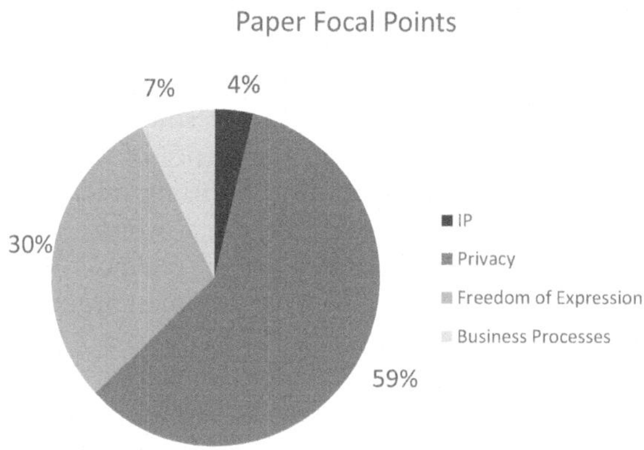

Fig. 2 Sorin Adam Matei and Larry Kilman, *Paper Focal Points* (2020)

are very different. Four papers found the regulatory regimes somewhat similar and two indicated deep similarities.

Our surprise was not that so many students found the two regimes different, but the depth of these differences, which were sometimes seen in very stark terms. Paper 6, for example, commented in very eloquent terms about the core stakeholding differences in defining freedom of expression across the Atlantic. While freedom of expression in the United States was more of an absolute:

> The French Government version is more blurred. They state that it's a precious right to all people but continues on saying the right is dictated by law. The right is not absolute and there is no guarantee if a citizen's opinion and expression will be guaranteed. Each respective country Freedom of Opinion and Expression declaration could cause one to pause and ask who has control, the people, the government or shareholders. [Paper 6]

Speaking about privacy, the most commonly discussed topic across the papers, Paper 10 described two different loci of control for the privacy policies, individual-internal in the United States and state-external in France:

> Privacy is a relevant topic discussed in France and taken as a high priority by the French government and their citizens. The French government has established laws and regulations to protect the privacy of their citizens. In the United States, citizens are expected to be responsible to protect their own privacy. They do this by signing agreements and authorizing organizations to keep their information. This can usually be found in the fine print of the agreements and privacy section of websites. United States citizens are typically more open to share personal information online through social media sites and disclose financial information to make purchases online. These examples display how privacy in France is better protected and placed as a priority by their citizens and government. [Paper 10]

What accounts for these profound perceived differences? Here, the surprise is that the students identified "degree of regulation" (15 papers) rather than the nature of regulation, as the main point of departure, followed by cultural differences (13 papers). The fact that the students focused often on degree of regulation, while claiming that the two regimes are very different, reveals a surprising fact. At the level of mature learners, knowledgeable about communication and regulatory issues, the devil is in the details. In effect, the United States and France have privacy regulatory regimes, laws, and bodies to track compliance, but the methods of pursuing privacy-related goals were seen as very different. For example, Paper 12 suggests that

> the French philosophy is that their people come first in all they do [...] while the French business community comes next. Meanwhile in America it is a much different philosophy where more thought and more power are given to the business community. Many laws and regulations are put into place in the U.S. to ultimately protect the businesses, while rarely a second thought is given to how the actual consumer will fare in this. [Paper 12]

Paper 18 sees equal desire on both sides of the Atlantic to protect privacy, with a difference in how it is approached:

> On a deeper level, both countries care about the protection of personal information for government, businesses, and citizens. The primary differences are how the government addresses these concerns, who decides how personal information is shared, and how personal information is used. [Paper 18]

Cultural differences were also very important, an unsurprising discovery given the focus of the course, which was meant to communicate that differences are often rooted in human and cultural values and group perceptions and experiences. Thus, a certain amount of "over-enthusiasm" for identifying cultural values might explain their interest in this topic. The most frequently cited reasons for these cultural differences were those related to the peculiar nature of French culture, which values and protects private affairs with a vengeance. For example, Paper 14 mentioned the concept of general interest as the main lens through which French regulation should be seen:

> France is a country with a more collectivist culture, which it protects with the concept of the intérêt général, or the common good. The intérêt général is structured in a way to balance collective demands and individual interests... Data protection and privacy is crucial as everyone becomes more interconnected than ever. Broadening the umbrella serves the intérêt général as it protects individuals from having their personal data connected

> to other people or having their data sold or otherwise given to other companies. [Paper 14]

Paper 26 makes the astute observation that core, empirically observable differences in cultural values might explain the differences between the two regulatory regimes:

> In the United States, a country that ranks higher than France on Hofstede's scale in terms of Individualism, it makes sense that freedom of individual rights and freedom of the press have been placed before regulating information—fact or fiction—on the Internet. In contrast, France rates higher than the United States in terms of Power Distance and Uncertainty Avoidance. It's little wonder then that the French government is currently voting on regulation specifically targeted at stopping the purposeful dissemination of fake news prior to elections. [Paper 26]

Finally, Paper 1 makes this excellent observation about differences in education, which precede and reinforce cultural differences:

> While other countries—such as the U.S.—slash funding for arts initiatives, France perseveres and continues to fund them. The French hold education and cultural diversity near and dear to their hearts. The French media's coverage of Bac exams is extensive; students are invited on talk shows to discuss the exams in great detail. I couldn't help but think of how American media often informs us of a high school student's college choice only if he or she is a star athlete signing a letter of intent for a university program. [Paper 1]

The evaluative conclusions derived from these observations fork in three directions. On the one hand, there is enthusiasm for the European statist model. Given the organizational and intellectual context of many of the students this would be expected. Paper 23 simple exclaims "France has an amazing set up to protect its citizens," while Paper 27 asks this rhetorical question followed by a laudatory answer regarding the French policies:

> Should the U.S. follow France in imposing stricter data privacy regulations? Yes. The U.S. is at risk and is not doing enough to protect its citizens. The U.S. should, indeed, impose stricter data privacy regulations because studies show that: 1. Americans don't feel their data is sufficiently protected. Over half of Americans would like more done to protect their data, and over two thirds of Americans believe data privacy laws should be

more stringent; 2. Countries in the European Union who abide by stricter data regulations lose less money to cyber-attacks; and 3. The large number of cyber-attacks indicates that the U.S.'s current model of having companies self-regulate protecting data has not been successful with keeping personal data safe. [Paper 27]

Yet, the papers make many critical arguments. The most articulated of these point to the necessary trade-offs implicit in the French-statist tradition. Some of the papers see the trade-offs in terms of losses when analyzing privacy and attempts to limit freedom of expression in the name of staving off social media fake news posts.

As paper 15 puts it:

> Many [French] individuals have voiced concerns that the [anti-fake news] legislation will limit free speech. Specifically, critics have challenged how fake news will be defined and by whom. Additionally, critics have raised the point regarding the difficulty judges will encounter in trying to quickly verify whether or not information is factual.... [Paper 15]

The opinions offered by the papers are quite nuanced, such as this one, which proposes that while

> Americans would be well-served if the United States followed France's lead and were influenced by France's unwavering support for the privacy of their citizens" it is quite possible that embracing "privacy at the expense of prosperity" may be too high a price for the United States to bear.... [Paper 16]

Speaking specifically about the French business environment, Paper 24 observes critically:

> To create an environment for an innovative, communication-related, tech startup economy to thrive, the nation's culture and government policies must support incentives that motivate entrepreneurs to take risks, create, and build. In the current state of French culture and regulations, that environment is not possible. Burdensome government regulations prevent new entrants into the market from being competitive with larger companies that can absorb the increased cost of following the bureaucratic red tape. [Paper 24]

However, the analytic framework proposed by the students goes beyond dual or even trade-off perspectives. Some of the students very insightfully noticed the French ability to adapt and innovate within their given cultural and political framework. Paper 11 proposes that the French tradition is not inimical to innovation:

> In analyzing the impact [of] the digital revolution has on the French Identity, [this paper] concludes [that] social media and the internet revolution have caused the French Identity to adapt, but these adaptations are not unusual to the French. They have been adapting their identity for centuries. Cultural Tradition is deeply rooted in the French Identity, and these changes will not change the core notion of "being French." [Paper 11]

Throughout these comments, we notice a constant return to themes of consequential differences. The learners felt with great acuity that the world in which they live and work is multifaceted and divided. While this perception might be exaggerated, in this space it might be reality. Our students felt and expressed feelings and thoughts of difference, focusing on the notion of protecting national values and ideas, as Paper 25 suggested:

> that France's digital innovation will likely thrive in the future, given 1) France's desire to intelligently innovate, 2) France's cultural values surrounding privacy and protection and finally, 3) France's familiarity and leadership in the area of institutionalized regulation in the sectors of media and communication. [Paper 25]

While a learning exercise, these comments and ideas are important for understanding where we are going, since our students are the US communication workers and leaders of tomorrow. In their commentary and reflections, we captured a continental drift of the large cultural and political blocks that might just as well converge or diverge. Which direction should we go in?

4 Conclusion—Learning from the Past and Looking at the Future

This chapter aimed to provide an overview of the main trends in the regulatory regimes in France and the United States as seen through the eyes of educators and students. The goal was both to provide a perspective on where we are going and on where learners and educators think we are going. The overall conclusions indicate the possibility of divergence, led both by the on-the-ground realities in regulatory regimes, and in terms of cultural and intellectual perceptions. The goal of future educational activities should be to sensitize the learners to similarities, while instilling in them a critical attitude toward simplistic understanding of cultural and value differences. Furthermore, we need to focus on revealing and working toward new models of educating about regulation, which include a more diverse view, including the possibility of co-regulation. It is interesting that none of the students mentioned this possibility, despite the fact of being exposed to it throughout the course. Neither did the students propose alternative, third ways for overcoming current differences. This lack of discussion on possible solutions to regulatory divergence is evidence that the question should be emphasized in future courses.

References

Alesina, Alberto, and Edward L. Glaeser. 2006. Why Are Welfare States in the US and Europe So Different? What Do We Learn? *Horizons Stratégiques* 2 (2): 51–61.

Blair, Dennis, and John Huntsman. 2017. *Update to the IP Commission Report*. Washington, DC: National Bureau of Asian Research.

Bogen, David. 1983. The Origins of Freedom of Speech and Press. *Maryland Law Review* 42 (3): 429.

Brannon, Valerie. 2019. Free Speech and the Regulation of Social Media Content. R45650. Washington, DC: Congressional Research Service. https://doi.org/10.1201/b22397-4.

Deb, Anamitra, Stacy Donohue, and Tom Glaisyer. 2017. Is Social Media a Threat to Democracy? The Omidyar Group. https://fronteirasxxi.pt/wp-content/uploads/2017/11/Social-Media-and-Democracy-October-5-2017.pdf.

"Déclaration Des Droits de l'Homme et Du Citoyen de 1789." 1789. 1789. https://www.legifrance.gouv.fr/contenu/menu/droit-national-en-vigueur/constitution/declaration-des-droits-de-l-homme-et-du-citoyen-de-1789.

EU Commission. 2015. The EU Copyright Legislation. Text. Shaping Europe's Digital Future—European Commission. August 28. https://ec.europa.eu/digital-single-market/en/eu-copyright-legislation.

Faulkner, William. 2011. *Requiem for a Nun*. New York: Vintage Books. http://search.ebscohost.com/login.aspx?direct=true&scope=site&db=nlebk&db=nlabk&AN=746113.

Giorello, Marco. 2016. Modernisation of the EU Copyright Rules. Text. Shaping Europe's Digital Future—European Commission. September 14. https://ec.europa.eu/digital-single-market/en/modernisation-eu-copyright-rules.

Hawkins, Derek. 2018. Analysis | The Cybersecurity 202: Why a Privacy Law like GDPR Would Be a Tough Sell in the U.S. *Washington Post*, May 2018. https://www.washingtonpost.com/news/powerpost/paloma/the-cybersecurity-202/2018/05/25/the-cybersecurity-202-why-a-privacy-law-like-gdpr-would-be-a-tough-sell-in-the-u-s/5b07038b1b326b492dd07e83/.

Hudson, David L. 2018. Free Speech on Public College Campuses Overview | Freedom Forum Institute. Freedom Forum Institute. March 2018. https://www.freedomforuminstitute.org/first-amendment-center/topics/freedom-of-speech-2/free-speech-on-public-college-campuses-overview/.

Hughes, Trevor J. 2013. Bridging the EU-U.S. Privacy Gap. 2013. https://iapp.org/news/a/bridging-the-eu-u-s-privacy-gap/.

Jørgensen, Rikke Frank, and Lumi Zuleta. 2020. Private Governance of Freedom of Expression on Social Media Platforms: EU Content Regulation Through the Lens of Human Rights Standards. *Nordicom Review* 41 (1): 51–67. https://doi.org/10.2478/nor-2020-0003.

Kelly, Christopher. 1997. Rousseau and the Case for (and Against) Censorship. *The Journal of Politics* 59 (4): 1232–1251. https://doi.org/10.2307/2998599.

Leloup, Damien. 2020. Téléchargement illégal : une partie des pouvoirs de la Hadopi contraire au droit constitutionnel. Le Monde.fr, May 20. https://www.lemonde.fr/pixels/article/2020/05/20/telechargement-illegal-une-partie-des-pouvoirs-de-la-hadopi-contraires-au-droit-constitutionnel_6040294_4408996.html.

Loi N° 72-546 Du 1 Juillet 1972 Relative à La Lutte Contre Le Racisme - Légifrance. 1972. 1972. https://www.legifrance.gouv.fr/jorf/id/JORFTEXT000000864827?isSuggest=true.

LOI N° 2009-669 Du 12 Juin 2009 Favorisant La Diffusion et La Protection de La Création Sur Internet. 2009. June 12. https://www.legifrance.gouv.fr/loda/id/JORFTEXT000020735432/2020-10-22/.

Nadeau, Jean-Benoit, and Julie Barlow. 2003. *Sixty Million Frenchmen Can't Be Wrong: Why We Love France but Not the French*, 1st ed. Naperville, IL: Sourcebooks.

Neilstein, Vincent. 2016. Why It's Harder to Be a Successful Musician Than Ever Before. Online Magazine. Metal Sucks. February 16. https://www.metalsucks.net/2016/02/16/why-its-harder-to-be-a-successful-musician-than-ever-before/.

Oh, Sunny. 2018. Why Is the U.S. Accusing China of Stealing Intellectual Property? MarketWatch. April 6. https://www.marketwatch.com/story/why-is-the-us-accusing-china-of-stealing-intellectual-property-2018-04-05.

Peeler, Calvin D. 1999. From the Providence of Kings to Copyrighted Things (and French Moral Rights). *Indiana International & Comparative Law Review* 9 (2): 423–456. https://doi.org/10.18060/17468.

Pelet, Jean-Éric, and Basma Taieb. 2017. Privacy Protection on Social Networks: A Scale for Measuring Users' Attitudes in France and the USA. https://doi.org/10.1007/978-3-319-56538-5_77.

Perotti, Elena. 2019. HADOPI, Copyright and Privacy. Presentation presented at the Presentation for Purdue University Online MA program in strategic communication, Course SA590, Global Internet Communication, Paris, October.

Rozin, Paul, Abigail K. Remick, and Claude Fischler. 2011. Broad Themes of Difference between French and Americans in Attitudes to Food and Other Life Domains: Personal Versus Communal Values, Quantity Versus Quality, and Comforts Versus Joys. *Frontiers in Psychology* 2. https://doi.org/10.3389/fpsyg.2011.00177.

The Economist. 2016. Free Speech—Under Attack, June 4. https://www.economist.com/leaders/2016/06/04/under-attack.

The President of the United States. 2020. Executive Order on Preventing Online Censorship. White House Official Page. White House. May 28. https://www.whitehouse.gov/presidential-actions/executive-order-preventing-online-censorship/.

UN General Assembly. 1948. "Universal Declaration of Human Rights." Information. United Nations. December 10. https://www.un.org/en/universal-declaration-human-rights/.

United States Intellectual Properety Enforcement Coordinator. 2019. Annual Intellectual Property Report to Congress. Washington, DC: Executive Office of the President of the United States. https://www.whitehouse.gov/wp-content/uploads/2019/02/IPEC-2018-Annual-Intellectual-Property-Report-to-Congress.pdf.

Waxman, Olivia. 2018. GDPR—Disturbing History Behind the EU's New Data Privacy Law. *Time*, May 24. https://time.com/5290043/nazi-history-eu-data-privacy-gdpr/.

Weber, Andrew. 2015. FALQs: Freedom of Speech in France | In Custodia Legis: Law Librarians of Congress. Blog. March 27. https://blogs.loc.gov/law/2015/03/falqs-freedom-of-speech-in-france/.

Instead of Conclusions: Short- and Long-Term Scenarios for Media Regulation

Sorin Adam Matei, Françoise Benhamou, Maud Bernisson, Nicolas Curien, Larry Kilman, Marko Milosavljević, Iva Nenadić, and Franck Rebillard

Even the most insightful academic texts dealing with political and social trends only maintain their currency for a limited time. A decade or a generation, at the most, and most books are left behind in the dust of time. While many books could be seen after that period as witnesses to

S. A. Matei (✉)
Purdue University, West Lafayette, IN, USA
e-mail: smatei@purdue.edu

F. Benhamou
Université Sorbonne Paris Nord, Villetaneuse, France

M. Bernisson
Karlstad University, Karlstad, Sweden
e-mail: maud.bernisson@kau.s

N. Curien
Conservatoire National Des Arts et Métiers, Paris, France

L. Kilman
WAN-IFRA, Paris, France

S. A. Matei et al. (eds.), *Digital and Social Media Regulation*,
https://doi.org/10.1007/978-3-030-66759-7_9

their time, few guide us into the future. We acknowledge that some chapters in this collection will maintain their relevancy longer than others; our contributors are keenly aware of the limitations intrinsic in any scholarly pursuit. Aggregated from the individual and personal expectations of the contributors comes this forecast, which was gathered not only from our analytic exercise, but from what we didn't include in our personal contributions.

Each of us possesses an understanding of the world we live in that is contained in the pages of this collection—viewpoints which extend beyond the media and regulatory regimes we were invited to discuss. This understanding is subterraneously connected not only to our scholarship, but also to that which we saw, the organizations we work for, the situations we encountered, the student questions we answered, the businesses, organizations, or governments we advised at different points in our careers. These experiences, beyond scholarship, inform our deepest concerns and research questions. With that in mind, this final chapter aims to replace bland recapitulation of what was already said in each chapter with more daring, personal, future-oriented collective answers to two questions:

1. What do you think will be the greatest regulatory challenge in the near future (5–10 years)? and
2. Considering the current discernible trends in media technologies and business models, what would be a potential "hidden" threat or opportunity for the more distant future—beyond 25 years?

M. Milosavljević
Department of Journalism, University of Ljubljana, Ljubljana, Slovenia
e-mail: Milosavljevic@fdv.uni-lj.si

I. Nenadić
Zagreb University, Zagreb, Croatia

F. Rebillard
Institut de la Communication des Médias, Université Sorbonne Nouvelle, Paris, France
e-mail: franck.rebillard@sorbonne-nouvelle.fr

These questions are not comfortable for an academic. They openly invite speculation. Yet, they are necessary. Looking at the future through them, as if through a binocular, we could at the very least tell what there is to see ahead—be it something or nothing. We invited our contributors to combine the power of imagination with their deep and solid knowledge of the topic to break through the glass wall of the future. Needless to say, that we consider these opinions to be the first springboard for future exploration and definitive solutions to the challenges of the present.

The two questions were asked after the chapters were written and answers were provided, informally, through email, as "personal communication." For that reason, the tone, at times, is conversational and imbued with a note of emotional engagement. Again, this is expected, as we did not mean to re-write the book, but to add the personal experiences and insights of our collaborators to the conversation so that we could offer a fuller picture.

Let us start with the answers about the short-term challenges.

1 The Immediate Future: Convergence and Threats to Liberties

Regarding the near future, we obtained a coherent group answer: We expect a drift toward global alignment of regulatory regimes, especially in the West, but at the possible cost of a more mellow version of the most comprehensive and controlling regulatory frameworks.

The need and possible drift toward greater integration is remarked by Nenadić and Milosavljević, who emphasize:

> The development of individual responses to individual issues (such as taxation or hate speech or moderation) by individual EU countries is far from comprehensive, even though digital stakeholders today completely dominate specific and general markets. Thus, the greatest regulatory challenge in the near future seems to be a development of a comprehensive digital media regulation and governance: one that will take into account economic, political, societal and psychological aspects and implications of digital environment and digital media.

Curien also noted that, regarding data management and privacy, there is a trend toward new for tighter synthesis between the industries. At the same time, he recommends a careful calibration of transborder regulatory instruments:

> The rulings which frame the collection, the usage and the cession of personal data (GDPR in Europe), while being restrictive enough to guarantee a suitable consumer protection, should also be permissive enough as not to hinder the service innovation process, as concerns interactivity and personalized access to content.

Similarly, Bernisson affirms:

> In an international context, levers of action to defend freedoms and rights are more efficient at the EU level. Yet freedom of expression and information is considered as a national matter, not an EU matter. The EU has strengthened the right to privacy against international private companies. Concerning electronic communications, it would be useful to strengthen freedom of expression and information likely.

She is particularly concerned about the over-reach of the current attempts to curtail freedom of expression in the name of protecting national security:

> The attempts to reinforce the campaign against terrorism threatens freedom of expression and information. There are multiple examples in the European Union, but France provides a striking example with the law against hate speech (Avia law). Briefly, the law entailed to remove manifest *or not manifest* terrorist or child pornographic content online in less than twenty-four hours, without a judge's prior authorization. In June 2020, the French Constitutional Court struck down the key elements of the law because it would breach freedom of expression. Yet the French state is trying to pass it through another channel, EU laws. Although safeguards exist, the trend towards more security [at the cost of] fundamental rights is worrisome.

Kilman is even more pointed in his analysis of the present situation. In his recommendations for more careful considerations of the many calls for more stringent regulation, especially of freedom of expression he states:

> The multiple, and often incompatible, regulatory environments around the world will continue to be a challenge for some time to come. As regulations concerning privacy, freedom of expression and copyright are largely set by

> individual nations, with differing political, legal and cultural environments, this patchwork of regulations is proving to be inadequate for the demands of digital media that transcend national borders.
>
> This issue is being addressed through intergovernmental mechanisms, and will, to some extent, likely move toward greater compatibility in coming years. We are already seeing regional agreements such as the European General Data Protection Regulation having an impact far beyond European borders. Recognition that international cooperation is inevitable for internet regulation is likely to lead to a more coherent regulatory environment.
>
> Protection of freedom of expression, which is under threat not only in repressive regimes but in democratic countries as well, is also a serious regulatory challenge when it comes in conflict with protection of privacy as well as the growing calls to regulate hate speech and "offensive" and "aggressive" speech.
>
> This is likely to be much more difficult to resolve. Privacy regulations, such as the "right to be forgotten" in Europe, have attempted to protect freedom of expression by making exceptions for legitimate news interest. But the rising concern about speech that is hateful or hurtful is a trend that potentially leads to increasing censorship. New regulations to protect against hate and hurtful speech could potentially damage freedom of expression. Unfortunately, the pendulum is swinging in this direction.
>
> This challenge can be met by regulation that recognizes the importance of freedom of expression and seeks to balance this basic human right against other concerns. But it is not solely a question for the regulatory mechanisms. The fast-changing digital environment is leaving societies with little time to assess the impact of emerging technologies on their basic rights. Technological developments must therefore be accompanied by better media literacy education that emphasizes the importance of freedom of expression to society, and how seemingly well-meaning regulations can have unintended impacts.

At the same time, Benhamou explains no amount—no matter how much—of regulation can ignore the media titans looming in the background. There is one important reality: "the market power of Internet giants, taking into account the characteristics of digital markets [and the fact that most] media depend deeply on [social media] platforms' power." In the same vein, Rebillard sees the need to mitigate the power of the leading platforms (Facebook, Instagram, Twitter, YouTube) proposing the vigorous pursuit and implementation of the EU Digital Services Act, which will demand that social media platforms should allow the users to take their profiles and activities from platform to platform. His answer deserves to be cited in extenso:

> For a few months now, an interesting proposal has been making its way [in the public conversation]. It consists in setting up interoperability between major social media platforms. Operators of these platforms stand in a monopoly or oligopoly position for several reasons. One of them is quite decisive. It stems from network effects, stimulating users to join the platform that is already the most popular. As a result, the platform benefits from positive externalities that strengthen its monopoly and dominant position, and make users more dependent on it. Such a chain -a virtuous circle for platform operators, but a vicious circle for users- should be broken. Users should be empowered to move from one platform to another without losing the data and relationships they have built up on each platform. To do this, an interoperability mechanism would have to be put in place. This proposal is put forward by several organizations and even supported by some political leaders. It might be taken into account during the debates surrounding the implementation of the Digital Services Act, which will renovate a European Union directive dating from 2000. If so, we would be returning to a more decentralized form of the Internet, which had shown its advantages during the 20th century and which undoubtedly still owns an innovative potential for society in the 21st century.

Matei, on the other hand, believes the greatest regulatory challenge will come with the growing crisis of an open Internet that made possible the concentration of social media and search companies that benefit from network effects:

> The Internet was created to allow anyone, anywhere, not only to connect-to but also add value and services to the Internet community. Yet, for any given service that takes advantage of our social nature and needs, one or at the most a handful of companies are sufficient. Furthermore, useful services are often outcompeted by nefarious pursuits of the same kind. Think email and spam. Think free downloads and malware. Think news and fake news. Given the network effects, all connectivity-based services work better for the consumers who are on the same network. At the same time, competing network services may differentiate themselves by heightened level of security, privacy control, or by reduced footprint. For this, however, we need to accept the necessary trade-off implicit in radically new network structures and infrastructures that can allow federated interconnection between nodes, while not forcing all the nodes to work with each

> other the same way. Imagine a security-first, encrypted, network, blockchain style, on which access is filtered by verifying identity, credibility, and creditability in a material sense, possibly by bioscans. For this, however, we need a new way to think about regulation, more local, more pragmatic, and less interested in universal rules of universal access if such access makes it easier for terrorists, phishers, hackers, drug dealers, pornographers, and scammers of all kinds to pollute our computers and networks with their schemes.

Likewise, our scholars also took their predictions further into the future.

2 The Longer View: The Regulatory Cycle Might Go Through a Trough While Technology Might Advance at a Higher Pace

While our contributors see the immediate needs relatively similar in terms of a need to create a more flexible, inclusive, and permissive regulatory infrastructure—especially with respect to freedom of expression—the distant future presents several diverging paths. On the one hand, there is a sense of over-abundant possibility, which challenges the imagination and the outer edges of the possible.

Curien sees the future in terms of another technological revolution, one that will erase modes of production and consumption:

> Sooner or later, we might attend a technological, industrial and usage convergence between (i) historical audiovisual services, (ii) video games, (iii) virtual/augmented reality glasses. The driving force of this likely convergence is the growing consumer appetite for an immersive, global and proactive media experience: e.g. becoming oneself a character in a movie, playing a virtual game in the middle of a real crowd, or creating one's own composite mediatic scenery, made of both real and virtual pieces...
>
> In the long run, the combination of information and biological technologies could even lead to the supremacy of an ultimate and universal screen and consumer device, namely the human retina!
>
> On the industry side, this hybridization process will gradually reshape the market: it will cause horizontal mergers across suppliers of different types of content, beforehand separated by distinct business models.
>
> On the regulatory side, the globalization of content, facilitated and complemented by the generalization of artificial intelligence, will raise critical ethical concerns, far beyond today's current ones. Think of under-skin

> implantation of perceptive prostheses, the liability of avatars, the legal redefinition of identity and privacy, etc.

Although it sounds like a scene from Blade Runner, it is not beyond the realm of possibility, or concern. Curien's vision in fact forces us to imagine the unimaginable and to regulate the "unregulable," at least by today's standards.

In a similar vein, Rebillard warns about the unbridled and over-enthusiastic free reign of AI technologies, which may:

> [a]ffect all sectors of activity, with likely upheavals in the coming decades in transportations (autonomous cars) or housing (domestic tasks carried out).
>
> Overall regulation will be necessary, but it will be difficult and time-consuming to implement – instead very general guidelines may be put in place initially. This makes it more necessary to support citizens facing these changes and, just as much as the regulation of activities, ambitious actions in the area of education would be welcome.
>
> Media literacy has taken a long time to enter basic school curricula and still occupies a marginal place in them. Beyond this, learning of computer code and programming is still reserved for specialized courses, and does not sufficiently take into account the way in which these technologies are now embedded into many human activities.
>
> An introduction to the rudiments of artificial intelligence, notably making neural networks less opaque, should be implemented in both initial and continuing education. Benefiting from a more detailed understanding of the social issues resulting from IA technologies, citizens would be aware of the possibility of changing them to aim for a better society.

To help us navigate a space without apparent boundaries of measurable parameters, Bernisson invites us to ignore, for a moment, the content of the future technologies. Instead, our responsibility is to think about the form of the technological development curves and the attendant regulatory responses. Adroitly, she proposes that we should look at the future as a space of cyclical development, following a wave pattern:

> The rise and fall of communication infrastructures work as a cycle (Spar 2015; Wu 2010), especially in a self-regulatory environment. The current situation follows a similar logic. The information society has been focused on telecommunications, which was meant to strengthen the EU market. It came with a wave of liberalization of public companies in the EU,

> capable of competing on the global market of telecommunications (Vedel 1999). This regulatory environment left room for a few tech giants to dominate electronic communications in Western societies. With the rise of big data, the focus has shifted from infrastructure (telecommunications) to data (online companies). Ownership of data by these few tech giants leads to a strong dependency on private companies by a huge number of actors, including public institutions, who need to access the data collected (e.g. health) but also to scrutinize the practices of these organizations. No matter what the next technological development is (it could be the 5G), it is likely that it will follow a similar pattern.

At the same time Bernisson sees in technological developments a screen that might hide deeper and more serious concerns:

> However, scrutinizing technology alone is misleading. Technology serves goals. The future of electronic communications depends on the hierarchization of these goals. Security seems to rank higher in several cases, which weakens the right to privacy and freedom of expression. For example, the current regulatory framework for privacy provides more leeway to the EU member states to strengthen security measures against the right to privacy. Another example is the redefinition of freedom of expression and information online by private companies like Facebook, who could self-regulate for a long time. If technological trends support mainly A) the current movement towards protecting public security, B) the Digital Single Market and C) the substitution of public institutions by private actors, fundamental rights and freedoms will be put in serious jeopardy in the EU.

Nenadić and Milosavljević take a similar critical view of a technology-driven world. However, they see more disruption and turmoil. In this, they rely on the displacement we have seen over the past 25 years :

> Twenty-five years have passed since Nicholas Negroponte published "Being Digital" (Negroponte 1995). It was a highly significant book that correctly predicted a number of events or developments—such as demise of Blockbuster and possible emergence of companies like Netflix – even if they actually happened only 10 or 20 years later… [T]he next 25 years can also be marked by a replaying of the past 25 years [at another scale] so unpredictable that even our wildest forecasts may turn out to be lackluster or wholly false.

> [The future might be] even quicker, more radical, more virtual, and less materialistic with less physical units and more digital transportation /streaming. Services and information will play even greater role, putting even more power in the hands of digital global companies. The main regulatory questions [...] will focus on how to control, curb the overwhelming digital behemoths, especially in the political realm [and] how to empower people and businesses and not just a small circle of tycoons and politicians.
>
> This will most likely need to include attempt to safeguard market competition and fair political process in all of their aspects: competition policy, tax policy, transparency, prevention of abuses (particularly regarding content), ensuring adequate plurality in sources of information, in distribution, and in consumption.

Benhamou offers one of the most pessimistic scenarios, though not very different from what she has seen in the immediate past or in the present:

> I'm afraid of the consequences of the twofold movement of industrial concentration and migration to digital formats: a drop in value, the bankruptcy of many media companies, the stranglehold on media by billionaires, with a threat for democracy.
>
> Regulatory environments must be stronger and agile, but one of the stakes is the ability to build an international cooperation and harmonization of some aspects of regulation (ex. regulation of personal data)

Matei looks at the problem from a longer historical perspective. For him, media concentration is part of a historical trend that is coeval with modernity, amplifying its trends and contradictions:

> If we think that modernity is all about "organic solidarity," as described by Durkheim, as a form of universal dependency due to our increased personal specialization, the trend toward tight connection via networking can only lead to more and stronger technological infrastructures of communication. However, their centralization, either by commercial oligopolies or by governmental over-regulation, will ultimately lead to ossification and decay. A period of balkanization and even withdrawal from the world of connectivity that we have today could be a natural consequence of this recoil. During this period, it will be important to reduce and push the interconnection protocols and regulatory measures that control them back to the idea of interconnectivity, rather than to that of tight vertical integration of production and consumption. The future should be more federated, with localized socio-technical networks of all kinds relatable but not reducible

> to either of them. In this world, regulation will return to the role of a technical arbiter rather than of prosecutor, judge, and jury of the nature of the content and services offered to the public, as is the trend right now.

Of course, these forecasting exercises will meet reality only halfway. The future is as unpredictable as the past is unbelievable. Kilman offers one other way to think about this alternate future, which gives the readers of this volume the space and time to imagine their own scenarios:

> Any attempt to forecast 25 years in the future is entering the realm of speculative fiction, as current discernible trends in media technologies and business models are irrelevant for such a large time frame. Facebook is only 16 years old (2004). Twitter is 14 (2006). Tik Tok is only 4 (2016). Google is the elderly one of this group – 22 years (1998). The same question asked 25 years ago would have failed to consider any of these platforms, and their central role in the media (and regulatory) environment. So too for the iPad (2010) or today's mobile technologies.
>
> Regulatory environments are ill-equipped to deal with the pace of change. The rapidity of innovation is perhaps the one constant that is likely to remain far into the future. Therefore, one hopes that regulatory environments will continue to evolve and become better equipped to deal with both the pace of change and the conflicting regimes.

References

Negroponte, Nicholas. 1995. *Being Digital*, 1st ed. New York: Knopf.

Spar, Debora L. 2015. *Pirates, Prophets and Pioneers*. London, UK: Cornerstone.

Vedel, Thierry. 1999. De la régulation internalisée à la régulation externalisée dans le domaine des télécommunications. *Droit et Société* 41 (1): 47–62. https://doi.org/10.3406/dreso.1999.1463.

Wu, Tim. 2010. *The Master Switch: The Rise and Fall of Information Empires*, 1st ed. New York: Alfred A. Knopf.

Correction to: Digital and Social Media Regulation

Sorin Adam Matei, Franck Rebillard, and Fabrice Rochelandet

Correction to:
S. A. Matei et al. (eds.),
***Digital and Social Media Regulation*,**
https://doi.org/10.1007/978-3-030-66759-7

The original version of the book was inadvertently published with incorrect author's name "Fabienne Graff" in Chapters 1, 3, 8 and Front matter, which has now been corrected to "Fabienne Graf". The book has been updated with the changes.

The updated version of the book can be found at
https://doi.org/10.1007/978-3-030-66759-7

S. A. Matei et al. (eds.), *Digital and Social Media Regulation*,
https://doi.org/10.1007/978-3-030-66759-7_10

Correction to: Digital and Social Media Regulation

Sorin Adam Matei, Franck Rebillard, and Fabrice Rochelandet

Correction to:
S. A. Matei et al. (eds.),
***Digital and Social Media Regulation*,**
https://doi.org/10.1007/978-3-030-66759-7

The original version of Chapters 1, 6 and 7 was previously published as non-open access, which has now been changed to open access under a CC BY 4.0 license, and the copyright holder has been updated to 'The Author(s)'. The book has been updated with the changes.

The updated version of these chapters can be found at
https://doi.org/10.1007/978-3-030-66759-7_1
https://doi.org/10.1007/978-3-030-66759-7_6
https://doi.org/10.1007/978-3-030-66759-7_7

S. A. Matei et al. (eds.), *Digital and Social Media Regulation*,
https://doi.org/10.1007/978-3-030-66759-7_11

Index

S. A. Matei et al. (eds.), *Digital and Social Media Regulation*, https://doi.org/10.1007/978-3-030-66759-7

The manufacturer's authorised representative in the EU is Springer Nature Customer Service Centre GmbH, Europaplatz 3, 69115 Heidelberg, Germany. If you have any concerns regarding our products, please contact ProductSafety@springernature.com

Printed and bound by CPI Group (UK) Ltd, Croydon, CR0 4YY
22/09/2026
02221054-0002